Discourses of
Thomas S. Monson
Pathways to Perfection

Discourses of
Thomas S. Monson

Pathways to Perfection

Published by Deseret Book Company
Salt Lake City, Utah

Library of Congress Catalog Card Number 73-88634

ISBN 0-87747-511-3

Printed in the United States of America

10   9   8   7   6   5   4

*To Frances, my eternal companion,
and to our children Tom, Ann, and Clark*

FOREWORD

It gives me pleasure and is a source of satisfaction to add my word of commendation to this publication of materials which have been taken from talks given by Elder Thomas S. Monson of the Council of the Twelve at general conferences, BYU addresses, or from other addresses, such as commencement exercises.

It has been my good fortune to know Elder Monson from his earlier boyhood days while I was president of the Pioneer Stake and he was a young man living in that stake who was rapidly coming to the attention of those with whom he was associated.

Elder Monson became a bishop at the age of 22 and, so far as I know, was one of the youngest bishops of the Church at that time, and possibly as far as one has any memory. As a young bishop in a ward which required much attention to needy persons, with many widows who, except for the attention of the bishop, would have nowhere to look for care and encouragement, he rose to the occasion; and from his intimate association with the problems of the everyday world, he developed a sensitivity which has characterized his life and comes out in the expressions we have heard and you now read from this publication as excerpts from his sermons.

Herein the reader will find a wealth of interesting illustrations, which have been delivered as only one gifted with his special talents could portray, with such vividness that the reader, or the listener, could easily put himself as an intimate spectator in the events he portrays.

To listen to him is to be inspired. To work with him is to be uplifted; and to feel of his devotion and the strength of his conviction and powerful testimony is to know that there is no doubt but that his calling as a special witness as an apostle of the Lord, Jesus Christ, is well merited.

Fortunately for the Church and for those of us who are associated with him, he is only in the midday of his life and his service. As we watch him grow and develop from the experiences that he has gleaned from worldwide contacts, he has an overview and a perspective that qualify him to be a teacher, and a leader, and an inspirer of those who sit under the sound of his voice.

I can only say that I will wait with eagerness to obtain a reading of the sermons that I have heard him deliver, to again have refreshed the lessons he has so ably taught.

Harold B. Lee

President Harold B. Lee

CONTENTS

THE PATHWAY OF FAITH

THE PATHWAY OF SERVICE

THE PATHWAY OF LOVE

THE PATHWAY OF PRAYER

THE PATHWAY OF
FAITH

"Remember that without faith you can do nothing;
therefore ask in faith."
D & C 8:10

1

I know that my Redeemer lives

MICHAEL PAUL SHUMWAY
BORN
OCTOBER 24, 1965
DIED
MARCH 14, 1966

pring has returned to the community of Franklin, Idaho. One can hear the ever-welcome chirp of the robin and see the beauty of the first daffodil. Seemingly overnight, the drab brown grass of winter turns to a verdant green. Soon plows will turn the earth, seeds will be planted, and a new cycle of life will commence. Tucked away from the bustle of activity and snuggled against the friendly hills is the town cemetery.

It was there one spring that a new grave was opened —not a large one—and a tiny casket was lowered into mother earth. Three lines appear on the attractive headstone:

MICHAEL PAUL SHUMWAY
Born: October 24, 1965
Died: March 14, 1966

May I introduce you to the Shumway family. They are my neighbors here in Salt Lake City, Utah. Mark and Wilma Shumway and each of the children always greet you with a friendly smile or a wave of the hand. They brighten a neighborhood. They are good people.

Can you imagine the happiness in the family home on that 24th day of October when little Michael was born? Father was proud, brothers and sisters were excited, mother was humble, as they welcomed this sweet new blossom of humanity, fresh fallen from God's own home, to flower on earth. Happy months followed.

Then came that fateful night in March when little Michael was called to his heavenly home and the breath of life was gone. As I visited with Mark and Wilma, so bowed down with grief from the loss of their precious son, I noticed one of Michael's tiny toys as it rested near the crib. I remembered the words of Eugene Field's masterpiece, "Little Boy Blue":

> *The little toy dog is covered with dust,*
> *But sturdy and stanch he stands;*
> *And the little toy soldier is red with rust,*
> *And his musket molds in his hands.*
> *Time was when the little toy dog was new,*
> *And the soldier was passing fair;*
> *And that was the time when our Little Boy Blue*
> *Kissed them and put them there.*
>
> *"Now, don't you go till I come," he said,*
> *"And don't you make any noise!"*
> *So toddling off to his trundle-bed,*
> *He dreamed of the pretty toys.*
> *And as he was dreaming, an angel song*
> *Awakened our Little Boy Blue,—*
> *Oh, the years are many, the years are long,*
> *But the little toy friends are true.*
>
> *Ay, faithful to Little Boy Blue they stand,*
> *Each in the same old place,*
> *Awaiting the touch of a little hand,*
> *The smile of a little face.*
> *And they wonder, as waiting these long years through,*
> *In the dust of that little chair,*
> *What has become of our Little Boy Blue*
> *Since he kissed them and put them there.*

My Redeemer lives

There are many toy dogs and many toy dolls that belonged to many boys and girls who lived and then were taken from us. And while the toys may wonder while they wait, anxious parents need not wonder. The revealed word of a loving Heavenly Father provides answers to questions of the heart.

Mark and Wilma, could you gather your little ones around as we discuss some of these answers. There are many hundreds of thousands of others, perhaps millions, who also may benefit from our conversation, for who hasn't lost a mother, a father, a sister, a brother, a son, or a daughter?

Every thoughtful person has asked himself that question best phrased by Job of old: "If a man die, shall he live again?" (Job 14:14.) Try as we may to put the question out of our thoughts, it always returns. Death comes to all mankind. It comes to the aged as they walk on faltering feet. Its summons is heard by those who have scarcely reached midway in life's journey, and often it hushes the laughter of little children.

While death is inevitable, it can best be understood when we learn of life, even eternal life.

Life on earth does not mark the beginning of our existence. The poet, William Wordsworth, wrote:

> Our birth is but a sleep and a forgetting;
> The soul that rises with us, our life's Star,
> Hath had elsewhere its setting
> And cometh from afar:
> Not in entire forgetfulness,
> And not in utter nakedness,
> But trailing clouds of glory do we come
> From God, who is our home:
> Heaven lies about us in our infancy.[1]

In the wisdom of God, an earth was created

3

upon which man might dwell. Genesis records that the earth was without form and void, and darkness was upon the face of the deep. Then God said, "Let there be light," and there was light; "Let there be a firmament," and there was a firmament; "Let the earth bring forth grass," and the earth brought forth grass. He made the fowls of the air, the creatures of the water, the beasts of the earth. (See Genesis 1.)

And then God created man in his own image, in the image of God created he him; male and female created he them. To man was given dominion over every living thing. Earth became a proving ground, a testing station, a provider of needed experience.

We laugh, we cry, we work, we play, we love, we live. And then we die. And dead we would remain but for one man and his mission, even Jesus of Nazareth. Born in a stable, cradled in a manger, his birth fulfilled the inspired pronouncements of many prophets. He was taught from on high. He provided the life, the light, and the way. Multitudes followed him. Children adored him. The haughty rejected him. He spoke in parables. He taught by example. He lived a perfect life. Through his ministry, blind men saw, deaf men heard, and lame men walked. Even the dead returned to life.

Though the King of kings and Lord of lords had come, he was accorded the greeting given to an enemy or a traitor. There followed a mockery that some called a trial. Cries of "Crucify him, crucify him," filled the night air. (John 19:6.) Then commenced the climb to Calvary's hill.

He was ridiculed, reviled, mocked, and jeered, nailed to a cross amidst shouts of "Let Christ the King of Israel descend now from the cross, that we may see and believe" (Mark 15:32); "He saved others; himself he cannot save" (Matthew 27:42); "If thou be Christ, save thyself" (Luke

23:39). His response: "Father, forgive them; for they know not what they do." (Luke 23:34.)

Death came. His body was placed by loving hands in a sepulcher hewn of stone.

On the first day of the week, very early in the morning, Mary Magdalene and the other Mary came unto the sepulcher. To their astonishment, the body of their Lord was gone. Luke records that two men in shining garments stood by them and said: "Why seek ye the living among the dead? He is not here, but is risen. . . ." (Luke 24:1, 5-6.) Job's question, "If a man die, shall he live again?" had just been answered.

The sacred scripture records the events following his ascension. However, today, as always, the skeptic's voice challenges the word of God, and each man must choose to whom he shall listen. Clarence Darrow, the famous lawyer and agnostic, declared, "No life is of much value, and every death is but a little loss." Schopenhauer, the German philosopher and pessimist, wrote: "To desire immortality is to desire the eternal perpetuation of a great mistake." And to their words are added those of new generations as foolish men crucify the Christ anew. For they modify his miracles, doubt his divinity, and reject his resurrection.

Robert Blatchford, in his book *God and My Neighbor,* attacked with vigor the accepted Christian beliefs, such as God, Christ, prayer, and immortality. He boldly asserted: "I claim to have proved everything I set out to prove so fully and decisively that no Christian, however great or able he may be, can answer my arguments or shake my case." He surrounded himself with a wall of skepticism. Then a surprising thing happened. His wall suddenly crumbled to dust. He was left exposed and undefended. Slowly he began to feel his way back to the faith he had scorned and ridiculed. What had caused this profound change in his outlook? *His wife died.* With a broken heart, he went into the room where all that was mortal of her lay. He looked again at the face he loved so well. Coming out he said to a friend: "It is she and yet it is not she. Everything is changed. Something that was there before is taken away. She is not the same. What can be gone if it be not the soul?"

Later he wrote: "Death is not what some people imagine. It is only like going into another room. In that other room we shall find . . . the dear women and men and the sweet children we have loved and lost."[2]

Against the philosophy rampant in today's world, a doubting of the authenticity of the Sermon on the Mount, an abandonment of Christ's teachings, a denial of God, and a rejection of his laws, we seek a point of reference, an unimpeachable source, even a testimony of eye witnesses. Stephen, doomed to the cruel death of a martyr, looked up to heaven and cried: "Behold, I see the heavens opened, and the Son of man standing on the right hand of God." (Acts 7:56.) Saul, on the road to Damascus, had a vision of the risen, exalted Christ. Peter and John also testified of the risen Christ.

Who can help but be penetrated by the stirring testimony of Paul at Corinth. He declared:

> . . . Christ died for our sins according to the scriptures;
> And . . . was buried, and . . . he rose again the third day according to the scriptures;
> And . . . was seen of Cephas, then of the twelve;
> After that, he was seen of above five hundred brethren at once; of whom the greater part remain unto this present. . . .
> After that, he was seen of James; then of all the apostles . . . and he was seen of me. (1 Corinthians 15:3-8.)

To the agnostic, the skeptic, the reviler, I ask, "Agnostic, can you answer?" "Skeptic, can you save?" "Reviler, can you redeem?"

God the Eternal Father spoke to the multitude on this continent and said:

> Behold my beloved Son, in whom I am well pleased, in whom I have glorified my name—hear ye him.
>
> And . . . as they understood they cast their eyes up again towards heaven; and behold, they saw a Man descending out of heaven. . . .
>
> . . . he stretched forth his hand and spake unto the people, saying:
>
> Behold, I am Jesus Christ, whom the prophets testified shall come into the world.
>
> . . . I am the light and life of the world; and I have drunk out of that bitter cup which the Father hath given me, and have glorified the Father in taking upon me the sins of the world. . . .
>
> Arise and come forth unto me, that ye may thrust your hands into my side, and also that ye may feel the prints of the nails in my hands and in my feet, that ye may know that I am the God of Israel, and the God of the whole earth, and have been slain for the sins of the world.
>
> And when they had all gone forth and had witnessed for themselves, they did cry out with one accord, saying:
>
> Hosanna! Blessed be the name of the Most High God! And they did fall down at the feet of Jesus, and did worship him. (3 Nephi 11:7-11, 14, 16-17.)

This loving God who introduced his crucified and resurrected Son was not a God lacking in body, parts, or passions—the God of a man-made philosophy. Rather, God our Father has ears with which to hear our prayers. He has eyes with which to see our actions. He has a mouth with which to speak to us. He has a heart with which to feel compassion and love. He is real. He is living. We are his children made in his image. We look like him and he looks like us.

This is the God who so loved the world that he gave his Only Begotten Son that we might have everlasting life.

To you, Wilma and Mark Shumway, and to all who

have loved and lost a dear one, he provides the courage to say, ". . . the Lord gave and the Lord hath taken away; blessed be the name of the Lord." (Job 1:21.) As you and your children journey to the family home in Franklin, Idaho, where tenderly and lovingly you place flowers of springtime on that tiny grave, your eyes may be moist with tears, but your hearts will burn with the knowledge that the bands of death have been broken and that members of your family, though now separated by death, will one day be reunited to share the blessings of eternal life.

With all my heart and the fervency of my soul, I testify as a special witness that God does live. Jesus is his Son, the Only Begotten of the Father in the flesh. He is our Redeemer; he is our mediator with the Father. He it was who died on the cross to atone for our sins. He became the firstfruits of the resurrection. Oh, sweet the joy this sentence gives, "I know that my Redeemer lives!"

---

[1]"Ode on Intimations of Immortality from Recollections of Early Childhood."
[2]*God and My Neighbor* (Chicago: Charles H. Kerr and Company).

2

Meeting your Goliath

On June 5, 1967, the stillness of Sinai's desert air was shattered. Jet-powered aircraft streaked toward specified targets, cannons roared, tanks lumbered, men fought and died, women wept, and children cried. The Holy Land, once the personal province of the Prince of Peace, now was engulfed by war.

This troubled land has witnessed much conflict; its peoples have suffered terrible trial and tribulations. No single battle is better remembered, however, than occurred in the Valley of Elah during the year 1063 B.C. Along the mountains on one side, the feared armies of the Philistines were marshaled to march directly to the heart of Judah and the Jordan Valley. On the other side of the valley, King Saul had drawn up his armies in opposition.

Historians tell us that the opposing forces were about evenly matched in number and in skill. However, the Philistines had managed to keep secret their valued knowledge of smelting and fashioning iron into formidable weapons of war. The sound of hammers pounding upon anvils and the sight of smoke rising skyward from many bellows as the smiths went about the task of sharpening weapons and fashioning new ones must have struck fear into the hearts of Saul's warriors, for even the most novice of soldiers could know the superiority of iron weapons to those of brass.

As often happened when armies faced each other, individual champions challenged others from the opposing forces to single combat. There was considerable precedent for this sort of fighting; and on more than one occasion, notably during the tenure of Samson as judge, battles had been decided by individual combat.

Now, however, the situation was reversed as far as Israel was concerned, and it was a Philistine who dared to challenge all others—a veritable giant of a man called Goliath of Gath. Old accounts tell us that Goliath was ten feet tall. He wore brass armor and a coat of mail. And the staff of his spear would stagger a strong man merely to lift, let alone hurl. His shield was the longest ever seen or heard of, and his sword a fearsome blade.

This champion from the Philistine camp stood and cried unto the armies of Israel: "Why are ye come out to set your battle in array? am not I a Philistine, and ye servants to Saul? choose you a man for you, and let him come down to me." (1 Samuel 17:8.)

His challenge was that if he were overpowered by the Israelite warrior, then all the Philistines would become servants to the Israelites. On the other hand, if he were victorious, the Israelites would become their slaves. Goliath roared: "I defy the armies of Israel this day; give me a man, that we may fight together." (1 Samuel 17:10.)

And so, for forty days came the challenge, met only by fear and trembling. And all the men of Israel, when they saw the man Goliath, "fled from him, and were sore afraid." (1 Samuel 17:24.)

There was one, however, who did not quake with fear nor run in alarm. Rather, he stiffened the spine of Israel's soldiers by his piercing question of rebuke toward them: ". . . Is there not a cause? . . . Let no man's heart fail because of him; thy servant will go and fight with this Philistine."

10

(1 Samuel 17:29, 32.) David, the shepherd boy, had spoken. But he did not speak just as a shepherd boy. For the hands of Samuel, God's prophet, had rested upon his head and anointed him; and the Spirit of the Lord had come upon him.

Saul said to David: "Thou art not able to go against this Philistine to fight with him: for thou art but a youth, and he a man of war from his youth." (1 Samuel 17:33.) But David persevered; and bedecked with the armor of Saul, he prepared to meet the giant. Realizing his helplessness so garbed, David discarded the armor, took instead his staff in his hand, chose five smooth stones out of the brook, and put them in a shepherd's bag; and with his sling in hand, he drew near to the Philistine.

All of us remember the shocked exclamation of Goliath: "Am I a dog, that thou comest to me with staves? . . . Come to me, and I will give thy flesh unto the fowls of the air, and to the beasts of the field." (1 Samuel 17:43-44.)

Then David said: "Thou comest to me with a sword, and with a spear, and with a shield; but I come to thee in the name of the Lord of hosts, the God of the armies of Israel, whom thou hast defied.

"This day will the Lord deliver thee into mine hand . . . that all the earth may know that there is a God in Israel.

"And all this assembly shall know that the Lord saveth not with sword and spear: for the battle is the Lord's, and he will give you into our hands.

"And it came to pass, when the Philistine arose, and came and drew nigh to meet David, that David hasted, and ran toward the army to meet the Philistine.

"And David put his hand in his bag, and took thence a stone, and slang it, and smote the Philistine in the forehead, that the stone sunk into his forehead; and he fell upon his face to the earth.

"So David prevailed over the Philistine with a sling

11

and with a stone, and smote the Philistine and slew him.
. . ." (1 Samuel 17:45-50.)

The battle had thus been fought. The victory had been
won. David emerged a national hero, his destiny before
him.

Some of us remember David as a shepherd boy divinely
commissioned by the Lord through the prophet Samuel.
Others of us know him as a mighty warrior, for doesn't the
record show the chant of the adoring women following his
many victorious battles, "Saul has slain his thousands and
David his ten thousands"? Or perhaps we look upon him
as the inspired poet or as one of Israel's greatest kings. Still
others recall that he violated the laws of God and took that
which belonged to another—the beautiful Bathsheba. He
even arranged the death of her husband Uriah. I like to
think of David as the righteous lad who had the courage
and the faith to face insurmountable odds when all others
hesitated, and to redeem the name of Israel by facing that
giant in his life—Goliath of Gath.

Well might we look carefully into our own lives and
judge our courage, our faith. Is there a Goliath in your life?
Is there one in mine? Does he stand squarely between you
and your desired happiness? Oh, your Goliath may not
carry a sword or hurl a verbal challenge of insult that all
may hear and force you to decision. He may not be ten feet
tall, but he likely will appear equally as formidable, and his
silent challenge may shame and embarrass.

One man's Goliath may be the stranglehold of a cigarette or perhaps an unquenchable thirst for alcohol. To another, his Goliath may be an unruly tongue or a selfish
streak which causes him to spurn the poor and the downtrodden. Envy, greed, fear, laziness, doubt, vice, pride, lust,
selfishness, discouragement—all spell Goliath.

The giant you face will not diminish in size nor in
power or strength by your vain hoping, wishing, or wait-

ing for him to do so. Rather, he increases in power as his hold upon you tightens.

The poet truly describes this truth:

> *Vice is a monster of so frightful mien,*
> *As, to be hated, needs but to be seen;*
> *Yet seen too oft, familiar with her face,*
> *We first endure, then pity, then embrace.*

> —ALEXANDER POPE

The battle for our immortal souls is no less important than the battle fought by David. The enemy is no less formidable, the help of Almighty God no farther away. What will our action be? Like David of old, "our cause is just." We have been placed upon earth not to fail or fall victim to temptation's snare, but rather to succeed. Our giant, our Goliath, must be conquered.

David went to the brook and carefully selected five smooth stones with which he might meet his enemy. He was deliberate in his selection, for there could be no turning back, no second chance—this battle was to be decisive.

Just as David went to the brook, well might we go to our source of supply—the Lord. What polished stones will you select to defeat the Goliath that is robbing you of your happiness by smothering your opportunities? May I offer suggestions.

The stone of COURAGE will be essential to your victory. As we survey the challenges of life, that which is easy is rarely right. In fact, the course that we should properly follow appears at times impossible, impenetrable, hopeless.

Such did the way appear to Laman and Lemuel. When they looked upon their assignment to go unto the house of Laban and seek the records according to God's command, they murmured, saying it was a hard thing that was required of them. Thus, a lack of courage took from them

13

their opportunity, and it was given to courageous Nephi, who responded, "I will go and do the things which the Lord hath commanded, for I know that the Lord giveth no commandments unto the children of men, save he shall prepare a way for them that they may accomplish the thing which he commandeth them." (1 Nephi 3:7.) Yes, the stone of courage is needed.

Let us not overlook the stone of EFFORT—mental effort and physical effort.

> *The heights by great men reached and kept*
> *Were not attained by sudden flight,*
> *But they, while their companions slept,*
> *Were toiling upward in the night.*

> —HENRY WADSWORTH LONGFELLOW

The decision to overcome a fault or correct a weakness is an actual step in the process of doing so. "Thrust in thy sickle with thy might" was not spoken of missionary work alone.

Then there must be in our selection the stone of HUMILITY, for haven't we been told through divine revelation that when we are humble, the Lord, our God, will lead us by the hand and give us answer to our prayers?

And who would go forth to battle his Goliath without the stone of PRAYER, remembering that the recognition of a power higher than oneself is in no way debasing; rather, it exalts.

Finally, let us choose the stone of LOVE OF DUTY. Duty is not merely to do the thing we ought to do, but to do it when we should, whether we like it or not.

Armed with this selection of five polished stones to be propelled by the mighty sling of faith, we need then but to take the staff of virtue to steady us; and we are ready to meet the giant Goliath, wherever, and whenever, and however we find him.

For the stone of COURAGE will melt the Goliath of fear. The stone of EFFORT will bring down the Goliath of indecision and procrastination. And the Goliaths of pride, of envy, of lack of self-respect will not stand before the power of the stones of HUMILITY, PRAYER, and DUTY.

Above all else, may we ever remember that we do not go forth alone to battle against the Goliaths of our lives. As David declared to Israel, so might we echo the knowledge, ". . . the battle is the Lord's, and he will give [Goliath] into our hands." (1 Samuel 17:47.)

But the battle must be fought. Victory cannot come by default. So it is in the battles of life. Life will never spread itself in an unobstructed view before us. We must anticipate the approaching forks and turnings in the road.

However, we cannot hope to reach our desired journey's end if we think aimlessly about whether to go east or west. We must make our decisions purposefully. Our most significant opportunities will be found in times of greatest difficulty.

The vast, uncharted expanse of the Atlantic Ocean stood as a Goliath between Christopher Columbus and the New World. The hearts of his comrades became faint, their courage dimmed, hopelessness engulfed them; but Columbus prevailed with his watchword, "Westward, ever Westward, sail on, sail on."

Carthage jail, an angry mob with painted faces, certain death faced the Prophet Joseph Smith. But from the wellsprings of his abundant faith he calmly met the Goliath of death. "I am going like a lamb to the slaughter; but I am calm as a summer's morning. I have a conscience void of offense toward God, and toward all men."

Gethsemane, Golgotha, intense pain and suffering beyond the comprehension of mortal man stood between Jesus the Master and victory over the grave. Yet he lovingly assured us, "I go to prepare a place for you, . . . that where I am, there ye may be also." (John 14:2-3.)

And what is the significance of these accounts? Had there been no ocean, there would have been no Columbus. No jail, no Joseph. No mob, no martyr. No cross, no Christ!

Should there be a Goliath in our lives, or a giant called by any other name, we need not "flee" or be "sore afraid" as we go up to battle against him. Rather we can find assurance and receive divine help from that inspired psalm of David: "The Lord is my shepherd; I shall not want. . . . Yea, though I walk through the valley of the shadow of death, I will fear no evil: for thou art with me. . . ." (Psalm 23:1, 4.) Victory will be ours.

3

God's gifts to Polynesia's people

ave you ever heard Polynesian people sing? Their voices sound a message of hope, of gratitude, of peace. However, the daily newspaper from distant Tahiti tells of fear, frustration, and conflict. For on the atolls of Muruoa and Fangataufa, thermonuclear testing has begun. Atomic and hydrogen explosions thrust a new dimension upon Polynesia. One native was heard to say, "The kiss of death has been bestowed upon Tahiti, the queen of the islands of the Pacific." Well might we who love these people most ask the perplexing question, "Has paradise caught up with progress, or has progress overtaken paradise?"

But then, the people of Polynesia have survived a variety of threats from a multitude of sources through many periods of time.

When Captain James Cook and his ship's crew of the *Endeavor* first sailed into Matavai Bay in the mid-1700s, they found a literal Polynesian paradise, with fresh water in torrents and flowers and fruit everywhere. They found a people every bit as beautiful as their surroundings. There was food all around them: fish in the lagoons, breadfruit and coconuts in the branches overhead, bananas, yams, and sugar cane growing wild in prolific abundance. For the most part, the people knew no sickness except the gentle decline into old age and death. But then came what has been called the "fatal impact" of European civilization. Firearms, disease, alcohol, an alien code of laws became a threat to the people and their culture, just as the current products of our advanced society pose the threats of today.

But Polynesia remains synonymous with paradise. The word itself, meaning "many islands," is descriptive of the area of Polynesia which covers a major portion of the Pacific Ocean. Geographically, it is bounded roughly by an imaginary triangle drawn from Hawaii southward to New Zealand, thence eastward to Easter Island, and thence back to Hawaii. Here we find major island groups, large volcanic islands, smaller coral atolls, and tiny, uninhabited islets.

Robert Louis Stevenson described the Polynesian sky as "immoderately blue," but for the Polynesians themselves, he reserved the fitting tribute: ". . . the sweetest people God ever made." Polynesians are friendly, loving, handsome, and intelligent people. Their history is exciting, their spoken words like a beautiful melody, their hospitality genuine and their beauty legendary.

Many ask, "Why are these people so bounteously blessed?" "Why do returning missionaries always retain in their hearts a love for the islands and their people?" "Why do Polynesia's people so love the Lord?" The answer is found recorded in sacred scripture: ". . . Know ye not that I, the Lord your God, have created all men, and that I remember those who are upon the isles of the sea. . . . ?" (2 Nephi 29:7.) ". . . great are the promises of the Lord unto them who upon the isles of the sea." (2 Nephi 10:21.)

These promises, these gifts from God, are apparent to those who visit Polynesia. May I invite you to accompany me on a journey to the islands of the Pacific and look in on

Polynesia's people, that we might learn of God's gifts to them. Whether we stop at New Zealand among the Maori, in Samoa, "the heart of the South Seas," Nuku'alofa, Tonga, in the Friendly Islands, at Papeete in Tahiti, or at beautiful Rarotonga, we find people who are recipients of choice and cherished gifts.

Five such gifts are the gift of song, the gift of faith, the gift of love, the gift of obedience, and the gift of gratitude.

First, the gift of SONG:

Polynesians need no formal lessons in music. Their voices are naturally resonant, their ears tuned to melody. A ukulele is as common to a lad there as a jacknife is here. Dancing and song become parts of a way of life.

A few years ago in New Zealand a tragic drowning claimed the lives of two instructors of the Church College at Temple View. The young widows and their children were overcome by grief and heartache. Many well-wishing and sympathetic friends offered words of consolation, but the remorse remained. There came a soft knock at the door; a group of Maori Saints entered the room. Not a word was spoken, but song came forth from their lips and hearts. The bereaved families received a sustaining influence that accompanied them through the lonely and long journey homeward and even today turns tears of sorrow to warm smiles of gratitude. ". . . the song of the righteous is a prayer unto me, [sayeth the Lord,] and it shall be answered with a blessing upon their heads." (D&C 25:12.) The Polynesians have the gift of song.

The gift of FAITH, which they also enjoy, at times takes the form of miraculous healings of body and mind. In other instances it is reflected by simple trust and calm assurance that God will provide.

On my first visit to the fabled village of Sauniatu, so loved by President David O. McKay, my wife and I met with a large gathering of small children. At the conclusion of our messages to these shy, yet beautiful, youngsters, I suggested to the native Samoan teacher that we go forward with the closing exercises. As he announced the final hymn, I suddenly felt compelled to personally great each of these 247 children. My watch revealed the time was too short for such a privilege, so I discounted the impression. Before the benediction was to be spoken, I again felt this strong impression to shake the hand of each child. This time I made the desire known to the instructor, who displayed a broad and beautiful Samoan smile. He spoke in Samoan to the children, and they beamed their approval of his comments.

The instructor then revealed to me the reason for his and their joy. He said, "When we learned that the president of the Church had assigned a member of the Council of the Twelve to visit us in far-away Samoa, I told the children if they would each one earnestly and sincerely pray and exert great faith like the Bible accounts of old, that the apostle would visit our tiny village at Sauniatu, and through their faith, he would be impressed to greet each child with a personal handclasp."

Tears could not be restrained as each of these precious boys and girls walked by shyly and whispered softly to us a sweet "*talofa lava.*" The gift of faith had been evidenced.

The gift of LOVE is found throughout Polynesia. A love of God, a love of sacred things, and love for family, friends, and fellowmen. At Papeete, Tahiti, I met a distinguished yet humble man, extraordinarily blessed with the gift of love. He was eighty-four-year-old Tahauri Hutihuti from the island of Takaroa in the Taumotu island group. A faithful Church member all his life, he had longed for the day when there would be in the Pacific a holy temple of God. He had a love for the sacred ordinances he knew could only be performed in such a house. Patiently, and with purpose, he carefully saved his meager earnings as a pearl diver. When the New Zealand Temple was completed and opened, he took from beneath his bed his life savings of $600, accumulated over a forty-year span; and together with loved ones, he journeyed to the temple and thereby brought a fond dream to final fulfillment.

As I said a tender goodbye to the Tahitians, each one would come forward, place an exquisite shell lei about my neck, and leave an affectionate kiss upon my cheek. Tahauri, who did not speak English, stood by my side and spoke to me through an interpreter. The interpreter listened attentively and then, turning to me, reported: "Tahauri says he has no gift to bestow except the love of a full heart." Tahauri clasped my hand and kissed my cheek. Of all the gifts received that memorable night, the gift of this faithful man remains the brightest.

Allied with the gift of love is the gift of OBEDIENCE. When a Polynesian hears God's prophet speak, he obeys. When he sings, "We thank thee, O God, for a prophet," he sings with his heart, as well as his voice; and the walls resound.

A choice counselor in the Samoa Mission presidency typifies the spirit of obedience. He is handsome in appearance, sincere in his testimony, and responds to each call with seldom-equaled enthusiasm. A convert to the Church, he formerly studied for the ministry of another faith. Intelligent, educated, keen thinking and fearless, his actions demonstrate his love for the newly found truth that is his very life. Since his baptism in 1961, he has taught the gospel to many hundreds of persons and has himself baptized 174 as they have entered the kingdom of God.

Ridiculed by the unbelievers for lifting his voice in testimony, stoned for his teaching of the truth, mocked for his adherence to a rigid code of conduct, he courageously tells others of an apostasy from the Church that followed the death of the Lord and his apostles, and of the restoration of the gospel in this dispensation through the Prophet Joseph Smith.

I asked, "What provides your incentive, your strength to carry on such a missionary crusade amidst such a storm of protest?"

He replied: "Our prophet, God's mouthpiece, has asked that every member be a missionary. My desire is to be obedient to the prophet."

I thought of the words of Samuel: ". . . to obey is better than sacrifice, and to hearken than the fat of rams." (1 Samuel 15:22.) I heard the clarion call of Joshua: ". . . as for me and my house, we will serve the Lord." (Joshua 24:15.) To these people obedience is a gift, and they honor it.

I introduce next the gift of GRATITUDE. Late one evening on a Pacific isle, a small boat slipped silently to its berth at the crude pier. Two Polynesian women helped Meli Mulipola from the boat and guided him to the well-worn pathway leading to the village road. The women marveled at the bright stars which twinkled in the midnight sky. The friendly moonlight guided them along their way. However, Meli Mulipola could not appreciate these delights of nature—the moon, the stars, the sky—for he was blind.

His vision had been normal until that fateful day when, while working on a pineapple plantation, light turned suddenly to darkness and day became perpetual night. He had learned of the restoration of the gospel and teachings of The Church of Jesus Christ of Latter-day Saints. His life had been brought into compliance with these teachings. He and his loved ones had made this long voyage, having learned that one who held the priesthood of God was visiting among the islands. He sought a blessing under the hands of those who held the sacred priesthood. His wish was granted, a blessing provided. Tears streamed from his sightless eyes and coursed down his brown cheeks, tumbling finally upon his native dress. He dropped to his knees and prayed: "Oh God, thou knowest I am blind. Thy servants have blessed me that my sight may return. Whether in thy wisdom I see light or whether I see darkness all the days of my life, I will be eternally grateful for the truth of thy gospel, which I now see and which provides the light of my life."

He arose to his feet, thanked us for providing the blessing, and disappeared into the still of the night. Silently he came. Silently he departed. But his presence I shall never forget. I reflected upon the message of the Master: "I am the light of the world: he that followeth me shall not walk in darkness, but shall have the light of life." (John 8:12.)

There came to me an appreciation of these gifts of God to Polynesia's people: the gift of song, the gift of faith, the gift of love, the gift of obedience, and the gift of gratitude. But such gifts were suddenly dwarfed as I remembered God's greatest gift, given not only to the Polynesians, but to you, to me and to all persons everywhere—the gift of his Only Begotten and precious Son, Jesus Christ.

We may never open gates of cities or doors of palaces, but we will find true happiness and lasting joy when there enters our heart and soul a knowledge and understanding of this supreme gift. He may come to us as one unknown, without a name, as of old, by the lakeside, he came to those men who knew him not. He speaks to us the same words, "Follow thou me," and sets us to the tasks which he has to fulfill for our time. He commands, and to those who obey him, whether they be wise or simple, he will reveal himself in the toils, the conflicts, the sufferings that they shall pass through in his fellowship; and they shall learn in their own experience who he is.

Like a bright searchlight of truth, his gospel will direct

our journey along the pathways of life. Oh, how blessed are we to have this never-dimming, always-glowing hope and the eternal knowledge that belongs to us and that we share with the world, that the gospel has been restored to earth, that God lives, that Jesus is his Son, our Elder Brother, our mediator with the Father, our Lord and our Savior, God's greatest gift to us.

4

Our trust in the Lord

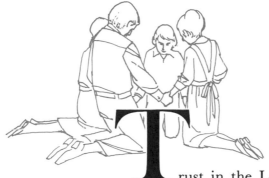

Trust in the Lord with all thine heart; and lean not unto thine own understanding. In all thy ways acknowledge him, and he shall direct thy paths." (Proverbs 3:5-6.) So spoke the wise Solomon, the son of David, King of Israel.

On this, the American continent, Jacob, the brother of Nephi, declared: "Look unto God with firmness of mind, and pray unto him with exceeding faith. . . ." (Jacob 3:1.)

In this dispensation, in a revelation given to the Prophet Joseph Smith, the Lord said, "Look unto me in every thought; doubt not, fear not." (D&C 6:36.)

This divinely inspired counsel comes to us today as crystal-clear water to a parched earth.

We live in troubled times. Doctors' offices throughout the land are filled with individuals who are beset with emotional problems, as well as physical distress. Our divorce courts are doing a land-office business because people have unsolved problems. Personnel workers and grievance committees in modern industry work long hours in an effort to assist people with their problems.

One personnel officer, assigned to handle petty grievances, concluded an unusually hectic day by placing facetiously a little sign on his desk for those with unsolved

25

problems to read. It read, "Have you tried prayer?" What that personnel director did not know when he placed such a sign upon his desk was that he was providing counsel and direction that would solve more problems, alleviate more suffering, prevent more transgression, and bring about greater peace and contentment in the human soul than could be obtained in any other way.

A prominent American judge was asked what we, as citizens of the countries of the world, could do to reduce crime and disobedience to law and to bring peace and contentment into our lives and into our nations. He carefully replied, "I would suggest a return to the old-fashioned practice of family prayer."

As a people, aren't we grateful that family prayer is not an out-of-date practice with us? There is no more beautiful sight in all this world than to see a family praying together. There is real meaning behind the oft-quoted adage: "The family that prays together stays together."

The Lord directed that we have family prayer when he said: "Pray in your families unto the Father, always in my name, that your wives and your children may be blessed." (3 Nephi 18:21.)

Will you join me as we look in on a typical Latter-day Saint family offering prayers unto the Lord? Father, mother, and each of the children kneel, bow their heads, and close their eyes. A sweet spirit of love, unity, and peace fills the home. As father hears his tiny son pray unto God that his dad will do the right things and be obedient to the Lord's bidding, do you think that such a father would find it difficult to honor the prayer of his precious son? As a teenage daughter hears her sweet mother plead unto the Lord that her daughter will be inspired in the selection of her companions, that she will prepare herself for a temple marriage, don't you believe that such a daughter will seek to honor this humble, pleading petition of her mother whom she so dearly loves? When father, mother, and each of the children earnestly pray that these fine sons in the family will live worthy that they may in due time receive a call to serve as ambassadors of the Lord in the mission fields of the Church, don't we begin to see how such sons grow to young manhood with an overwhelming desire to serve as missionaries?

As we offer unto the Lord our family and our personal prayers, let us do so with faith and trust in him. Let us remember the injunction of Paul to the Hebrews: ". . . for he that cometh to God must believe that he is, and that he is a rewarder of them that diligently seek him." (Hebrews 11:6.) If any of us have been slow to hearken to the counsel to pray always, there is no finer hour to begin than now. William Cowper declared, "Satan trembles when he sees the weakest saint upon his knees." Those who feel that prayer might denote a physical weakness should remember that a man never stands taller than when he is upon his knees. We cannot know what faith is if we have never had it, and we cannot obtain it as long as we deny it.

If our desire is to discard all doubt and to substitute, therefore, an abiding faith, we have but to accept the invitation extended to you and to me in the Epistle of James: "If any of you lack wisdom, let him ask of God, that giveth to all men liberally, and upbraideth not; and it shall be given him. But let him ask in faith, nothing wavering. For he that wavereth is like a wave of the sea driven with the wind and tossed." (James 1:5-6.) This promise motivated the young man, Joseph Smith, to seek God in prayer. He declared to us in his own words:

At length I came to the conclusion that . . . I must do as James directs, that is, ask of God. I at length came to the determination to ask of God, concluding that if he gave wisdom to them that lacked wisdom, and would give liberally, and not upbraid, I might venture.

So, in accordance with this, my determination to ask of God, I retired to the woods to make the attempt. . . . It was the first time in my life that I had made such an attempt, for amidst all my anxieties I had never as yet made the attempt to pray vocally. (Joseph Smith 2:13-14.)

Now, if we have hesitated in supplicating God, our Eternal Father, simply because we have not as yet made the attempt to pray, we certainly can take courage from the example of the Prophet Joseph. But let us remember, as did the Prophet, that our prayer must be offered in faith, nothing wavering.

It was by faith, nothing wavering, that the brother of Jared saw the finger of God as He touched the stones in response to his plea.

It was by faith, nothing wavering, that Noah erected an ark in obedience to the command from God.

It was by faith, nothing wavering, that Abraham was willing to offer up his beloved Isaac as a sacrifice.

It was by faith, nothing wavering, that Moses led the children of Israel out of Egypt and through the Red Sea.

It was by faith, nothing wavering, that Joshua and his followers brought the walls of Jericho tumbling down.

It was by faith, nothing wavering, that Joseph saw God, our Eternal Father, and Jesus Christ, his Son.

Now, the skeptic may say that these mighty accounts of faith occurred long ago—that times have changed.

Have times really changed? Don't we today, as always, love our children and want them to live righteously? Don't we today, as always, need God's divine, protecting care? Don't we today, as always, continue to be at his mercy and in his debt for the very life he has given us?

Times have not really changed. Prayer continues to provide power—spiritual power. Prayer continues to provide peace—spiritual peace.

Wherever we may be, our Heavenly Father can hear and answer the prayer offered in faith. This is especially true in the mission fields throughout the world. While presiding over the Canadian Mission, Sister Monson and I had the opportunity of serving with the finest young men and women in all this world. Their very lives exemplified faith and prayer.

There sat in my office one day a newly arrived missionary. He was bright, strong, filled with enthusiasm and a desire to serve, happy and grateful to be a missionary. As I spoke with him, I said, "Elder, I imagine that your father and mother wholeheartedly support you in your mission call." He lowered his head and replied, "Well, not quite. You see, president, my father is not a member of the Church. He doesn't believe as we believe, so he cannot fully appreciate the importance of my assignment." Without hesitating, and prompted by a source—not my own—I said to him, "Elder, if you will honestly and diligently serve God in proclaiming his message, your father will join the Church before your mission is concluded." He clasped my hand in a vice-like grip; the tears welled up in his eyes and began to roll forth down his cheeks, and he declared, "To see my father accept the truth would be the greatest blessing that could come into my life."

This missionary did not sit idly by hoping and wishing that the promise would be fulfilled; but, rather, he followed the example of Abraham Lincoln, of whom it has been said, "When he prayed, he prayed as though everything depended upon God, and then he worked as though everything depended upon himself." Such was the missionary service of this young man.

At every missionary conference I would seek him out before the meetings would ever commence and ask, "Elder, how's dad progressing?" His reply would invariably be, "No progress, president, but I know the Lord will fulfill the promise given to me through you as my mission president." The days turned to weeks and the weeks to months, and finally, just two weeks before we ourselves left the mission field to return home, I received the following letter from the father of this missionary:

Dear Brother Monson:

I wish to thank you so much for taking such good care of my son who recently completed a mission in Canada. He has been an inspiration to us.

My son was promised when he left on his mission that I would become a member of the Church before he returned. This promise was, I believe, made to him by you, unknown to me.

I am happy to report that I was baptized into the Church one week before he completed his mission and am at the present time athletic director of the MIA and have a teaching assignment.

My son is now attending BYU and his younger brother was also recently baptized and confirmed a member of the Church.

May I again thank you for all the kindness and love bestowed upon my son by his brothers in the mission field during the past two years.

Yours very truly,
A grateful father

The humble prayer of faith had once again been answered.

There is a golden thread that runs through every account of faith from the beginning of the world to the present time. Abraham, Noah, the brother of Jared, the Prophet Joseph, and countless others wanted to be obedient to the will of God. They had ears that could hear, eyes that could see, and hearts that could know and feel.

They never doubted. They trusted.

Through personal prayer, through family prayer, by trusting in God with faith, nothing wavering, we can call down to our rescue his mighty power. His call to us is as it has ever been, "Come unto me."

5

In search of truth

ast fall I heard a school-bell ring. I saw scores of boys and girls of every age hurry and scurry to the classrooms of learning. They were in search of truth. It was the season of the year, too, when the colleges and universities throughout the land opened wide their doors, that eager students might continue this search for truth. Their teachers, and scientists of all fields, pursue their constant labor of studying, experimenting—ever continuing this same search.

Is the search for truth really this important? Is it so vital? Must it span the ages of time, encompass every field of endeavor, and penetrate every human heart? Fortunately, there is a natural feeling which urges men and women toward truth. It is a responsibility placed upon mankind.

Even the law of the land jealously safeguards the principle of truth. In our courts of law, before a witness takes the stand to testify, he is placed under solemn oath: ". . . the testimony you are about to give . . . is the truth, the whole truth, and nothing but the truth. . . ."

The poet captured the real significance of the search for truth when he wrote these immortal lines:

In search of truth

Oh say, what is truth? 'Tis the brightest prize
To which mortals or Gods can aspire;
Go search in the depths where it glittering lies,
Or ascend in pursuit to the loftiest skies.
'Tis an aim for the noblest desire.

Then say, what is truth? 'Tis the last and the first,
For the limits of time it steps o'er.
Though the heavens depart and the earth's fountains burst,
Truth, the sum of existence, will weather the worst,
Eternal, unchanged, evermore.

—JOHN JACQUES

The Prophet Joseph Smith received the definition of truth in a revelation from the Lord at Kirtland, Ohio, May 6, 1833: ". . . truth is knowledge of things as they are, and as they were, and as they are to come." (D&C 93:24.)

Thousands of honest, searching souls continue to be confronted by that penetrating question which coursed through the mind of Joseph Smith as he surveyed the declarations made by the churches of his community concerning who was right and who was wrong. Joseph said: "In the midst of this war of words and tumult of opinions, I often said to myself: . . . Who of all these parties are right. . . ? If any one of them be right, which is it, and how shall I know it? . . . I at length came to the determination to ask of God." (Joseph Smith 2:10, 13.)

He prayed. The results of that prayer are best described in Joseph's own words: ". . . I saw two Personages, whose brightness and glory defy all description, standing above me in the air. One of them spake unto me, calling me by name and said, pointing to the other—*This is My Beloved Son. Hear Him!*" Joseph listened. Joseph learned. His question, "What is truth?" was answered.

Perhaps one of the most significant exchanges of question and answer occurred when Jesus was taken before

Pilate. Pilate asked the Master, "Art thou a king. . . ?"
Jesus answered, "Thou sayest that I am a king. To this end
was I born, and for this cause came I into the world, that
I should bear witness unto the truth. Every one that is of
the truth heareth my voice." (John 18:37.)

Is the voice of the Lord heard today? How does it
come to man? Can your search for truth be guided by his
voice? Can mine? Today, as always, when the true church
of Christ is on the earth, there stands at its head a prophet.
And just as the voice of the Lord came to Jeremiah, Ezekiel, and Isaiah, it has likewise come to latter-day prophets.

"Surely the Lord God will do nothing, but he re-
vealeth his secret unto his servants the prophets." (Amos
3:7.)

Do we need a prophet today? Does God regard his
children today as dearly as he did when Amos, Jeremiah,
and Ezekiel were on the earth? One of the foremost educa-
tors in America, Dr. Robert Gordon Sproul, describes the
need in these words:

We have the peculiar spectacle of a nation, which to a limited
extent practices Christianity without actively believing in Christianity.
We are asked to turn to the church for enlightenment, but when we do,
we find that the voice of the church is not inspired. The voice of the
church today is the echo of our own voices. And the result of this experience already manifest is disillusionment. The way out is the sound
of a voice, not our voice, but a voice coming from somewhere not ourselves in the existence of which we cannot disbelieve. It is the task of
the pastors to hear this voice, cause us to hear it, and tell us what it
says. If they cannot hear it, or if they fail to tell us what it says, we as
laymen are wholly lost. Without it we are no more capable of saving
the earth than we were capable of creating it in the first place.

From still another field of endeavor, Sir Winston
Churchill described the need:

I have lived perhaps longer experience than almost anyone, and
I have never brooded over a situation which demanded more patience,
composure, courage and perseverance than that which unfolds itself
before us today. The need of a prophet.

How grateful we should be that revelation, the clear and uncluttered channel of truth, is still open. Our Heavenly Father continues to inspire his prophets. This inspiration can serve as a sure guide in making life's decisions. It will lead us to truth.

You do not find truth groveling through error. Truth is found by searching, studying, and living the revealed word of God. We learn truth when we associate with truth. We adopt error when we mingle with error.

Some time ago I attended a large youth conference at Edmonton, Alberta, Canada. A part of the conference was a testimony meeting where the young men and young women could express the feelings of the heart.

A shy boy from Saskatchewan, standing before such an imposing audience for the first time, said, "Before I attended this youth conference, I could say, 'I think the gospel is true.' Then I received instruction, participated in the activities, and felt of the spirit of all of you. Today at the conclusion of these inspired events, I proudly, yet humbly, declare: 'I know the gospel is true.' " He had been edified. He had been enlightened. He had found the truth.

In July 1964, I visited the World's Fair at New York City. I found the fair most interesting and took special note of the religious exhibits. At the Mormon Pavilion I sat by an alert young man of perhaps thirty-five years. We spoke about the other exhibits at the fair. Then the lights dimmed. The film *Man's Search for Happiness* commenced. At the conclusion of this portrayal of the plan of salvation, the lights again brought the present to our view. Silently the crowd filed out, some stopping to wipe a tear from a moist eye. Others were visibly impressed. My visitor did not arise. I asked if he enjoyed the film. He answered, "This is the truth." One man's search for truth had just ended.

To those who humbly seek, there is no need to

stumble or falter along the pathway leading to truth. It is well marked by our Heavenly Father. We must first have a desire to know for ourselves. We must study; we must pray. We must do the will of the Father. And then we will know the truth and the truth shall make us free. Divine favor will attend those who humbly seek it.

A few years ago I was privileged to set apart William Agnew for his mission. I reviewed with him his conversion and that of his family some five years before in eastern Canada. The family had been seeking truth. The missionaries called and presented the teachings of the gospel. The family studied. They loved what they learned. They were approaching the decision to be baptized. One Sunday morning, by previous appointment, they were preparing to attend the Mormon Sunday School. Mother and the children readied themselves but were disappointed when Dad concluded not to attend. They even argued somewhat about the decision. Then mother and the children went to Sunday School and Dad angrily stayed at home. He first attempted to forget the misunderstanding by reading the newspaper, but to no avail. Then he went to his daughter Isabel's room and turned on the radio on her nightstand, hoping to hear the news. He didn't hear the news. Rather, he heard the Tabernacle Choir. Elder Richard L. Evans' message, it seemed, was directed personally to him. The theme was "Let not the sun go down on thy wrath." Brother Agnew realized the futility of his anger. He was now over-powered by a feeling of gratitude for the message he had just received.

When his wife and family returned home, they found him pleasant and happy. His children asked how this change came about. He told them how he had turned to the radio, hoping to get the news, only to be humbled by the message of the choir in word and song. His daughter said, "Which radio did you use, Dad?" He answered, "The one on your nightstand." She replied, "That radio is broken. It hasn't played for weeks." He led them to the room to prove that this radio did indeed function. He turned the proper dial. But that radio didn't play. Yet, when an honest seeker after truth needed the help of God, that radio did play. The message which led to conversion was received. Needless to say, the family became stalwart members of the Church.

There will be those who doubt, who scoff, who ridicule, who scorn. They will turn from the pathway leading to eternal truth and rather travel the slippery slopes of error and disillusionment.

But to those who honestly seek, those to whom so much has been given, to the faithful, the Lord, our God, has promised: ". . . they that are wise and have received the truth, and have taken the Holy Spirit for their guide, and have not been deceived—verily I say unto you, they . . . shall abide the day." (D&C 45:57.)

6

"Come, follow me"

To the east and a little south from the Tabernacle on Temple Square, marking the entrance to the valley of the Great Salt Lake, standing as a sentinel pointing the way, is located "This Is the Place" monument. Here we see featured Brigham Young—his back turned to the privations, hardships, and struggles of the long desert way, his outstretched arm pointing to the valley of precious promise.

Miles that once took months are now traveled in minutes. The many hundreds of thousands of visitors who each year pause at the monument tingle with the spirit of pioneer tradition. Such tradition reaches its high point on Pioneer Day, July 24th of each year. A grateful posterity sets aside the busy cares of our fast-moving world and reflects for a moment on the everlasting principles which helped to guide those noble pioneers to their promised land.

That first trek of 1847, organized and led by Brigham Young, is described by historians as one of the great epics of United States history. Mormon pioneers by the hundreds suffered and died from disease, exposure, or starvation. There were some who, lacking wagons and teams, literally walked the 1300 miles across the plains and through the mountains, pushing and pulling handcarts. In these groups, one in six perished.

For many, the journey didn't begin at Nauvoo, Kirtland, Far West, or New York, but rather in distant England, Scotland, Scandinavia, and Germany. Tiny children could not fully comprehend nor understand the dynamic faith which motivated their parents to leave behind family, friends, comfort, and security. A little one might inquiringly ask, "Mommy, why are we leaving home? Where are we going?"

"Come along, precious one; we're going to Zion, the city of our God."

Between the safety of home and the promise of Zion stood the angry and treacherous waters of the mighty Atlantic. Who can recount the fear that gripped the human heart during those perilous crossings? Prompted by the silent whisperings of the Spirit, sustained by a simple, yet abiding faith, they trusted in their God and set sail on their journey. Europe was behind, America ahead.

On board one of those overcrowded and creaking vessels of yesteryear were my great-grandparents, their tiny family, and a few meager possessions. The waves were high, the voyage long, the quarters cramped. Tiny Mary had always been frail, but now with the passage of each day, her anxious mother knew the little one was becoming especially weak. She had taken seriously ill. No neighborhood drugstore. No doctor's prescription. No modern hospital. Just the steady roll of the tired old ship. Day after day worried parents peered for land, but there was no land. Now Mary could not stand. Lips that were too weak to speak just trembled with silent but eloquently expressed wonderment and fear. The end drew near. Little Mary peacefully passed beyond this veil of tears.

As the family and friends crowded around on the open deck, the ship's captain directed the service; and that precious, ever-so-small body, placed tenderly in a tear-stained canvas, was committed to the angry sea. Strong father, in emotion-choked tones, comforted grieving mother, repeating, " 'The Lord gave, and the Lord hath taken away; blessed be the name of the Lord.' [Job 1:21.] We'll see our Mary again!"

Such scenes were not uncommon. Tombstones of sage and rock marked tiny graves the entire route from Nauvoo to Salt Lake City. Such was the price some pioneers paid. Their bodies are buried in peace, but their names live on evermore.

Tired oxen lumbered, wagon wheels squeaked, brave men toiled, Indian war drums sounded, and coyotes howled. Our faith-inspired and storm-driven ancestors pressed on. They, too, had their cloud by day and pillar of fire by night.

Often they sang:

> *Come, come ye Saints, no toil nor labor fear;*
> *But with joy wend your way.*
> *Though hard to you this journey may appear,*
> *Grace shall be as your day. . . .*
> *All is well. All is well.*
>
> —WILLIAM CLAYTON

These pioneers remembered the words of the Lord: "My people must be tried in all things, that they may be prepared to receive the glory that I have for them, even the glory of Zion. . . ." (D&C 136:31.)

As the long, painful struggle approached its welcomed end, a jubilant spirit filled each heart. Tired feet and weary bodies somehow found new strength.

Time-marked pages of a dusty pioneer journal speak movingly to us: "We bowed ourselves down in humble prayer to Almighty God with hearts full of thanksgiving to

Him, and dedicated this land unto Him for the dwelling place of His people."

The crude homes were described by a small boy in these terms: "There was no window of any kind whatever in our house. Neither was there a door. My mother hung up an old quilt, which served as a door for the first winter. This was our bedroom, our parlor, our sitting room, our kitchen, our sleeping room, everything in this room of about 12 x 16 feet. How in the world we all got along in it I do not know. I recollect that my dear old mother stated that no queen who ever entered her palace was ever more happy or proud of shelter and the blessings of the Lord than was she when she entered that completed dugout."

Such were the trials, the hardships, struggles, and heartaches of a former day. They were met with resolute courage and an abiding faith in a living God. The words of their prophet leader provided their pledge: "And this shall be our covenant—that we will walk in all the ordinances of the Lord." (D&C 136:4.)

The passage of time dims our memories and diminishes our appreciation for those who walked the path of pain, leaving behind a tear-marked trail of nameless graves. But what of today's challenge? Are there no rocky roads to travel, no rugged mountains to climb, chasms to cross, trails to blaze, or rivers to ford? Or is there a very present need for that pioneer spirit to guide us away from the dangers that threaten to engulf us and lead us rather to a Zion of safety?

In the nearly three decades since the end of World War II standards of morality have lowered and lowered. Today we have more people in jail, in reformatories, on probation, and in trouble than ever before. From the padded expense account to grand larceny, from petty crimes to crimes of passion, the figures are higher than ever and going higher. Crime spirals upward! Decency careens downward! Many are on a giant roller coaster of disaster, seeking the thrills of the moment while sacrificing the joys of eternity. We conquer space but cannot control self. Thus we forfeit peace.

Can we somehow muster the courage, that steadfastness of purpose, which characterized the pioneers of a former generation? Can you and I, in actual fact, be pioneers today? The dictionary defines a pioneer as "one who goes before, showing others the way to follow." Oh, how the world needs such pioneers today!

We forget how the Greeks and Romans prevailed magnificently in a barbaric world and how that triumph ended, how a slackness and softness finally came over them to their ruin. In the end, more than they wanted freedom, they wanted security, a comfortable life; and they lost all—security and comfort and freedom. From the confusion of our modern world, sincere persons searchingly ask themselves: "To whom shall we listen? Whom shall we follow? Whom shall we serve?"

Today chronic strife even permeates the personal province of the Prince of Peace. Contention thrives where taught he who declared, ". . . contention is not of me, but is of the devil. . . ." (3 Nephi 11:29.) However, when we have ears that truly hear, we will be mindful of the echo from Capernaum's past. Here multitudes crowded around Jesus, bringing the sick to be healed; a palsied man picked up his bed and walked, and a Roman centurion's faith restored his servant's health.

Many turn away from our Elder Brother, who said, "I am the way, the truth, and the life" (John 14:6), and rather follow blindly after that Pied Piper of sin who would lead us down the slippery slopes to our own destruction. He cunningly calls to troubled youth in truly tempting tones.

Do not yield to his enticements; rather, stand firm for truth.

The unsatisfied yearnings of the soul will not be met

by a never-ending quest for joy midst the thrills of sensation and vice. Vice never leads to virtue. Hate never points to love. Cowardice never reflects courage. Doubt never inspires faith.

It is not difficult to withstand the mockings and unsavory remarks of foolish ones who would ridicule chastity, honesty, and obedience to God's commands. The world has ever belittled adherence to principle. Times change. Practices persist. When Noah was instructed to build an ark, the foolish populace looked at the cloudless sky, then scoffed and jeered—until the rain came.

On the American continent, those long centuries ago, people doubted, disputed, and disobeyed until the fire consumed Zarahemla, the earth covered Moronihah, and water engulfed Moroni. Jeering, mocking, ribaldry, and sin were no more. They had been replaced by sullen silence, dense darkness. The patience of God had expired, his timetable fulfilled.

Must we learn such costly lessons over and over again? When we fail to profit from the experiences of the past, we are doomed to repeat them with all their heartache, suffering, and anguish. Haven't we the wisdom to obey him who knows the beginning from the end—our Lord, who designed the plan of salvation, rather than that serpent who despised its beauty?

In the words of the poet, "Wouldst thou be gathered to Christ's chosen flock,/Shun the broad way too easily explored,/And let thy path be hewn out of the rock,/The living rock of God's eternal word." (William Wordsworth, Inscription on a Rock at Rydal Mount.)

Can we not follow the Prince of Peace, that pioneer who literally showed the way for others to follow? His divine plan can save us from the Babylons of sin, complacency, and error. His example points the way. When faced with temptation, he shunned it. When offered the world, he

42

declined it. When asked for his life, he gave it!

> *"Come, follow me," the Savior said,*
> *Then let us in his footsteps tread,*
> *For thus alone can we be one,*
> *With God's own loved, begotten Son.*
>
> *For thrones, dominions, kingdoms, powers,*
> *And glory great and bliss are ours*
> *If we throughout eternity,*
> *Obey his words, "Come, follow me."*
>
> —JOHN NICHOLSON

Now is the time. This is the place. Let us follow him.

7

The key of faith

A few years ago it was my good fortune to respond to a call to serve as a member of the Priesthood Genealogy Committee and to have the privilege of visiting stakes and missions, speaking to the membership of the Church relative to this sacred subject—one that is perhaps the most misunderstood among all of the programs of the Church.

Our chief responsibility at that time was to convince the members that they need not be specialists, they need not be in their eighties, they need not be exclusively genealogists in order to understand the responsibility that rests upon each member of the Church to seek out his kindred dead and to perform the work that must necessarily be accomplished in their behalf.

I believe there is and has been a feeling that genealogy is for a select few and not for the general membership of the Church. I know that out of the series of conferences we held then, one of the great measures of good was the development of family organizations. Throughout the Church we have an increasing awareness of the responsibility one has toward his family members.

Since I have a mixed genealogy (part of my ancestry coming from Sweden, with the great problems of patronym-

ics, and others of my ancestry coming from Scotland and
England), I feel I have inherited all of the problems and all
of the challenges of one who must seek after his kindred
dead.

Just to give you who are not Scandinavian an insight
into some of our problems, my grandfather's name was
Nels Monson; his father's name was not Monson at all, it was
Mons Okeson; and his father's name was Oke Pederson;
and his father's name was Peter Monson—right back to
Monson again—and his father's name was Mons Lustig,
which was a Swedish army name to differentiate the Peter-
sons, the Johnsons, and the Monsons from one another as
they entered military service.

Yet I am amazed at the record of achievement of our
family association in our family line, and similarly on the
lines that my mother's forebears gave to us—the Condie
and the Watson lines.

To me it is particularly significant that I have had the
opportunity to have walked where my forebears walked,
where they worked, where they prayed, where they studied
the gospel, and where they embraced the truth. I felt that
I was on sacred ground.

It was Sister Monson's and my opportunity to visit the
land of Sweden and there to go to a little country village of
Smedjebacken where her father, his eleven brothers and
sisters, and his mother and father lived in a little two-room
farmhouse. And then to think that it was my privilege to
have a great-uncle who took the gospel to this choice family! I recreated in my own mind the experience those missionaries must have had—sitting before the open fire, eating
food to which they were unaccustomed; greeting people
who were friendly, but perhaps a little suspicious; and then
praying together, that the light of heaven might bless their
mutual understanding and that conversion to the gospel

of Christ might be the result. I thanked our Heavenly Father for his divine help.

The mission president in Sweden at the time of our visit was a cousin to my wife, President Reid H. Johnson. As he and our group were journeying throughout that area, we went to a large Lutheran church. As we walked into the building, President Johnson said, "I think you would be interested in an experience my companion, Donald Timpson, and I had in this city, Granjarde, at the termination of our missions back in 1949."

He said, "We came to this town because we knew that our family history was steeped here and had been lived here. As we entered this large church, we were met by a most apprehensive keeper of the archives. Upon hearing that we had completed our missions and had a few precious days in which we would like to seek out the records that he maintained in his church building, he said that no one had ever been given the opportunity to peruse those valuable records, far less a Mormon. He declared they were under lock and key, and he held up to view the large key to the vault in which the records were stored. He said, 'My job and my future, and the sustenance of my family, depend upon how well I safeguard this key. No, I am afraid it would be impossible for you to peruse these records. But if you would like to see the church, I'll be happy to show you through. I'll be pleased to show you the architecture and the cemetery which surrounds the church, but not the records, for they are sacred.'"

President Johnson indicated they were stunned and their hopes had vanished into thin air. He said to the keeper of the archives, "We will accept your kind offer." All of this time he and his companion were praying fervently and earnestly that somehow something would change this keeper's mind, that he would let them view the records.

After a lengthy journey through the cemetery and looking at the church building, the keeper of the archives said to them, "I'm going to do something I have never done before. It may cost me my job, but I'm going to let you borrow this key for fifteen minutes."

President Johnson thought, "Fifteen minutes! All we can do in fifteen minutes is open the lock!"

But he let them take the key. They turned the key, thereby opening the lock, and had made available to their view records that were priceless for their genealogical value. Fifteen minutes later the keeper arrived. He looked at them and found they were still in a state of Christmas wonder over the find they had discovered.

They said, "Can't we stay longer?"

He said, "How much longer?" And he looked at his watch.

They responded, "About three days."

He said, "I've never done anything like this before. I don't know why, but I feel I can trust you. Here is the key; you keep it, and when you are through, return it to me. I'll be here every morning at eight o'clock and every evening at five o'clock."

For three consecutive days those two missionaries literally studied and recorded for our current use information that could have been obtained in no other way. President Johnson filled with emotion as he explained this experience to us. He said, "The Lord does move in a mysterious way, his wonders to perform." As he made this statement of testimony to me, I realized that this was a blessing that had come to me and my wife, because this happened to be our family lines.

I thought of that key that the keeper of the archives gave to those two missionaries. While it opened the lock which revealed and released to their information the names they needed, there is a greater key—a key that each one of us earnestly seeks to obtain and that will open the locks to the treasure houses of the knowledge we desire to acquire. That key is the *key of faith*. In this work, no lock will open without it.

I testify that when we do all we can to accomplish the work that is before us, the Lord will make available to us that sacred key to unlock the treasure which we so much seek. (See Ether 12:6-22.)

President Hugh B. Brown declared to a group of us when the Priesthood Genealogy Committee was first organized that missionary work is going forward in the spirit world at an accelerated pace, compared to how it is going forward in our earthly existence. Then he quoted the statement of President Joseph F. Smith, to the effect that all those who have not had an opportunity in mortality to hear the everlasting gospel are hearing it now. President Smith declared:

This gospel revealed to the Prophet Joseph is already being preached to the spirits in prison, to those who have passed away from this stage of action into the spirit world without the knowledge of the gospel. Joseph Smith is preaching that gospel to them. So is Hyrum Smith. So is Brigham Young, and so are all the faithful apostles that lived in this dispensation under the administration of the Prophet Joseph. (*Gospel Doctrine*, p. 471.)

And as President Smith indicated in 1916:

Through our efforts in their behalf their chains of bondage will fall from them, and the darkness surrounding them will clear away, that light may shine upon them and they shall hear in the spirit world of the work that has been done for them by their children here, and will rejoice with you in your performance of these duties. (*Gospel Doctrine*, pp. 469-70.)

I like that word *duty*. He did not say "rejoice with you in the fulfillment of an *assignment*, in response to a *calling*." He said, ". . . in the performance of your *duty*."

The person who is working on his genealogy fits that description of one who is fulfilling his duty. I know the effort, I know the expense, I know the difficulties through which one may go to uncover one name. I know our Heavenly Father is aware of these efforts. And those for whom we perform these sacred ordinances are aware of our efforts. Oftentimes, in a miraculous way, there shall appear before us a clear pathway through a field of turbulence.

I remember so well the secretary of our genealogy committee of one of our fine districts in Canada. How she labored in her assignment! This dear woman was responsible for much of the genealogical research that had been done in her area of Canada. But she had come to an iron wall, to a curtain she could not penetrate. She went to her Heavenly Father and poured out her soul to him and literally made a plea that somehow he would intervene, somehow the way would be opened. Without waiting for a specific answer, she continued her research.

One day she was traveling down the main street of Belleville, Ontario, and came to an old bookstore. She felt compelled to enter the bookstore, and when she did, the clerk said, "May I help you?"

She replied, "No, I'm just browsing around." Her eye caught a two-volume set on the top shelf and she knew she had to see those books. She said to the clerk, "What are the names of those two volumes?"

He replied, "I'll have to see; I haven't looked lately."

With the aid of a ladder, he withdrew the two volumes and read their titles: *Pioneer Life on the Bay of Quinte, Volumes 1 and 2*. She then turned to the first page, the second, and the third. Those two volumes contained nothing but genealogy from the first page to the last. One volume supplied that key which opened the lock to the mystery which had frustrated her work.

She was elated, so she asked the price. Then her elation turned to doubt. "Two hundred dollars for the two rare volumes," said the clerk. Well, I am proud to say that the quorum of elders in that district purchased those two volumes after their worth had been verified. The books were sent to the genealogical archives in Salt Lake City, and I am told that they also provided some of the missing keys to the research of President Henry D. Moyle, for some of his forebears had come from the Bay of Quinte, near Belleville, Ontario. A great blessing had been realized because a dear woman with "faith, nothing wavering" had performed her duty.

The oft-quoted epistle of James was not meant exclusively for investigators. It was meant for you and for me as well:

> If any of you lack wisdom, let him ask of God, that giveth to all men liberally, and upbraideth not; and it shall be given him. But let him ask in faith, nothing wavering. For he that wavereth is like a wave on the sea driven with the wind and tossed. (James 1:5-6.)

Should any Latter-day Saint encounter obstacles, may I plead with him to follow her worthy example, to seek the companionship of the Holy Spirit to guide him in the solution of the problem he faces. I testify that the Spirit will come, the way will be opened, and the key will be provided. Let us not think that all of these keys and all of this inspiration are going to remain confined to one group.

Let us not think the Lord looks only upon English and Scottish genealogy and ignores some of the less-known nations and family lines. One of the great missions of the Church is the Tonga Mission. I do not know how much you know about the islands of Tonga. It is a kingdom. It has a great king, great in size and great in that which he accomplishes. He stands 6 feet 2 inches and weighs 325 pounds. This gives you an idea of the size of the Tongan people. They have never been subjugated. They are a powerful people. They are a prayerful people. When they accept the gospel they love it and they live it. This mission is making significant accomplishments.

The key of faith

The Tonga Mission was presided over by John H. Groberg, a man who lives close to God. On one occasion he went down to the docks to welcome home the forty members of the Church who had just returned from the New Zealand Temple. They had sacrificed all they had to go to the temple, and that is considerable for those poor people. For years they had lived under modest circumstances to save the money, that they might go and receive their own endowments and their sealing blessings.

As they returned, they expected President Groberg to greet them with enthusiasm and to commend them for their journey. He said to me, "I didn't feel that impression; rather, I felt to chastise them a little."

As they landed and were all smiles, they said, "What do you think of our accomplishments, President Groberg?"

He responded, "I think they are many. You have journeyed long and have endured much, and you have contributed greatly to the happiness of those for whom you officiated. But how many were Tongan names? How many were your ancestors?"

As he spoke to them so beautifully and so fluently in Tongan, the people admitted that other than their own endowments and maybe one or two family names, the ordinance work they had performed in the New Zealand Temple was the same ordinance work you and I could perform in the Salt Lake Temple, or in the Logan Temple, or in the Manti Temple. A vision of eternity came to their view as President Groberg spoke to them for a full hour about their responsibility to their own kindred dead.

This experience has prompted such an active interest in genealogy in the Tongan Islands that when I was there last, I saw some of the finest genealogy committees I have ever seen. I saw men from district councils step to chalkboards and trace family group lines and point out pedigree information better than I have seen in many of the large stakes of Zion. These people have literally caught the spirit, and now when they go to the New Zealand Temple, not one Caucasian name goes with them—all Tongan names, much to the consternation of the temple president, who cannot pronounce them, but to the glory of God, and to the glory of those people who have waited so long.

I am a man of simple faith. I do not believe that John Groberg in and of himself received this inspiration. I testify that this inspiration came as a result of the pleadings of those who have waited long and have yearned to be "loosed from the chains which hold them captive," as President Joseph Fielding Smith has said; who have remained in darkness, but who now desire to see the light of heaven shine upon them, that they may go forward to their exaltation.

Oh, my brothers and sisters, do not be weary in well-doing. If we feel that our contribution is small or insignificant, remember that the worth of souls is precious in the sight of God.

Our opportunity is to prepare the way and to accomplish the ordinance work, after faithful research, that these souls may prepare for the glory which is their divine opportunity. Is it any wonder, then, that when one has received a testimony of this work, he desires to give so much to its progress and advancement? Is it any wonder that barriers in due time evaporate, as mists before the morning sun, when one has performed his work, when he has experienced that test of his faith, when he has qualified for the desired blessings?

All through the scriptures the key of faith has proved to be a prerequisite to receiving desired and needed blessings. Abraham experienced the tortuous ordeal of being willing to sacrifice his precious son Isaac before he heard the words, "Lay not thine hand upon the lad, neither do thou any thing unto him: for now I know that thou fearest

The key of faith

God, seeing thou hast not withheld thy son, thine only son from me." (Genesis 22:12.) Abraham's faith had to be tested.

The prophet Daniel was to be thrown to those lions in the pit before there came to fruition his God-given blessings. The three Hebrew children were cast into the fiery furnace, that their faith might be tested. Joseph Smith entered a quiet grove and bowed in prayer as a test of his faith.

Isn't it significant that when Abraham's faith was tested there was no lamb in the thicket that *he* could see? Isn't it significant that when Daniel was threatened to be thrown into the den of lions there were no muzzles binding those lions? Isn't it significant that the three Hebrew children had no asbestos suits of clothing when they were cast into the fiery furnace? Isn't it significant that when Joseph, the boy prophet, went down upon bended knee to seek the help of Almighty God, that God, the Father, and Jesus, the Son, did not appear until after his faith had been tested?

The key to the archives that was handed to President Johnson in Sweden, which opened the latch thereby revealing the names he desired, may be the key you will need and the key those who are associated with us will need. That key is the key of faith. No locked door can withstand its opening capacity. Faith is a requisite to this work. There is within our grasp this same key, which shall unlock to our view that which we earnestly seek.

In section 76 of the Doctrine and Covenants, there is recorded a vision given to Joseph Smith the Prophet and Sidney Rigdon at Hiram, Ohio, February 16, 1832. This revelation contains the promise of the Lord to the faithful:

> Hear, O ye heavens, and give ear, O earth, and rejoice ye inhabitants thereof, for the Lord is God, and beside him there is no Savior.
>
> Great is his wisdom, marvelous are his ways, and the extent of his doings none can find out.
>
> His purposes fail not, neither are there any who can stay his hand.

The key of faith

From eternity to eternity he is the same, and his years never fail.

For thus saith the Lord—I, the Lord, am merciful and gracious unto those who fear me, and delight to honor those who serve me in righteousness and in truth unto the end.

Great shall be their reward and eternal shall be their glory.

And to them will I reveal all mysteries. . . . (D&C 76:1-7.)

The key of faith can be ours. May we use it wisely, thus opening to the view of those who have gone before that great vision of their opportunity in the kingdom of our Heavenly Father.

Adapted from an address given to an annual genealogical seminar at Brigham Young University.

8

Decisions determine destiny

s each Latter-day Saint approaches the crisis of the crossroads of life, he perhaps recalls a particular passage of scripture, a relevant illustration, a testimony of truth heard and felt. As such a thought floods through his memory, that still, small voice will whisper, "Remember, remember, remember to be true!"

Have you ever stopped to consider that the prophet of God is counting on each one of us? Yes, he is counting on our conduct. He is confident of our courage. How I pray that each may declare, "I resolve to merit the prophet's trust." "I shall not deviate from my duty." "I shall not dishonor my divine destiny."

The way to exaltation is not a freeway featuring unlimited vision, unrestricted speeds, and untested skills. Rather, it is known by many forks and turnings, sharp curves, and controlled speeds. Our driving ability is being put to the test. Are we ready? We're driving. We haven't passed this way before. Fortunately, the Master Highway Builder, even our Heavenly Father, has provided a road map showing the route to follow. He has placed markers along the way to guide us to our destination.

Perhaps we may recognize some of his signs:

• Honor thy father and thy mother.

- Search the scriptures, for they are they
  which testify of me.
- Seek ye first the kingdom of God
  and his righteousness.
- Be ye clean.

That evil one, too, has placed roadsigns to frustrate our progress and to lead us from the path of truth into detours of sin. His detours all lead to a dead end. These are some of his markers:

- Times have changed.
- My love is mine to give; my life is mine to live.
- It can't hurt anyone but me.
- Just this once won't matter.

Now we see coming into focus the responsibility to choose: that inevitable crisis at the crossroads of life. He who would lead us down waits patiently for the dark night, a wavering will, a confused conscience, a mixed-up mind. Are we prepared to make the decision at the crossroads?

You may ask, "Are decisions really that important?" Decisions determine destiny. One can't make eternal decisions without eternal consequences. May I provide a simple formula by which we can measure the choices that confront us. It's easy to remember; sometimes difficult to apply: "You can't be right by doing wrong; you can't be wrong by doing right."

Some foolish persons turn their backs on the wisdom of God and follow the allurement of fickle fashion, the attraction of false popularity, and the thrill of the moment. Their course of conduct so resembles the disastrous experience of Esau, who exchanged his birthright for a mess of pottage.

And what are the results of such action? I testify to you

that turning away from God brings broken covenants, shattered dreams, vanished ambitions, evaporated plans, unfulfilled expectations, crushed hopes, misused drives, warped character, and wrecked lives.

Such a quagmire of quicksand must be avoided. We are of a noble birthright. Eternal life in the kingdom of our Father is our goal.

Such a goal is not achieved in one glorious attempt, but rather is the result of a lifetime of righteousness, an accumulation of wise choices, even a constancy of purpose. Like the coveted A grade on the report card of a difficult and required college course, the reward of eternal life requires effort. The A grade is the result of each theme, each quiz, each class, each examination, each library project, each term paper. So each Sunday School lesson, each MIA teacher, each prayer, each date, each friend, all precede the goal of temple marriage—that giant step toward an A grade on the report card of life.

Some time ago I returned from a month-long, thirty-thousand-mile journey to the stakes and missions of the South Pacific. As the great jet plane hurtled through the heavens, I gazed out the window and marveled at the stars by which the navigator charted our course. My thoughts were upon our glorious youth; I said to myself: "Ideals are like the stars—you can't touch them with your hands, but by following them you reach your destination."

What ideals when followed will bring to us those blessings we so much seek, even a quiet conscience, a peace-filled heart, a loving husband or wife, a healthy family, a contented home?

May I suggest these three:

- *Choose your friends with caution.*
- *Plan your future with purpose.*
- *Frame your life with faith.*

First, choose your friends with caution

In a survey made in selected wards and stakes of the Church, we learned a most significant fact. Those persons whose friends married in the temple usually married in the temple, while those persons whose friends did not marry in the temple usually did not marry in the temple. The influence of one's friends appeared to be a more dominant factor than parental urging, classroom instruction, or proximity to a temple.

We tend to become like those whom we admire. Just as in Nathaniel Hawthorne's classic account "The Great Stone Face," we adopt the mannerisms, the attitudes, even the conduct of those whom we admire—and they are usually our friends. We should associate with those who, like us, are planning not for temporary convenience, shallow goals, or narrow ambition, but rather for those things that matter most—even eternal objectives.

Inscribed on the wall of Stanford University Memorial Hall is this truth: "We must teach our youth that all that is not eternal is too short, and all that is not infinite is too small."

Beyond the friends of our peer group, even our own age, will we make a friend of our father? Really, each of us has three fathers. First, we have our Heavenly Father. He stands ready to answer the prayers of our heart. Being the Father of our spirit, and having created us in his own image, knowing the end from the beginning, his wisdom faileth not and his counsel is ever true. Make a friend of him.

Second, we have our earthly father. He labors to insure our happiness. Together with our mother, he prays for our guidance and well-being. Make a friend of him.

Third, there is the father of our ward, even the bishop. He has been called of God by prophecy and the laying on of hands, by those who are in authority, to preach the gospel and administer in the ordinances thereof. In short, he is endowed to provide us with counsel and help. Make a friend of him.

How well I remember the challenges confronting the youth in the ward over which I once presided. One evening a lovely teenage girl came to the office with her boyfriend to talk things over with me. The two of them were very much in love, and temptation was beginning to make its inroad.

As we counseled together, each of my young friends made a pledge to the other to resist temptation and keep uppermost in his and her minds the goal of a temple marriage. I suggested a course of action to follow and then felt impressed to say: "If you ever find yourselves in a position of compromise and need additional strength, you call me regardless of the hour."

Early one morning at one o'clock, the telephone rang and a voice said: "Bishop, this is Nancy. Remember how you asked me to call if I found myself being tempted? Well, Bishop, I'm in that situation." I asked where she was, and she described one of the more popular moon-watching spots in the Salt Lake Valley. She and her fiancé had walked to a nearby phone booth to make the call. The setting wasn't ideal for providing counsel, but the need was great and the young couple was receptive.

Months later, when the mailman delivered her wedding announcement to our home and Sister Monson read, "Mr. and Mrs. _____ request the pleasure of your company at the wedding reception of their daughter, Nancy," she sighed, "Thank heaven! No more 1:00 A.M. telephone calls." When I noticed the small print at the bottom which read, "Married in the Salt Lake Temple," I said silently, "Thank heaven for the strength of Latter-day Saint youth!"

Choose your friends with caution.

Second, plan your future with purpose

The great Thomas Carlyle said: "A man without purpose in life is as a ship without a rudder, a waif, a nothing, a nobody. Have a purpose in life, and having it, throw such strength of muscle and brain into your work as God has given you."

Latter-day Saint young men seek for their companions young women who plan with a purpose. They admire such young women when they turn from mediocrity and set their course toward excellence. The Lord has warned, "Be not unequally yoked together." In youth's quest for the mate of his dreams and the dream of his life, he may well heed the counsel given by King Arthur in the popular musical *Camelot.* Faced with a particularly vexing dilemma, King Arthur was speaking to himself, but could well have been speaking to our youth, when he declared, "We must not let our passions destroy our dreams."

Some time ago several outstanding teachers were honored at the general Sunday School conference. It was my privilege to pay a tribute to a Sunday School teacher of my boyhood days—Lucy Gertsch Thomson.

Lucy was lovely and ever so sweet. She was deserving of a worthy companion. Yet such success evaded her. The years flew by and Lucy reached the worrisome twenties, the desperate thirties, even the frightful forties—and then she met Dick. It was a case of love at first sight. Just one problem—Dick was not a member of the Church. Did Lucy succumb to the age-old fallacy of marrying out of desperation, with the fleeting hope that one day he would become a member? Not Lucy. She was wiser than this. She simply told Dick: "Dick, I think you're wonderful, but we would never be happy dating together."

"Why not?" he countered.

"Because you're not a Mormon."

"How do I become a Mormon? I want to date you." He studied the gospel. She answered his questions. He was baptized.

Then he said, "Lucy, now that I'm a member, we can be married at last."

Lucy replied, "Oh, Dick, I love you so much. Now that you are a member of the Church, you wouldn't be content with anything but a temple marriage."

"How long will that take, Lucy?"

"About a year, if we meet the other requirements." One year later Lucy and Dick entered the House of the Lord. Lucy lived the truth of the verse:

> *Dare to be a Mormon;*
> *Dare to stand alone;*
> *Dare to have a purpose firm;*
> *Dare to make it known.*

Plan your future with purpose.

Third, frame your life with faith

Amidst the confusion of our age, the conflicts of conscience, and the turmoil of daily living, an abiding faith becomes an anchor to our lives.

My mind goes back to a day when I was approaching my eighteenth birthday. We were all very fearful. World War II was still being fought, and every young man knew that he had to make a choice. There was not much latitude to the choice: he could choose to go into the army or he could choose to go into the navy. I enlisted in the navy.

As forty-four of us young men stood there in the recruiting office, I shall never forget the chief petty officers coming up to us and presenting a choice. They said, "Now, you young men must make an important choice. On one hand, you can be wise and choose to join the regular navy.

You can enlist for four years. You will receive the finest schooling. You will be given every opportunity because the navy looks upon you as its own. If you choose not to follow this direction, you can go into the naval reserves. The navy does not have paramount interest in the naval reserves at this stage of the war. You will receive no schooling. You will be sent out to sea duty. No one knows what your future might be."

Then they asked us to sign on the dotted line. I turned to my father and said, "What should I do, Dad?"

In a voice choked with emotion, he replied, "I don't know anything about the navy."

That was the position of every father who was there that day.

Forty-two of the forty-four enlisted in the regular navy for four years. The forty-third one could not pass the regular navy physical, so he had to enlist in the reserves. Then they came to me; and I confess that with all the faith I could muster I sent a prayer heavenward, earnestly hoping that the Lord would answer it. And he did. The thought came to me just as clearly as though I had heard a voice, "Ask those chief petty officers which they chose."

I asked each of those veteran petty officers: "Did you choose the regular navy, or did you choose the reserves?"

Each of them had chosen the reserves.

I turned and said, "With all the wisdom and experience that you have, I want to be on your side."

I chose the reserves, which meant that I enlisted for the duration of the war, plus six months. The war ended, and within a year I was honorably discharged from the service. I was able to continue my schooling. I had the privilege of serving in many Church capacities. Who knows how the course of my life might have been changed had I not taken that moment to call in faith upon my Heavenly Father for guidance and direction in what might appear to some to be a minor decision!

No decision that young Latter-day Saints make is minor or unimportant. Exaltation is your goal.

Frame your life with faith.

When we choose our friends with caution, plan our future with purpose, and frame our life with faith, we merit the companionship of the Holy Spirit. Then we can testify through our own experience to the truth of the Lord's promise:

"I will be on your right hand, and on your left; and my spirit shall be in your hearts, and mine angels round about you to bear you up." (D&C 84:88.)

THE PATHWAY OF

SERVICE

". . . when ye are in the service of your fellow beings
ye are only in the service of your God."

MOSIAH 2:17

9
Building bridges

eaders of our young people fill a variety of roles. Some are trained executives and secretaries in the world of business, skilled physicians and nurses in the field of medicine, or competent teachers in the classrooms of learning. Others have studied sociology, psychology, languages, or history. Many are filling the vital role of homemaker. In reality, each is also engaged in the building trade. The product: building a bridge to the heart of a youth.

A good share are skilled journeymen, even master craftsmen, having had many years of service and experience in this significant trade, while others are just commencing their apprenticeship. All are needed. Where there is one leader who is willing and able to build a bridge to the heart of a youth, there are many more individuals who, through greed, selfishness, and warped thinking, lurk in the shadows of gloom, away from the light of truth, to tear a young person down. I speak of those who belittle morality, who violate law and, for filthy lucre, sell the youth those products that destroy; those who put sin on a pedestal, who conceal truth, who glamorize error, who look upon a lovely young person as a commodity for exploitation.

The "get rich quick" theories, the philosophy of something for nothing, confusion of proper goals and objectives, have all combined to make the leader's building task more difficult. The foundations of love- and life-established principles are crumbling before our very eyes. They are being eroded by the forces of Lucifer. Unfortunately, some of our precious youth are even now sliding to their destruction down the slippery slopes of sin.

This, then, is every leader's duty, responsibility, opportunity: to guide, to build, to inspire our youth. Over and over again we hear the frantic phrase of frustration: "How can I reach our youth?" One whose teacher succeeded in this quest wrote:

During my junior and senior high school years, illness kept me from school and church almost half the time. When I could attend, I couldn't participate in any activities. Since I couldn't make friends or enter into their lives very well under these circumstances, I was a "loner."

Only once did I try to break the pattern—by entering an MIA speech contest. I was the only one who entered from our ward, so without hearing my talk, the ward executives sent me to the stake contest, where I was a miserable failure. I decided then and there to stay within my shell and not get hurt again.

But my Gleaner teacher decided differently. For the first time, I had a teacher who was not willing to let me sit silent in my corner. She was given the chairmanship of a program for the stake Gleaner banquet and immediately assigned to me the job of being toastmistress, deciding the theme and suggesting topics for the responses. I told her I couldn't do it. "Yes, you can," she assured me time after time, "because I'll help you every step of the way."

I loved her so much I was willing to try for her although in my heart I knew I'd fail. First, she and I talked over possible themes. When we met with a committee of girls, however, she made me tell them my ideas. She claimed no part in them. I wrote out my continuity, and with her careful and loving suggestions, rewrote it many times until I could see that it was good.

"But," I told her, "I can't stand up before three hundred girls and give it. I'll make a poor impression, and I'm not pretty or attractive, and I'll spoil your whole evening." With an arm around me, she said, "That's utter nonsense; you'll be the star of the evening."

So she heard me say my part many times, once even taking me to the Empire Room of the Hotel Utah to rehearse it. She had arranged to have a microphone there so I could experience the actual setting. Then she asked to see the dress I would wear. She brought a corsage for me that night that not only matched the dress, but also lifted my spirits. She had her hairdresser do my hair in a way that would be more becoming to me.

But best of all, she knelt with me just before the event and explained to the Lord that I was a lovely girl who had worked hard and that I needed his help to do a good job. How could I fail with his and her love so surrounding me?

And so my wonderful teacher, through love and personal work and sacrifice, started me on the road to normal associations with young people and to activity in the Church.

What a lovely tribute to a devoted teacher!

How can we reach our youth? I answer, "Build a bridge to their hearts."

Some attempt to build a bridge with inferior materials, inadequate planning, and improper tools. The finished product may appear substantial, attractive, and be ready for use in a minimum of time. But then come the storms and the stresses of life and the tell-tale sign: "Danger! Bridge washed out!" We cannot risk such an occurrence in our bridge building. Our responsibility is too great, our influence too lasting, our opportunity too perishable. We must build wisely, skillfully, and, with meticulous care, follow our blueprint.

In any bridge-building project, the first requirement is a visit to the site, that we might get clearly in our minds the task which lies ahead and the problems likely to be encountered. How wide is the gulf? How firm is the base? What is the stress factor? What are the available resources? Where and when do we commence?

Bridge builder, do you know your youth? Do you understand their problems and their perplexities, yearnings, ambitions, and hopes? Do you know how far they have traveled, the troubles they have experienced, the burdens they have carried, the sorrows they have borne?

The shifting sands of popular opinion, the power of the peer group, in all too many intances become an irresistible magnet drawing downward to destruction the precious sons and daughters of God. We become the stable force, the port of safety in the storm-tossed seas, the watchman on the tower, even the guide at the crossroads:

He stood at the crossroads all alone,
The sunlight in his face.
He had no thought for the world unknown—
He was set for a manly race.
But the roads stretched east and the roads stretched west,
And the lad knew not which road was best.
So he chose the road that led him down,
And he lost the race and the victor's crown.
He was caught at last in an angry snare
Because no one stood at the crossroads there
To show him the better road.

Another day at the self-same place
A boy with high hopes stood.
He, too, was set for a manly race;
He, too, was seeking the things that were good.
But one was there who the roads did know,
And that one showed him which way to go.
So he turned from the road that would lead him down,
And he won the race and the victor's crown.
He walks today the highway fair
Because one stood at the crossroads there
To show him the better way.

—CENTRAL CHRISTIAN MONITOR

The Lord emphasized the worth of the human soul—this precious product we seek to reach—when he declared:

Building bridges

"Remember the worth of souls is great in the sight of God." (D&C 18:10.)

At a quarterly conference the priesthood committee representative discussed this scripture and asked the question, "Just what is the worth of a human soul?" One quorum officer responded, "The worth of a soul is its capacity to become as God." What a profound answer to a most penetrating question.

Then we must prepare. A blueprint is to be drawn. Nothing can be left to chance. If we fail to prepare, we prepare to fail. Trite? Perhaps, but ever so true.

Preparation will dispel that hidden and insidious enemy who lurks within and limits our capacity, destroys our initiative, and strangles our effectiveness. This enemy of whom I speak is fear. A fear to wholeheartedly accept our calling. A fear to provide direction to others. A fear to lead, to motivate, to inspire. In his wisdom, the Lord provided a formula whereby we might overcome the arch villain— *fear.* He instructed: ". . . if ye are prepared ye shall not fear." (D&C 38:30.)

Remember, we are all entitled to our Father's blessings. He did not call us to our privileged posts to build alone, without guidance, trusting to luck. On the contrary, he knows our skills, he realizes our devotion, and he will convert our supposed inadequacies to recognized strengths.

With a resolve in our heart, and our finished blueprint under our arm, we are ready to assemble our materials for bridge building.

Faith becomes steel, dedication to purpose provides cement, earnest prayers are as the bolts to hold the parts of the bridge in place, love furnishes connecting cables.

Are our fellow workers by our side? Are we organized and working as a united team? Teamwork eliminates the weakness of a person standing alone and substitutes, therefore, the strength of workers serving together.

Building bridges

We cannot perform all of the needed work by ourselves. Executive capacity is a quality to be cultivated. The renowned business leader, J. C. Penney, advised: "My definition of an executive's job is brief and to the point. It is simply this: Getting things done through other people." Cooperativeness is not so much learning how to get along with others as taking the kinks out of ourself, so that others can get along with us.

Now comes the actual work. "Thrust in thy sickle with thy might" was not an admonition reserved for missionary work alone. Our Father expects us to labor and to do so diligently and willingly. He counseled: "[I] the Lord requireth the heart and a willing mind. . . ." (D&C 64:34.)

As we proceed step by step, we must not deviate from the recognized plan of the Master Architect, even the Lord. We must follow the approved program, and know and apply the handbook guidelines and suggestions. Pet theories will not replace adopted principles. In short, we have to build the right kind of bridge. And what is the proper bridge to the heart of a youth?

Is it a drawbridge? Such a bridge is controlled exclusively by the operator. By command it moves up and out of place or down and into place. In Honolulu, I saw the weakness of such a bridge. While the operator raised the two portions high into the air to permit a vessel to pass beneath, long lines of automobiles and pedestrians waited impatiently. Their own onward course was halted abruptly. When our youth need our help, we cannot afford to have a disconnected bridge. The angry waters of discouragement and despair wait altogether too threateningly and menacingly to swallow the young person who would attempt a crossing to safety. The drawbridge is out.

What about a swinging bridge? Such a bridge is easily built. It is quaint and provides a sweeping view. But what happens to such a bridge when the winds of life whip up to tempest proportions? The bridge swings with the gale and can hurl an unsuspecting traveler to destruction.

When bridge builders are wavering in their testimony, when they yield to temptation or the way of the world, they hold out to young people the dangers of a swinging bridge. Wise youth will not trust such a bridge. And wise builders will not waste their time or energies on such an uncertain undertaking.

Should we consider the footbridge? Hastily erected, it permits limited traffic. There are no safety rails. It cannot carry the weight of present-day responsibility. It may reach to the opposite bank, but it won't reach to the heart of a youth. The leader in the Church who looks at his or her assignment as one night a week, four nights a month and no more, is guilty of such gross underbuilding. The footbridge cannot meet today's growing needs. It parallels narrow concepts, limited vision, inadequate communication, and unsatisfactory results.

What of the covered bridge? We see a few as we travel about the countryside. Usually they span small streams. Oh, the covered bridge may keep out a few storms, but have you noticed how the moss forms on the areas that never receive the sunlight? A musty odor and a dark passage await each person to cross over. To reach our youth, we need to permit the sunlight of truth to shine warmly on all parts of our bridge of understanding. We are to be optimistic, forward looking, abreast of these challenging times —and the old-fashioned covered bridge simply won't suffice.

Should we attempt to build a narrow bridge? The initial effort is modest, but inconvenience and hazardous travel will follow. One-way traffic, the curse of the narrow bridge, is like one-way communication. It is outmoded. A good leader must learn to listen. Listening is not a passive activity. To actively listen to another person requires will-power, concentration, and great mental effort. Its rewards are many, because only then do we really learn to understand our youth.

What, then, is the proper bridge to build? When I was in Sydney, Australia, I crossed over one of the world's truly great bridges. It is a tribute to human genius. I appraised its virtues:

1. There was two-way, multiple lane passage.
2. The bearing load could accommodate the smallest Volkswagen or any number of mammoth semi-trucks and trailers.
3. It was well supported and firmly anchored on both sides.
4. It had been constructed with care. It could withstand the most severe storm or heaviest burden. Its stress strength was above, as well as below, the surface. Some parts, like the giant cables, were exposed to view. Other portions, such as the bearing girders and underwater supports, were hidden, but nevertheless doing duty as required.
5. One felt safe in crossing such a bridge.

When our youth can discuss their challenges with us, rather than being relegated to the position of patient listener only, we have such multiple-lane passage. Understanding is enhanced and our work becomes our joy, for we see its effect in the lives of others. When the bearing load of our bridge is geared to accommodate minimum and maximum requirements, our youth trust our judgment and will unburden the heavy loads that sometimes weigh upon the human heart. When we have an abiding faith in the living God, when our outward actions reflect our inner convictions, we have the composite strength of exposed and hidden virtues. They combine to give safe passage for our youth.

Bridge builders, when we really love our youth, they will not find themselves in that dreaded "Never, Never Land." Never the object of concern. Never the recipient of needed aid. Rather, we will be present, serving diligently and devotedly in the cause of truth and the cause of youth.

Building bridges

We may never open gates of cities or doors of palaces, but true happiness and lasting joy will be ours as we achieve success in building a bridge to the heart of a youth.

We and our youth may be in the position described by Miss W. A. Dromgoole in her classic poem "The Bridge-builder":

An old man traveling a lone highway
Came at evening time cold and gray,
To a chasm vast and wide and steep,
With waters rolling cold and deep.
The old man crossed in the twilight dim,
For the sullen stream held no fears for him.
But he turned when he reached the other side,
And builded a bridge to span the tide.

"Old man," cried a fellow pilgrim near,
"You are wasting your strength with building here;
Your journey will end with the ending day,
And you never again will pass this way.
You have crossed the chasm deep and wide.
Why build you a bridge at eventide?"

And the builder raised his old gray head:
"Good friend, on the path I have come," he said,
"There followeth after me today
Youth whose feet will pass this way.
This stream which has been as naught to me
To fair-haired youth may a pitfall be;
They, too, must cross in the twilight dim—
Good friend, I am building this bridge for them."

I earnestly and sincerely pray our Heavenly Father will ever bless each builder of bridges to the hearts of youth.

Adapted from an address delivered to a group of Young Women's MIA leaders.

10

Yellow canaries
with gray on their wings

Some twenty-three years ago I was called as a young man to serve as the bishop of a large ward in Salt Lake City. The magnitude of the calling was overwhelming and the responsibility frightening. My inadequacy humbled me. But my Heavenly Father did not leave me to wander in darkness and in silence, uninstructed or uninspired. In his own way, he revealed the lessons he would have me learn.

One evening, at a late hour, my telephone rang. I heard a voice say, "Bishop Monson, this is the hospital calling. Kathleen McKee, a member of your congregation, has just passed away. Our records reveal that she had no next of kin, but your name is listed as the one to be notified in the event of her death. Could you come to the hospital right away?"

Upon arriving there, I was presented with a sealed envelope which contained a key to the modest apartment in which Kathleen McKee had lived. A childless widow seventy-three years of age, she had enjoyed but few of life's luxuries and possessed scarcely sufficient of its necessities. In the twilight of her life, she had become a member of The Church of Jesus Christ of Latter-day Saints. Being a quiet and overly reserved person, little was known about her life.

That same night I entered her tidy basement apartment, turned the light switch, and in a moment discovered a letter written ever so meticulously in Kathleen McKee's own hand. It rested face up on a small table and read:

Bishop Monson,
    I think I shall not return from the hospital. In the dresser drawer is a small insurance policy which will cover funeral expenses. The furniture may be given to my neighbors.
    In the kitchen are my three precious canaries. Two of them are beautiful, yellow-gold in color and are perfectly marked. On their cages I have noted the names of friends to whom they are to be given. In the third cage is "Billie." He is my favorite. Billie looks a bit scrubby, and his yellow hue is marred by gray on his wings. Will you and your family make a home for him? He isn't the prettiest, but his song is the best.

In the days that followed, I learned much more about Kathleen McKee. She had befriended many neighbors in need. She had given cheer and comfort almost daily to a cripple who lived down the street. Indeed, she had brightened each life she touched. Kathleen McKee was much like "Billie," her prized yellow canary with gray on its wings. She was not blessed with beauty, gifted with poise, nor honored by posterity. Yet her song helped others to more willingly bear their burdens and more ably shoulder their tasks. She lived the message of the verse:

> *Go visit the lonely, the dreary;*
> *Go comfort the weeping, the weary.*
> *Oh, scatter kind deeds on your way*
> *And make the world brighter today.*

The world is filled with yellow canaries with gray on their wings. The pity is that so precious few of them have learned to sing. Perhaps the clear notes of proper example have not sounded in their ears or found lodgment in their hearts.

Some are young people who don't know who they are,

80

what they can be or even want to be. They are afraid, but they don't know of what. They are angry, but they don't know at whom. They are rejected, and they don't know why. All they want is to be somebody.

Others are stooped with age, burdened with care, or filled with doubt—living lives far below the level of their capacities.

All of us are prone to excuse our own mediocre performance. We blame our misfortunes, our disfigurements, or our so-called handicaps. Victims of our own rationalization, we say silently to ourselves, "I'm just too weak," or "I'm not cut out for better things." Others soar beyond our meager accomplishments. Envy and discouragement then take their toll.

Can we not appreciate that our very business in life is not to get ahead of others, but to get ahead of ourselves? To break our own records, to outstrip our yesterdays by our todays, to bear our trials more beautifully than we ever dreamed we could, to give as we have never given, to do our work with more force and a finer finish than ever— this is the true idea: to get ahead of ourselves.

To live greatly, we must develop the capacity to face trouble with courage, disappointment with cheerfulness, and triumph with humility. You ask, "How might we achieve these goals?" I answer, "By getting a true perspective of who we really are!" We are sons and daughters of a living God in whose image we have been created. Think of that truth: "Created in the image of God." We cannot sincerely hold this conviction without experiencing a profound new sense of strength and power, even the strength to live the commandments of God, the power to resist the temptations of Satan.

True, we live in a world where moral character ofttimes is relegated to a position secondary to facial beauty or personal charm. We read and hear of local, national, and international beauty contests. Throngs pay tribute to

Miss America, Miss World, and Miss Universe. Athletic prowess, too, has its following. The winter games, the world Olympics, the tournaments of international scope bring forth the adoring applause of the enthralled crowd. Such are the ways of men!

But what are the inspired words of God? From a time of long ago, the counsel of Samuel the prophet echoes in our ears: ". . . the Lord seeth not as man seeth; for man looketh on the outward appearance, but the Lord looketh on the heart." (1 Samuel 16:7.)

Sham and hypocrisy found no place with the King of kings and the Lord of lords. He denounced the scribes and Pharisees for their vanity and shallow lives, their pretense and feigned righteousness. He called them "like unto whited sepulchres, which indeed appear beautiful outward, but are within full of dead men's bones. . . ." (Matthew 23:27.)

They, like the beautiful yellow canaries, were outwardly handsome, but a true song came not from their hearts.

To their counterparts on this continent, God's prophet declared:

"For behold, ye do love money, and your substance, and your fine apparel, and the adorning of your churches, more than ye love the poor and the needy, the sick and the afflicted.

". . . Why are ye ashamed to take upon you the name of Christ? . . .

"Why do ye adorn yourselves with that which hath no life, and yet suffer the hungry, and the needy, and the naked, and the sick and the afflicted to pass by you, and notice them not?" (Mormon 8:37-39.)

The Master could be found mingling with the poor, the downtrodden, the oppressed, and the afflicted. He brought hope to the hopeless, strength to the weak, and freedom to the captive. He taught of the better life to come—

even eternal life. This knowledge ever directs those who receive the divine injunction: "Follow thou me." It guided Peter. It motivated Paul. It can determine our personal destiny. Can we make the decision to follow in righteousness and truth the Redeemer of the world? With his help, a rebellious boy can become an obedient man, a wayward girl can cast aside the old self and begin anew. Indeed, the gospel of Jesus Christ can change men's lives.

In his epistle to the Corinthians, the apostle Paul taught: ". . . God hath chosen the weak things of the world to confound the things which are mighty." (1 Corinthians 1:27.)

When the Savior sought a man of faith, he did not select him from the throng of self-righteous who were found regularly in the synagogue. Rather, he called him from among the fishermen of Capernaum.

While teaching on the seashore, he saw two ships standing by the lake. He entered one and asked its owner to put it out a little from the land so he might not be pressed upon by the crowd. After teaching further, he said to Simon, "Launch out into the deep, and let down your nets. . . ."

Simon answered: "Master, we have toiled all the night, and have taken nothing: nevertheless at thy word I will let down the net.

"And when they had this done, they inclosed a great multitude of fishes. . . .

"When Simon Peter saw it, he fell down at Jesus' knees, saying, Depart from me; for I am a sinful man, O Lord." (Luke 5:4-6, 8.)

Came the reply: "Follow me, and I will make you fishers of men." (Matthew 4:19.) Simon the fisherman had received his call. Doubting, disbelieving, unschooled, untrained, impetuous Simon did not find the way of the Lord a highway of ease nor a path free from pain. He was to hear the rebuke: "O thou of little faith" (Matthew 14:31), and likewise the denunciation, "Get thee behind me, Satan: thou art an offence unto me" (Matthew 16:23). Yet, when the Master asked him, ". . . whom say ye that I am?" Peter answered: "Thou art the Christ, the Son of the living God." (Matthew 16:15-16.)

Simon, man of doubt, had become Peter, apostle of faith. A yellow canary with gray on his wings qualified for the Master's full confidence and abiding love.

When the Savior was to choose a missionary of zeal and power, he found him not among his advocates, but amidst his adversaries. Saul of Tarsus made havoc of the church and breathed out threatenings and slaughter against the disciples of the Lord. But this was before the experience of Damascus Way. Of Saul, the Lord declared: ". . . he is a chosen vessel unto me, to bear my name before the Gentiles, and kings, and the children of Israel. . . . I will shew him how great things he must suffer for my name's sake." (Acts 9:15-16.)

Saul the persecutor became Paul the proselyter. Like the yellow canary with gray on his wings, Paul, too, had his blemishes. He himself said: "And lest I should be exalted above measure through the abundance of the revelations, there was given to me a thorn in the flesh, the messenger of Satan to buffet me. . . .

"For this thing I besought the Lord thrice, that it might depart from me.

"And he said unto me, My grace is sufficient for thee: for my strength is made perfect in weakness. . . ." (2 Corinthians 12:7-9.)

Both Paul and Peter were to expend their strength and forfeit their lives in the cause of truth. The Redeemer chose imperfect men to teach the way to perfection. He did so then. He does so now—even yellow canaries with gray on their wings.

He calls you and me to serve him here below and sets

us to the tasks he would have us fulfill. The commitment is total. There is no conflict of conscience. And in our struggle, should we stumble, then let us plead: "Lead us, oh lead us, great Molder of men; out of the darkness to strive once again." (From the "Fight Song," Yonkers High School.)

Our appointed task may appear insignificant, unnecessary, unnoticed. We may be tempted to question:

> *"Father, where shall I work today?"*
> *And my love flowed warm and free.*
> *Then He pointed out a tiny spot*
> *And said, "Tend that for me."*
>
> *I answered quickly, "Oh no, not that!*
> *Why, no one would ever see,*
> *No matter how well my work was done.*
> *Not that little place for me."*
>
> *And the word He spoke, it was not stern;*
> *He answered me tenderly:*
> *"Ah, little one, search that heart of thine;*
> *Art thou working for them or for me?*
> *Nazareth was a little place,*
> *And so was Galilee."*
>
> —MEADE McGUIRE

My prayer is that we indeed will follow that Man of Galilee, that we will praise his name, that we will order our lives so as to reflect our love, that we will remember that to us God our Father gave his Son and that for us Jesus Christ gave his life.

11

True shepherds after the way of the Lord

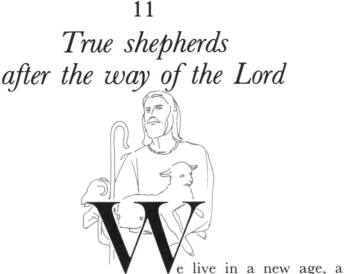

We live in a new age, a changing world. Many of the old traditions are being swept away. For example, we are no longer in rural, confined communities. Our young people are more mobile than they have ever been before. They think nothing of driving great distances, to new places, whereas a few generations ago they never left their own communities. It was: "Up in the morning, do the chores, go to work, then do the chores, then go to bed." It was a different world. We live in a society that is marked by change.

Young people do not want to wait to grow up. They want the answers now; and when they come to us, if we don't have the answers, they feel that we're from the old establishment, that we don't communicate, that there is a generation gap. We could say this is the "now" generation, but the need for wise counseling has never been more urgent.

As an example, may I share with you a letter from a young lady who wrote to me:

Dear Brother Monson:

I need counseling and advice *now*. [She underlined "now."] I need it from someone holding and honoring the priesthood who is in a position to have insight and give the right advice. I am a recent convert of eleven months and come from a stable home. My parents are very moral and ethical in their own way, but not by LDS standards. I come from a very rough neighborhood, and all of my previous standards directly oppose gospel teaching.

When I joined [the Church], I was engaged to a wonderful young man who had left for the service three months prior to my becoming a member. He has since returned, and I spent Christmas vacation with him. Brother Monson, I broke the Word of Wisdom. I was guilty of doubting the teachings of the Church, and I slept with the boy I love several times. I don't in the least regret or feel ashamed of having shared my love with him, but I truly am ashamed of having taken a taste of rum and Coke.

Now there is a letter from a very confused girl. It was written in sincerity. I think it reflected her honest feelings. She had rationalized within her mind that sexual sin with the person she loved was not so serious as breaking the Word of Wisdom. This type of young girl, demonstrating this type of confusion, may come to us in our capacity as a seminary or an institute teacher or priesthood or auxiliary leader and will hunger for wise counsel. I believe the letter indicates the need. Other illustrations could be given.

Let us turn for a moment from the need, and talk about the prize. I think if we are to be wise counselors, we must have within our minds constantly a picture of the true value of the young men and women whom we are teaching and whom we are counseling. These young men and women are precious in the sight of God. They have been reserved to come forth in this day and in this age. I think they are a royal generation, as it were, and a chosen and a choice generation. But they need counsel.

I believe that if we are to be wise counselors, we must appreciate the true worth of a human soul. You and I know that in the revelation the Lord gave the Prophet Joseph he said: "Remember, the worth of souls is great in the sight of God." (D&C 18:10.) And then he gave us a challenge, saying that if we should labor all our days and bring save it be one soul unto him, how great should be our joy. He added that if we should bring many souls unto the kingdom of our Father, how great should then be our joy. (See D&C 18:15-16.) We have that capacity to save human souls. Remember the injunction of the Lord: "Feed my lambs. . . . Feed my sheep." (John 21:15-16.) Let us feed our youth, and feed them the gospel of Jesus Christ.

We have talked about the need; and we have talked about the prize—the human soul. Now let's talk about the method of counseling.

First, in the art of counseling may I say this: *listen attentively.* If you are to be a good counselor, you must, of necessity, be a good listener. As a young boy or a young girl comes to you for advice, set the stage for the interview in such a fashion that he will not be inhibited in what he discusses with you. Let the interview be conducted in private. Likewise, assure him, as you listen attentively, that the interview will be strictly confidential. Assure him further that you are genuinely interested in his future. One way to do this is to ask questions intelligently as you guide the interview. It is a wise counselor who knows how to ask questions. And then be patient. It will take the young person a little time to put the wheat and the chaff on the table before you. And if you are to be a good counselor, you are not only to listen attentively, but you are to obtain the facts. This may require, as I have indicated, some effort through wise questioning and some patience through careful listening. *Listen attentively.*

Secondly, may I suggest that you *evaluate carefully.* Before you speak, consider what you have heard. Consider the course you are going to recommend that this young person take. Don't, in a willy-nilly fashion, speak from the top of your head. You have to be careful what you tell these young people to do, because they usually do it, since they have great respect for you as their teacher and as their counselor. So *listen attentively,* and then *evaluate carefully.*

Counsel wisely—that is the third step. And in giving wise counsel, I hope that first and foremost you will be in a position to determine those problems which, as you have observed in your interview, would require the young boy or girl to go to his or her bishop. I cannot emphasize this too much. You may be the most skillful of all counselors, but you are not the bishop of the ward; and it is the bishop of the ward who should listen to those confessions which relate to membership status in the Church. You will be a wise counselor if you will suggest how the young person may best get in touch with his or her bishop.

Frequently, we have young people who are frightened who come to our offices; and I think one of the kindest things that any one of us can do is to obtain permission from the person to get in touch with the bishop. I have often telephoned the bishop while a young couple is with me; and I have said to him: "Here is a young couple who would like to speak to you, bishop, about a matter which pertains to their future lives. When could they visit with you?" I believe every leader could follow that same course.

Now, to help you counsel wisely, may I add another thought—one about which I have strong feelings. Unfortunately, we find that sometimes a teacher, in his desire to attract and hold attention, turns to the dramatic. Sometimes he becomes somewhat like an actor on a stage, and he feels that the way to obtain and hold attention is to reveal past mistakes he may have made in his life. Our Heavenly Father said: "By this ye may know if a man repenteth of his sins—behold, he will confess them and forsake them." (D&C 58:43.) And then he said: ". . . though your sins be as scarlet, they shall be as white as snow; though they be red like crimson, they shall be as wool." (Isaiah 1:18.) As Brother Hugh B. Brown often said, "We should not try to remember what the Lord has indicated he is willing to forget." If we have erred in our lives and

90

have truly repented, then we do not bring before our youth a parade of experiences that indicate the sordidness of our past.

Another part of the changing world in which we live is that we find that some people, not motivated by the principles of Christ, believe in group confession. Some professional counselors follow this procedure. This is not the way of the Lord. I trust that we will *counsel wisely*.

Then I would turn to a fourth area. I would ask that each person, as a counselor, *pray fervently*. In and of yourself you may not have the capacity to be a wise counselor, but if you pray earnestly to the Lord, he will bless you. It matters little whether you be young, whether you be old, whether you be well-educated or not. If you will pray fervently, you will have that help.

Then a final element—*live righteously*. You can't teach the youth if you don't live the principles you teach. If you are not genuine, they can see through your facade. They recognize and want the real thing. You can fool some of your leaders, but you cannot fool the young people.

How might we as leaders live righteously? I believe first of all there should be a good relationship between each man and his wife. A man cannot be an effective teacher, leader, or counselor if at home there is bickering and quarreling, if his wife is forever nagging him and suggesting that he should have been an engineer, that he should have been an architect, or should have gone into this field or that field. But if the wife is supportive, if she lets her husband know that he is engaged in the greatest work that a man could possibly pursue, that she sustains him with all her heart and with all her soul, I have a feeling that he will do the same with her and sustain her in her role as a homemaker, as a companion, as a wife, as a mother.

The Lord said there should be no contention among men. In the book of Third Nephi he declared: "And there shall be no disputations among you." He further indicated that contention is not of God but is of the devil who "stirreth up the hearts of men to contend with anger, one with another." He said: ". . . this is not my doctrine, to stir up the hearts of men with anger, one against another; but this is my doctrine, that such things should be done away." (3 Nephi 11:28-30.) Let your home be blessed with beauty all around by incorporating within it the spirit of love.

Live righteously by honoring the leaders whom the General Authorities have appointed to direct your efforts and labors. I have a great deal of respect and admiration for men and women who have learned how to follow the leaders whom the Brethren have appointed. Part of living righteously is reflected in the manner in which you sustain the administration that directs your efforts. These persons have as their objective in life the advancement of the work of the Lord. A vital segment of living righteously is learning how to sustain the decisions of those who preside. I would hope that you could do so.

As you counsel young people, you must be in the frame of mind to be receptive to the Spirit of the Lord if you are to help them in their decision making. There are no small decisions in the life of a young person. Remember that the power to lead is also the power to mislead; and the power to mislead is the power to destroy. You have the power to destroy the souls of the young men and women under your charge. Conversely, you have the power to lift them closer to God as you live righteously and as your teaching reflects that righteous life.

I bear testimony to you today that as you *listen attentively,* as you *evaluate carefully,* as you *counsel wisely,* as you *pray fervently,* as you *live righteously,* you will be the counselor our Heavenly Father would have bless the lives of his precious youth. Provide that word of encouragement, that interview with the bishop, that example to follow which will bring young people upward and onward toward the celestial kingdom of God. You are indeed shepherds watching over Israel, and you must not be found sleeping when your services are needed.

One thing I remember best about Provo Canyon is the experience encountered when driving around a bend near Vivian Park—to meet on the road a large herd of sheep. Have you ever seen a sheepherder in one of our western mountain canyons directing the sheep? You have to look rather searchingly to find him. He is usually at the rear of the flock, slouched down on his horse, sound asleep. And doing the work are half a dozen small dogs yapping and barking at the heels of the sheep. He is a sheepherder.

A few months ago in Munich, Germany, I saw a true shepherd. There he was with staff in hand, singing, walking in front of his flock; and the flock followed behind him. When he turned to the left, the sheep turned to the left; when he went to the right, they went to the right. There were no dogs barking at the heels of his sheep. They indeed knew their shepherd and were following the pathway he took.

I would hope that each of our leaders would be not a sheepherder, but rather a true shepherd. Through wise counseling you will direct your young people far more effectively than by barking or yapping at their heels as together you move along life's highway. Be a true shepherd. There is no finer way to gain an unfaltering testimony of Jesus Christ than by serving his lambs and feeding them his gospel. There will come into such a leader's life a peace, a joy, and a contentment that always come when one has the testimony that Jesus Christ is the Son of God. Such a testimony is your message to the students who sit before you.

You need not go to Palestine to walk where Jesus

walked. You need simply to walk through the door of your classroom, walk to the front of your class, and bear your testimony, as did Jesus of old, that God our Heavenly Father lives, that the gospel of Christ is a reality, that it has the answers for the problems which vex our young people. Indeed, as you teach the precious youth, you may show them that these times are the best of times, that this age is the age of wisdom, that this epoch is the epoch of belief, that this season is not the season of despair but the season of hope, because they are on the threshold of great accomplishments in the work of their Heavenly Father.

Adapted from an address given to seminary and institute leaders.

12
Messengers of glory

More than 17,000 Latter-day Saints today, in response to a call from God's prophet, have left behind home, family, friends, and school and gone forward to serve in His harvest fields so wide. Men of the world ask the question: "Why do they respond so readily and willingly give so much?" Our missionaries could well answer in the words of Paul, that peerless missionary of an earlier day: "For though I preach the gospel, I have nothing to glory of: for necessity is laid upon me; yea, woe is unto me if I preach not the gospel!" (1 Corinthians 9:16.)

The Holy Scriptures contain no more relevant proclamation, no more binding responsibility, no more direct instruction than the injunction given by the resurrected Lord as he appeared in Galilee to the eleven disciples. Said he: "All power is given unto me in heaven and in earth. Go ye therefore, and teach all nations, baptizing them in the name of the Father, and of the Son, and of the Holy Ghost: Teaching them to observe all things whatsoever I have commanded you: and, lo, I am with you alway, even unto the end of the world." (Matthew 28:18-20.)

This divine command, coupled with its glorious promise, is our watchword today as in the meridian of time. Missionary work is an identifying feature of The Church of Jesus Christ of Latter-day Saints. It has always been so; it shall ever be. As the Prophet Joseph Smith declared: "After all that has been said, the greatest and most important duty is to preach the Gospel." (*History of the Church,* vol. 2, p. 478.)

Within eighteen months or two years, all of these missionaries in this royal army of God will conclude their full-time labors and return to their homes and loved ones. Their replacements are found in the ranks of the converted and devoted members of the Church. Young men and women, are you ready to respond? Are you willing to work? Are you prepared to serve? Mediocrity is not in fashion. Excellence is the order of the day.

President John Taylor summed up the requirements:

The kind of men we want as bearers of the gospel message are men who have faith in God; men who have faith in their religion; men who honor their priesthood; men in whom the people who know them have faith, and in whom God has confidence. . . . We want men full of the Holy Ghost and the power of God. . . . Men who bear the words of life among the nations ought to be men of honor, integrity, virtue and purity; and this being the command of God to us, we shall try to carry it out.

Now that is quite an order. Especially is it so when I reflect upon several of the young and inexperienced missionaries who came to the mission over which I had the privilege to preside. I shall ever remember the bewilderment of one boy from down on the farm when he first gazed at the skyscrapers of Toronto. He inquired of me: "President, how many people in this here town?" I answered: "Oh, about a million and a half." To which he responded, "Goll-ee! There are only eighty in my home town."

That evening in our traditional get-acquainted testimony meeting, some of the veteran missionaries expressed themselves regarding the difficulty of the work. "Doors will slam in your face, abusive language will be hurled toward you, you'll get discouraged and downhearted, but when it's all over, you will say, 'These have been the happiest two years of my life.' " My missionary from the small town was more hesitant than ever as he spoke falteringly: "I'll be glad when the happiest two years of my life are over."

At best, missionary work necessitates drastic adjustment to one's pattern of living. No other labor requires longer hours or greater devotion, nor such sacrifice and fervent prayer. As a result, dedicated missionary service returns a dividend of eternal joy that extends throughout life and into eternity.

Today our challenge is to be more profitable servants in the Lord's vineyard.

May I suggest a formula that will insure a missionary's success:

1. *Search the scriptures with diligence!*
2. *Plan your life with purpose!*
3. *Teach the truth with testimony!*
4. *Serve the lord with love!*

Let us consider each of the four parts of this formula.

1. Search the scriptures with diligence

The scriptures testify of God and contain the words of eternal life. They become the strength of the missionary's message—even the tools of his trade. His confidence will be directly related to his knowledge of God's word. Oh, yes, there are some missionaries who are lazy, less than effective, and anxious for their missions to conclude. A careful examination of such instances will reveal that the actual culprit is not laziness nor disinterest, but is the foe known as *fear*. Our Father chastized such: ". . . with some I am not well pleased, for they will not open their mouths, but they hide the talent which I have given unto them, because of the *fear* of man. . . ." (D&C 60:2. Italics added.)

Had not this same loving Heavenly Father provided a prescription to overcome this malady, his words perhaps would appear overly harsh. In a revelation given through Joseph Smith the Prophet on January 2, 1831, the Lord declared: ". . . if ye are prepared ye shall not fear." (D&C 38:30.) This is the key. Will you use it?

How grateful am I that the family home evening manual places emphasis upon the scriptures. The seminary and institute curricula likewise stress the scriptures and help the student to internalize their vibrancy and meaning. The same holds true of the courses of study now used by the priesthood quorums and the auxiliary organizations, all programmed and coordinated through the correlation effort of the Church.

Let me provide but one reference that has immediate application to our lives. In the Book of Mormon, the 17th chapter of Alma, we read the account of Alma's joy as he once more saw the sons of Mosiah and noted their steadfastness in the cause of truth. The record describes these "missionaries."

> . . . they had waxed strong in the knowledge of the truth; for they were men of a sound understanding and they had searched the scriptures diligently, that they might know the word of God.
>
> But this is not all; they had given themselves to much prayer, and fasting; therefore they had the spirit of prophecy, and the spirit of revelation, and when they taught, they taught with power and authority of God. (Alma 17:2-3.)

Search the scriptures diligently!

2. Plan your life with purpose

Preparation for a mission begins early. It is a wise parent who encourages young Jimmy to commence even in boyhood his personal missionary fund. As the fund grows, so does Jimmy's desire to serve. He may well be encouraged as the years go by to study a foreign language, that if necessary his language skills could be utilized. Didn't the Lord say, "Teach all nations"? (Matthew 28:19.)

Then comes that glorious day when the bishop invites

Jim into his office. Worthiness is ascertained; a missionary recommendation is completed. There follow those anxious moments of wonderment and the unspoken question, "I wonder where I will be called?"

During no other crisis does the entire family so anxiously watch and wait for the mailman and the letter that contains the return address: 47 East South Temple, Salt Lake City, Utah. The letter arrives, the suspense is overwhelming, the call is read. Often the assigned field of labor is a far-away place with a strange-sounding name—Tonga, the Philippines, France-Belgium—to name but a few. More frequently, the assignment may be closer to home. The response of the prepared missionary is the same: *"I will serve."*

The experience at the Missionary Home in Salt Lake City is enjoyable, hectic, and helpful. Never has a young person had newer clothing, cleaner shirts, nor more uncomfortable shoes. He occupies the limelight. It is a touching scene to witness parents of modest means give so freely to outfit their sons and daughters. I hope our youth appreciate the sacrifice their parents so willingly make for them. Their labors will sustain the missionary, their faith will encourage him, their prayers will uphold him. A mission is a family affair. Though the expanse of oceans may separate, hearts are as one, as evidenced by this letter from a missionary son to his father:

Dear Dad:

This is my first Christmas away from my home and family. I wish that I could be home to share the joy, good cheer, and the love that come with this season; but I am grateful to be here in Sweden as a missionary.

I'm grateful for my father; I do so love, admire, and respect him. His life has always been a wonderful example to me and has helped me countless times to make the right decisions.

I'm grateful for his wisdom, which has counseled me; his love, which has disciplined me; and his testimony, which has inspired me.

How can a son show his love for his father? How can he fully express what he feels? How can he demonstrate his gratitude? I wish

99

I could answer these questions. There is, however, one way that I know I can show my gratitude, and that is by patterning my life after that of my father.

This, then, is my task—to live a life equal to that of my father's, that I may spend eternity together with him.

Merry Christmas and God Bless You,
Paul

As young Latter-day Saints plan with purpose their lives, they should remember that their missionary opportunities are not restricted to the period of a formal call. Time spent in military service can and should be profitable. Each year, our young men and women in uniform bring thousands of souls into the kingdom of God. How do they accomplish this marvelous feat? They themselves honor their priesthood, live the commandments of God, and teach to others his divine word. Many returned missionaries have testified that their missionary experiences in the military were equally as bountiful and richly rewarding as in the mission field itself.

And while pursuing their formal education, young people should not overlook their privilege to be missionaries. Their example as Latter-day Saints is being observed, weighed, and ofttimes will be emulated. They should make time in their lives and provide room in their hearts for school, a mission, the military and, of course, temple marriage.

Plan your life with purpose.

3. Teach the truth with testimony

We must obey the counsel of the apostle Peter, who urged: ". . . be ready always to give an answer to every man that asketh you a reason of the hope that is in you. . . ." (1 Peter 3:15.) We must lift up our voices and testify to the true nature of the Godhead, declare our witness concerning the Book of Mormon, convey the glorious and beautiful truths contained in the plan of salvation. Regarding one's testimony, remember, that which one willingly shares he keeps, while that which he selfishly keeps he loses. We must have the courage and the kindness, as did Jesus, to teach the Nicodemuses whom we may meet that baptism is essential to salvation. *Teach and testify.* There is no better combination.

Remember our boy from the rural community who marveled at the size of Toronto? He was short in stature but tall in testimony. Together with his companion, he called at the home of Elmer Pollard in Oshawa, Canada. Feeling sorry for the young men who, during a blinding blizzard, were going house to house, Mr. Pollard invited the missionaries into his home. They presented to him their message. He did not catch the spirit. In due time he asked that they leave and not return. His last words to the elders as they departed his front porch were spoken in derision: "You can't tell me you actually believe Joseph Smith was a prophet of God!"

The door was shut. The elders walked down the path. Our country boy spoke to his companion: "Elder, we didn't answer Mr. Pollard's question. He said we didn't believe Joseph Smith was a true prophet. Let's return and bear our testimonies to him."

At first the more experienced missionary hesitated, but finally he agreed to accompany his "green" companion. Fear struck their hearts as they approached the door from which they had been turned away. A knock, the confrontation with Mr. Pollard, an agonizing moment, then with power, a testimony born by the Spirit: "Mr. Pollard, you said we didn't really believe Joseph Smith was a prophet of God. Mr. Pollard, I testify that Joseph was a prophet; he did translate the Book of Mormon; he saw God the Father and Jesus the Son. I know it."

Mr. Pollard, now Brother Pollard, stood in a priesthood meeting sometime later and declared: "That night I could not sleep. Resounding in my ears I heard the words:

'Joseph Smith was a prophet of God. I know it. I know it. I know it.' The next day I telephoned the missionaries. Their message, coupled with their testimonies, changed my life and the lives of my family."

Teach the truth with testimony.

4. Serve the Lord with love

There is no substitute for love. Successful missionaries love their companions, their mission leaders, and the precious persons whom they teach. Often this love is kindled in youth by a mother, expanded by a father, and kept vibrant through service to God.

In the fourth section of the Doctrine and Covenants, the Lord established the qualifications for the labors of the ministry. Let us consider but a few verses:

> . . . O ye that embark in the service of God, see that ye serve him with all your heart, might, mind and strength, that ye may stand blameless before God at the last day.
>
> And faith, hope, charity and love, with an eye single to the glory of God, qualify him for the work.
>
> Remember faith, virtue, knowledge, temperance, patience, brotherly kindness, godliness, charity, humility, diligence. (D&C 4:2, 5-6.)

Well might each of us ask himself: Today, have I increased in faith, in virtue, in knowledge, in godliness, in *love?*

When our lives comply with God's own standard, those within our sphere of influence will never speak the lament: "The harvest is past, the summer is ended, and we are not saved." (Jeremiah 8:20.)

Through our dedicated devotion at home or abroad, those souls whom we help to save may well be those whom we love the most.

Several years ago, while touring the California Mission, I interviewed a missionary who appeared rather dejected and downcast. I asked him if he had been sending a letter home to his parents each week. He replied: "Yes, Brother Monson, each week for the last five months."

I responded: "And do you enjoy the letters you receive from home?"

Came his unexpected answer: "I haven't had a letter from home since I came on my mission. You see, my dad is inactive and mother is a nonmember. She didn't favor my accepting a mission call and said that if I went into the mission field she would never write nor send a dime." With a half smile which didn't really disguise the heartache, he said: "And she has kept her word. What can I do, Brother Monson?"

I prayed for inspiration. The answer came. "Keep writing, son, every week. Bear your testimony to mother and to dad. Let them know you love them. Tell them how much the gospel means to you. And serve the Lord with all your heart."

Six months later when I attended a stake conference in that area, this same elder ran up to me and asked: "Do you remember me? I'm the missionary whose parents didn't write." I remembered only too well and cautiously asked if he had received a letter from home. He reached into his pocket and held out to my view a large handful of envelopes. With tears streaming down his cheeks he declared proudly, "Not one letter, Brother Monson, but a letter every week. Listen to the latest one: 'Son, we so much appreciate the work you are doing. Since you left for your mission our lives have changed. Dad attends priesthood meeting and will soon be an elder. I have been meeting with the missionaries and next month will be baptized. Let's make an appointment to all be together in the Los Angeles Temple one year from now as you conclude your mission. Sincerely, Mother.' "

Love had won its victory. Serve the Lord with love.

May each one of us *search the scriptures with diligence;*

plan his life with purpose; teach the truth with testimony; and *serve the Lord with love.*

The perfect Shepherd of souls, the missionary who redeemed mankind, gave us his divine assurance:

> . . . if it so be that you should labor all your days in crying repentance unto this people, and bring, save it be one soul unto me, how great shall be your joy with him in the kingdom of my Father!
>
> And now, if your joy will be great with one soul that you have brought unto me into the kingdom of my Father, how great will be your joy if you should bring many souls unto me! (D&C 18:15-16.)

Of him who spoke these words, I declare my witness. He is the Son of God, our Redeemer and our Savior.

13

Constant truths in changing times

oday the classrooms of learning are vacant; textbooks with worn pages now have closed covers; the mammoth stadium, with its excitement of athletic contest, is strangely silent; no peal of the victory bell rings through the still air. Though it is morning, the beloved campus seems to echo the hymn:

> *Now the day is over; Night is drawing nigh,*
> *Shadows of the evening steal across the sky.*

Our emotion-filled hearts supply the reason: Graduation Day is here.

We honor our graduates for excellence in a world where mediocrity is commonplace. We welcome them to a brave new world. They will confront grievous uncertainties. We do not warn them of such a world—we welcome them to it. We admonish them: don't miss a second of it. Relish every moment. This big, wide, wonderful world we live in is yours.

In recent years the world has witnessed many changes —a population explosion of newly independent nations, an epidemic of international conflicts, and the steadily increasing role of government in society. We have observed the first glimpses of man's ultimate control over his environment—the unleashing of thermonuclear forces, the extension of the electron to virtually every human activity, the exploratory probings into the secrets of life, the reaching out to the moon and planets. If occasionally our older and younger generations have not been communicating on the same wave length, and there has been too much static in the air, it seems to me that this is due not so much to a difference in years, but to a fundamental difference in time.

The world has changed more in the nearly threescore years since World War II than in all the previous millennia of recorded history.

The dispersal of a mushroom cloud around the world moves us to awe at man's unlimited power and to dread at his limited wisdom. This is an age when man moves toward solving the mysteries of the highest heavens . . . and of the deepest oceans.

We are living in one of the most precious and privileged periods of all human history—a period of change and challenge and infinite promise. One cannot venture into the uncertainties of the future without reference to the certainties of the past. Our challenge is to join the forces of the old and the new—experience and experiment, history and destiny, the world of man and the new world of science.

We have observed in recent years the accelerating erosion of many of the restraints upon human conduct which have guided the lives of past generations. Theology has stretched its boundaries to embrace thinkers who proclaim the death of God, and God's orphans are freed to indulge their selfishness according to their whims.

There are those who declare chastity to be a state of mind rather than a physical condition. Integrity, which was once a fixed and absolute quality, has taken on a new flexibility; some seem to have accepted as their philosophy

Oscar Wilde's dictum that the best way to get rid of temptation is to give in to it.

Our intellectual and moral condition has fallen hopelessly behind our technical progress. Anxiously, and with sincere interest, youth may ask: Are there no constant truths to meet these changing times? Are there no islands of virtue amid seas of sin? For our answer we turn not to him who is applauded by the world for his scientific achievement, his cultural progress, or his degrees of learning. Rather, we seek an unfailing point of reference whereby we might orient our eternal course.

We turn backward in time that we might go forward with hope. Back, back beyond the silent generation, the beat generation, the lost generation. Back, back beyond the Space Age, the Computer Age, and Industrial Age. Back, back to him who walked the dusty paths of villages we now reverently call the Holy Land, to him who caused the blind to see, the deaf to hear, the lame to walk, and the dead to live. To him who tenderly and lovingly assured us, "I am the way, the truth, and the life."

His constant truths prevail in these changing times. He speaks to us today as he spoke to the multitudes who thronged about him those many years ago.

Do you remember his words? Do you recall his actions? Do you reflect his teachings in your life? His words and those of his apostles stand forth as rays of hope penetrating the dullness of despair.

Constant truth number 1

Jesus counseled, ". . . seek ye out of the best books words of wisdom; seek learning, even by study and also by faith." (D&C 88:118.)

Learning is not just an in-class activity, but an all-day, everywhere process. It is not all formal, is rarely neat, and is not at all cut-and-made-to-order. Maybe that is why it is so challenging. Schooling and education are not the same thing. Education is a process to which one is subjected throughout life. Schooling is only part of that process, an important part, but only a part and covering only a fraction of a normal life's span.

Remember, an educated man is not one whose memory is trained to carry a few dates in history—he is one who can accomplish things. A man who cannot think is not an educated man, however many college degrees he may have acquired. Thinking is the hardest work anyone can do, which is probably the reason why we have so few thinkers. As we pursue our careers and develop our purposes, we need to keep in mind the broader objectives of our time on earth, to achieve a balance and richness in our personal lives.

One must, having learned to learn, then go on learning. What the public takes for brilliance is really the result of thorough, painstaking investigation and downright hard work. Were we to be deprived of work, we should be robbed of our greatest field of enjoyment and be forever condemned to mediocrity.

Reading "out of the best books" stretches our mental muscles and expands our horizons. It takes us out of our mundane worlds and lets us travel as far as our imaginations and the picture-painting words of the authors can carry us. Reading keeps us vibrant; it keeps us alive and makes us far more interesting to our marriage mates and our families. It is also a form of insurance against mental aging. We are only as old as we think we are. Some people say that one way to keep alive is to keep interested in many things, and the way to keep interested is to read widely and wisely.

> *Books are keys to wisdom's treasure;*
> *Books are gates to lands of pleasure;*
> *Books are paths that upward lead;*
> *Books are friends; come, let us read.*

Reading is one of the true pleasures of life. In our age of mass culture, when so much that we encounter is abridged, adapted, adulterated, shredded, and boiled down, and commercialism's loudspeakers are incessantly braying, it is mind-easing and mind-inspiring to sit down privately with a good book. It is ennobling when that book contains the revealed word of God.

Constant truth number 2

James, a servant of God and of the Lord Jesus Christ, advised, "But be ye doers of the word, and not hearers only, deceiving your own selves." (James 1:22.)

Sloth is one of the seven deadly sins, responsible for a great deal of the failing and underachieving we see; but idling away one's time is not enjoying life. Emerson counseled: "God offers to every mind its choice between truth and repose. Take what you please—you can never have both."

To the Philippians the apostle Paul pleaded, "Finally, brethren, whatsoever things are true, whatsoever things are honest, whatsoever things are just, whatsoever things are pure, whatsoever things are lovely, whatsoever things are of good report; if there be any virtue, and if there be any praise, think on these things." (Philippians 3:8.)

But what comes next? What, beyond thinking, is so imperative? "Those things which ye have both learned, and received, and heard, . . . *do*: and the God of peace shall be with you." (Philippians 3:9. Italics added.)

With Paul, as he wrote to the Philippians, I plead with all Latter-day Saints to be doers, as well as thinkers, and thereby translate their thoughts into deeds and to live their thoughts to the highest level of their ideals.

Time is the raw material of life. Every day unwraps itself like a gift, bringing us the opportunity to spin a fabric of health, pleasure, and content and to evolve into something better than we are at its beginning. Success is contingent upon our effective use of the time given us. When we cease peering backwards into the mists of our past, and craning forward into the fog that shrouds the future, and concentrate upon doing what lies clearly at hand, then we are making the best and happiest use of our time. Success is the ratio of our accomplishments to our capacities.

We must not be beguiled by that enemy of accomplishment, even procrastination. More than two centuries ago Edward Young wrote, "Procrastination is the thief of time." In fact, procrastination is much more. It is the thief of our self-respect. It deprives us of the fullest realization of our ambitions and hopes.

Constant truth number 3

From the apostle Paul we are charged, ". . . be thou an example of the believers, in word, in conversation, in charity, in spirit, in faith, in purity."

What an all-encompassing challenge!

Leaders who lead by example are not in overabundant supply in our changing world. The international president of perhaps the largest trade union in the world was convicted and sentenced to a prison term for flagrantly violating the law of the land. His famous statement, "Every man has his price," finally led to his downfall, as he was given an eight-year prison sentence for tampering with a jury-hearing charge that he had accepted more than one million dollars in illegal payments from one firm and of fraudulently diverting one million dollars of trust funds.

Nor is business immune. Not too long ago top executives from one of our oldest and most respected companies were convicted of illegal price fixing and sentenced to prison terms.

By listening carefully, we hear the echo from the apostle of old, even Peter, who declared, ". . . what manner of persons ought ye to be. . . ." (2 Peter 3:11.)

Can we not be men and women of integrity, of principle, of honor? Not fence straddlers, but men of courage and conviction. Seek not freedom from responsibility, but the freedom and the willingness to accept responsibility.

There were about three million people who lived in the American colonies at the time of the Revolution. They could only get fifty-six people to sign the Declaration of Independence. It took a lot of courage, because they knew if this failed, they were going to hang by the neck until dead.

When you stop to think of it, it is pretty wonderful that they got even fifty-six to meet in Philadelphia and pledge their lives, their fortunes, and their sacred honor. One of them, John Hancock, achieved a certain measure of immortality by signing his name so large that nobody could miss the fact that John Hancock was for this.

There were a lot of Carrolls in the colonies, but the Carroll who signed wanted everybody to know which Carroll was for this Declaration of Independence, and he signed it "Carroll of Carrollton, Maryland." Steadfastness of purpose provides a refreshing breeze amidst the stale winds of indecision and lethargy.

One of the fundamental objectives of any student's life will have been realized if he who enters to learn now goes forth to serve: to serve his God and to serve his fellowmen; to be an example of one who loves the Lord with all his heart and his neighbor as himself.

To all inspired examples in our changing world, I say:

> You will meet sin—*shun it.*
> You inherit freedom—*protect it.*
> You have a testimony—*share it.*
> You know the truth—*live it.*

Constant truth number 4

"Be ye therefore perfect," counseled the only perfect Man. Such perfection is not achieved simply by wishing or hoping for it to come. It is approached as we establish specific goals in our lives and strive for their successful accomplishment.

Without a goal there can be no real success. Indeed, a good definition of success is: "The progressive realization of a worthy ideal."

An ancient philosopher observed, "We become what we think about." And the Savior taught, "As a man thinketh in his heart, so is he."

As we strive for perfection, we seek excellence. Excellence may leave one sensitive in the face of the jaded; curious in the crowd of uninterested; quiet in groups of static and noise; caring in the company of the unconcerned; exact while all about us is approximation; refined in place of gross; exceptional instead of commonplace.

To achieve known landmarks on the way to perfection, keen vision is required. As the wise sage commented: "Where there is no vision, the people perish."

Signs of national weakness pose threats to our quest for the perfect life—and these threats grow more prevalent as each day goes by. Some of them are: (1) the growing trend toward personal non-involvement; (2) the rising tide of mediocrity; and (3) the choice of security over opportunity.

We must refuse to compromise with expedience; to maintain the courage to defy the consensus; to choose the harder right instead of the easier wrong. By so doing, we will not detour, but rather ever remain on the way to perfection.

To aid each of us is the Church, for as Paul declared to the saints at Ephesus:

And he gave some, apostles; and some, prophets; and some, evangelists; and some, pastors and teachers;
For the perfecting of the saints, for the work of the ministry, for the edifying of the body of Christ:
Till we all come in the unity of the faith, and of the knowledge

of the Son of God, unto a perfect man, unto the measure of the stature of the fulness of Christ. (Ephesians 4:11-13.)

The symbol of academic accomplishment, the traditional cap and gown, is placed aside as we enter the laboratories of science, the offices of commerce, the halls of justice, the classrooms of teaching. In the words of Shakespeare's *Tempest,* "What's past is prologue." In the play, Antonio completes his comment by saying, "What is to come is in our hands."

Our youth today not only enter their new world—they help to shape it. Ruskin provided sound counsel:

Wherefore, when we build, let us think that we build forever. Let it not be for present delight, nor for present use alone; let it be such work as our descendants will thank us for, and let us think as we lay stone on stone that a time is to come when those stones will be held sacred, because our hands have touched them; and men will say, as they look upon the labor and wrought substance of them, "See, this our fathers did for us."

Our Father gave his Only Begotten Son for you and me. Jesus Christ, the Lord, spilled his precious blood and gave his blessed life that we might live. He provided a summary of constant truths to meet changing times.

And seeing the multitudes, he went up into a mountain: and when he was set, his disciples came unto him:
And he opened his mouth, and taught them, saying,
Blessed are the poor in spirit: for theirs is the kingdom of heaven.
Blessed are they that mourn: for they shall be comforted.
Blessed are the meek: for they shall inherit the earth.
Blessed are they which do hunger and thirst after righteousness: for they shall be filled.
Blessed are the merciful: for they shall obtain mercy.
Blessed are the pure in heart: for they shall see God.
Blessed are the peacemakers: for they shall be called the children of God.
Blessed are they which are persecuted for righteousness' sake; for theirs is the kingdom of heaven.
Blessed are ye, when men shall revile you, and persecute you, and

shall say all manner of evil against you falsely, for my sake. (Matthew 5:1-11.)

. . . seek ye first the kingdom of God, and his righteousness. . . . (Matthew 6:33.)

Such constant truths, when applied in our lives, will provide a never-failing compass to guide us along life's journey through changing times. No wave will be too high, no storm too severe, no danger too threatening, no objective too difficult, no peril too great.

May all of us follow in the footsteps of him who lived the perfect life, that we too will "increase in wisdom and stature, and in favour with God and man." (Luke 2:52.)

Adapted from a commencement address delivered at Brigham Young University.

14

Yesterday, today, and tomorrow

cclesiastes, or the Preacher, declares: "To every thing there is a season, and a time to every purpose under heaven: A time to be born, and a time to die; . . . A time to weep, and a time to laugh; a time to mourn, and a time to dance. . . ." (Ecclesiastes 3:1-2, 4.)

The pilgrimage of life has the bittersweet urgency of a lad . . .

who turns from home,
   eagerly, but reluctantly,
   moving past the point of no return,
   realizing that he is now really on his own;

who becomes aware of the awesome magnitude of life,
   more vast and complex than his wildest dreams,
   confronting questions bigger than life itself,
   knowing the answers he gives will not be complete;

who realizes that the future is wide open and unmade,
   its opportunities breathtaking,
   its dilemmas increasing,
   its guarantees evaporating.

So shall his knowledge always be incomplete and a

safe future forever beyond his grasp. This is the rhapsody and rigor of life.

Every passing instant is a juncture of many roads open to our choice. Shall we do this or that? Go this way or that? We cannot stand still. Choosing between alternatives in the use of time is evidence of one of the noblest of God's gifts, freedom of choice.

You ask, "Has one who has gone before left a road-map, that I may find my way?"

I answer: "There is no guide which shows each super-highway, every fork and turning of the many country roads, the washed-out bridge, or the blocked mountain pass."

Yet, if we listen carefully, we seem to hear the voices of those who have walked this way before. They speak as one. Their message:

> The past is behind—*learn from it.*
> The future is ahead—*prepare for it.*
> The present is here—*live in it.*

At times, progressive, eager youth frown on the possibility of learning from the past. Remember that the roads we travel so briskly lead out of dim antiquity, and we study the past chiefly because of its bearing on the living present and its promise for the future. When one fails to learn from the lessons of the past, he is doomed to repeat the same mistakes and suffer their attendant consequences.

This is not to infer that we should think longingly of our yesterdays, with the hope that we can somehow return and un-do or re-do, un-live or re-live the experiences of the past. The wishful thinking expressed in the lilting melody "Yesterday" by John Lennon and Paul McCartney just isn't a reality. They wrote:

Yesterday, all my troubles seemed so far away.

Yesterday, today, and tomorrow

Now it looks as though they're here to stay.
Oh, I believe in yesterday.

From the yesterdays of recorded history come thrilling lessons for our lives. Ever so long ago the Psalmist wrote: "It is better to trust in the Lord than to put confidence in man. It is better to trust in the Lord than to put confidence in princes." (Psalm 118:8-9.)

One who learned this lesson too late was Cardinal Wolsey, who, according to Shakespeare, spent a long life of faithful service to three sovereigns and enjoyed wealth and power. Finally, he was shorn by an impatient ruler. From the anguish of his soul, he cried: "Had I but served my God with half the zeal I served my king, he would not in mine age have left me naked to mine enemies." (*Henry VIII*, Act III, sc. 2.)

The scripture summarizes succinctly: "Fear God, and keep his commandments: for this is the whole duty of man." (Ecclesiastes 12:13.) *The past is behind—learn from it.*

What a fantastic future is in store! Here are but a few predicted developments:

E. G. Sherbourne, of Science Service, says that "our present scientific knowledge could be placed in ten million volumes and is increasing one million volumes a year." But listen! "By 1977, we will find out more than we have from the beginning of time to the present."

Knowledge has advanced more rapidly in the past fifty years than in the previous 5,000 years. It is doubling every ten years. There is 100 times more to know today than there was in 1900. By the year 2000, there will be 1,000 times as much to be learned as today.

The world is advancing: Our challenge is to advance with it. To do so, we had better take time to be informed, or time will leave us behind.

We need to learn constantly; to cease learning is to

cease existing. And the best way to prepare for our future does not consist of merely dreaming about it. Great men have not been merely dreamers; they have returned from their visions to the practicalities of replacing the airy stones of their dream castles with solid masonry wrought by their hands.

The future will present insurmountable problems—only when we consider them insurmountable. Our challenge is to keep faith with the past while we keep pace with the future. With the help of God, we can do so. *The future is ahead—prepare for it.*

Unfortunately, there are those who wish their lives away, looking only for tomorrow. The Spanish word for tomorrow is *"mañana"* and a familiar way of postponing a present duty is to await *"mañana."* A line from a popular song of a decade ago read, *"Mañana, mañana, mañana* is good enough for me." *Mañana,* or tomorrow, is not good enough for us. Live only for tomorrow and we will have a lot of empty yesterdays today. *The present is here—live in it.*

And what a dynamic life is ours. This is an age when man moves toward solving the mysteries of the highest heavens—and of the deepest oceans. In our lifetime man has made greater strides in science, in physics, in medicine, and in engineering than did all his forebears in countless generations of struggle up the ladder of civilization.

To meet the combined demands of the accumulated past and of the accumulating future, we need—

> —to act, not just react,
> —to program, not just protest,
> —to solve, not just resolve,
> —to perform, not just proclaim.

Man has made remarkable strides in conquering outer space, but how futile have been his efforts in conquering inner space—the space in the hearts and minds of men. Our

118

intellectual and moral condition has fallen hopelessly behind our technical progress. Our youth are the hope to restore the balance.

I can almost hear their unspoken question voiced in unison—HOW?

My answer:

> Be true to yourself.
> Be fair with your neighbor.
> Be faithful to your God.

Perhaps the word *character* best describes one who is true to himself. For character takes no account of what you are thought to be, but what you are. Character is having an inner light and the courage to follow its dictates.

One who is true to himself develops the attributes needed to survive errors, to keep marching on a road that seems to be without end, and to rise above disappointment and distress. His motto: to strive, to seek, to find—but never to yield.

Oh, how we need basic honesty! When discovered it is as a beautiful pearl. Its rarity has increased its value. May I illustrate?

Recently, while visiting in New Zealand we were showing a film to a group of missionaries. Operating the projector was Dick Nemelka, an all-American college and professional basketball star. During the course of showing the movie the film was broken. The sound stopped. The lights went on. Dick went about his task of applying a quick splice so the movie could continue. Someone reached over and whispered to him, "Did the film break?" He replied, "No, the film didn't break—I broke it." No performance on the basketball court ever marked Dick Nemelka more as an all-American than did his basic honesty, demonstrated so naturally that night.

When one is true to himself he is naturally fair with

his neighbor. He lives the sermon expressed in the song based on the words of John Donne:

> *No man is an island,*
> *No man stands alone;*
> *Each man's joy is joy to me,*
> *Each man's grief is my own.*
> *We need one another,*
> *So I will defend*
> *Each man as my brother,*
> *Each man as my friend.*[1]

Not so well phrased, but equally as moving, was the conversation between a man and a boy. Noticing a small lad carrying his lame brother upon his back and struggling with the burden, the man asked: "Isn't he too heavy for you to carry, son?" "Nah," came the reply. "He's not heavy—he's my brother."

True to ourselves, fair with our neighbors, we will not find it difficult to be faithful to our God.

"Created in the image of God" is not an idle phrase, but rather a noble truth. When this knowledge becomes ours, we will have achieved what the great English statesman, William H. Gladstone, declared as the world's greatest need: "A living faith in a personal God."

With such a living faith we will hear spoken from Mount Sinai for our guidance the law of God—even the Ten Commandments. We will know that the Savior's sermon given on the Mount is for us. The citizens of Capernaum, Bethsaida, Chorazin turned from him in disappointment as he offered them the kingdom of God rather than a kingdom of man. Destruction followed.

Philip, Peter, Matthew turned toward him and responded to his beckoning invitation, "Come, follow me." Joy resulted.

Lessons from the past, challenges of the future display

dramatically the need for God's help today. If we earnestly seek it, we shall surely find it. In the words from Proverbs: "I love them that love me; and those that seek me early shall find me. . . . For whoso findeth me findeth life, and shall obtain favour of the Lord." (Proverbs 8:17, 35.)

---

[1]"No Man Is an Island," by Joan Whitney and Alex Kramer. Published by Shawnee Press Inc., Delaware Water Gap, Pa. Copyright 1950 by Bourne, Inc. All rights reserved.

15

In quest of the abundant life

What an exciting life is available for each one of us today! We may not be a John Cabot, sailing off into the blue with the king's patent to discover new lands, nor a Captain James Cook, whose voyages of discovery carried him to the known ends of the earth. Captain Cook declared: "I had ambition not only to go farther than any man had ever been before, but as far as it was possible for a man to go."

But we can be explorers in spirit, with a mandate to make this world better by discovering improved ways of living and of doing things. The spirit of exploration, whether it be of the surface of the earth, the vastness of space, or the principles of living greatly, includes developing the capacity to face trouble with courage, disappointment with cheerfulness, and triumph with humility.

God left the world unfinished for man to work his skill upon. He left the electricity in the cloud, the oil in the earth. He left the rivers unbridged and the forests unfelled and cities unbuilt. God gives to man the challenge of raw materials, not the ease of finished things. He leaves the pictures unpainted and the music unsung and the problems unsolved, that man might know the joys and glories of creation.

Carl Sandburg described our possibilities: "I see America, not in the setting sun of a black night of despair ahead of us. I see America in the crimson light of a rising sun, fresh from the burning creative hand of God. I see great days ahead, great days possible to men and women of will and vision."

However, during the last half century, there has been in this country a gradual but continual retreat from standards of excellence in many phases of our life.

We observe business without morality; science without humanity; knowlege without character; worship without sacrifice; pleasure without conscience; politics without principle; and wealth without works.

Perhaps the renowned author Charles Dickens, without really realizing his prophetic powers, described our day when he spoke of a period two centuries ago. His classic *A Tale of Two Cities* begins:

> It was the best of times, it was the worst of times, it was the age of wisdom, it was the age of foolishness, it was the epoch of belief, it was the epoch of incredulity, it was the season of Light, it was the season of Darkness, it was the spring of hope, it was the winter of despair; we had everything before us, we had nothing before us. . . .

To measure the goodness of life by its delights and pleasures and safety is to apply a false standard. The abundant life does not consist of a glut of luxury. It does not make itself content with commercially produced pleasure, the nightclub idea of what is a good time, mistaking it for joy and happiness.

On the contrary—

> *Obedience to law,*
> *Respect for others,*
> *Mastery of self,*
> *Joy in service*
> —these constitute the *abundant life.*

Perhaps we would understand these essentials best if

we discussed them on an individual basis.

1. Obedience to law

We turn at once to that revered and renowned code of conduct which has guided mankind through every conceivable turmoil. In so doing, we seem to hear the echo of the voice from Mt. Sinai speaking to us today, here and now:

> *Thou shalt have no other gods before me.*
> *Thou shalt not make unto thee any graven image. . . .*
> *Thou shalt not take the name of the Lord thy God in vain. . . .*
> *Remember the sabbath day, to keep it holy. . . .*
> *Honour thy father and thy mother. . . .*
> *Thou shalt not kill.*
> *Thou shalt not commit adultery.*
> *Thou shalt not steal.*
> *Thou shalt not bear false witness. . . .*
> *Thou shalt not covet. . . .*
>
> *(Exodus 20:3-4, 7-8, 12-17.)*

The late Cecil B. DeMille stated, after exhaustive research for the epic motion picture, *The Ten Commandments:* "Man can't break the Ten Commandments—only break himself against them."

Years after the law of Moses was given, there came the meridian of time, when a great endowment emerged—a power stronger than weapons, a wealth more lasting than the coins of Caesar; for the King of kings and Lord of lords introduced into the principles of law the concept of love.

Do you remember the penetrating question of the inquiring lawyer? "Master, which is the great commandment in the law?" More importantly, do you recall the divine answer? "Thou shalt love the Lord thy God with all thy heart, and with all thy soul, and with all thy mind. This is the first and great commandment. And the second is like unto it, Thou shalt love thy neighbour as thyself." (Matthew 22:36-39.)

These are the laws of God. Violate them and we suffer lasting consequences. Obey them and we reap everlasting joy.

Let us not overlook obedience to the laws of the land. They do not restrict our conduct so much as they guarantee our freedom, provide us protection, and safeguard all that is dear to us.

In our time when otherwise honorable men bend the law, twist the law, and wink at violations of the law, when crime goes unpunished, legally imposed sentences go unserved, and irresponsible and illegal conduct soars beyond previously recorded heights, there is a very real need to return to the basic justice which the laws provide when honest men sustain them.

Coming as I do from the world of business, I cannot move on without pausing to mention obedience to the laws, not theories, of economics. One cannot continually spend more than he earns and remain solvent. This law applies to nations as well as to men. A worker cannot, in the long run, adhere to a philosophy of something for nothing as opposed to something for something. Nor can management dismiss as optional the necessity of an adequate corporate profit and a reasonable return to shareholders if our economy of free enterprise is to flourish.

When economic decisions are based on theory rather than law, we find the chaos experienced in Uruguay:

Labor wanted higher wages; industrialists wanted bigger income; but nobody wanted to do any work. Citizens thought more of their rights than of their obligations. The country's vast web of social legislation redistributed wealth but did not create it. . . . Nobody had the vision to see that what Uruguay needed was production. (John Gunther, *Uruguay—Utopia Gone Wild.*)

One person of wisdom observed, "Laws are the rules by which the game of life is played." In reality, they are

much more; for obedience to law is an essential requirement if you are to be successful in your quest for the abundant life.

2. Respect for others

Second, let us learn respect for others if we are to realize the abundant life. Man, by nature, is tempted to seek
only his own glory and not the glory of his neighbor or the
glory of his God. None of us lives alone—in our city, our
nation, or our world. There is no dividing line between
our prosperity and our neighbor's wretchedness.

It is an immutable law that the more you give away,
the more you receive. You make a living by what you get,
but you make a life by what you give.

As the apostle Paul observed in his charge to the elders, ". . . remember the words of the Lord Jesus, how he
said, It is more blessed to give than to receive." (Acts 20:35.)
This is a truth more profound than most of us realize. Fur-
thermore, it is a very practical truth. Many of the problems of our times arise out of an excess of receiving.

In no uncertain terms, the Lord spoke to us in the parable of the rich fool:

Take heed, and beware of covetousness; for a man's life consis-
teth not in the abundance of the things which he possesseth.
And he spake a parable unto them, saying, The ground of a cer-
tain rich man brought forth plentifully:
And he thought within himself, saying, What shall I do, because
I have no room where to bestow my fruits?
And he said, This will I do: I will pull down my barns, and build
greater, and there will I bestow all my fruits and my goods.
And I will say to my soul, Soul, thou hast much goods laid up for
many years; take thine ease, eat, drink, and be merry.
But God said unto him, Thou fool, this night thy soul shall be
required of thee: then whose shall those things be, which thou hast
provided?
So is he that layeth up treasure for himself, and is not rich
toward God. (Luke 12:15-21.)

Happiness abounds when there is genuine respect one

for another. Particularly to those not yet married I counsel: Those who marry in the hope of forming a permanent partnership require certain skills and attitudes of mind. They must be skillful in adapting to each other; they need capacity to work out mutual problems; they need willingness to give and take in the search for harmony; and they need unselfishness of the highest sort—thought for their partners taking the place of desire for themselves. This is respect. It is part of our quest for the abundant life.

3. Mastery of self

Perhaps the surest test of an individual's integrity is his refusal to do or say anything that would damage his self-respect.

One teacher commented, "In the last analysis, I have to be true to myself; but it is a little tough to do that when I am being false to my students, because I'm a teacher not for my sake, but for the sake of my students. And if I do them any mental, physical, emotional, or social harm, then I drag them down with me into what ought to be, but cannot be, my own private purgatory."

One of the imperative requirements of life is to be able to make choices. In order to do so, one must know how to look at things and oneself. One must also learn that to live means being able to cope with difficulties; problems are a normal part of life, and the great thing is to avoid being flattened by them.

The battle for self-mastery may leave a person a bit bruised and battered, but always a better man or woman. Self-mastery is a rigorous process at best; too many of us want it to be effortless and painless.

Some spurn effort and substitute an alibi. We hear the plea, "I was denied the advantages others had in their youth." And then we remember the caption that Webster, the cartoonist, placed under a sketch of Abraham Lincoln's log cabin: "Ill-housed, ill-fed, ill-clothed."

The abundant life

Others say, "I am physically limited." History is replete with people possessing physical limitations. Homer could have sat at the gates of Athens, have been pitied and fed by coins from the rich. He, like Milton, the poet, and Prescott, the historian, had good alibis—they were blind. Demosthenes, greatest of all great orators, had a wonderful alibi —his lungs were weak, his voice hoarse and unmusical, and he stuttered. Beethoven was stone deaf at middle age. They all had good alibis—but they never used them.

Today's world moves at an increasingly rapid pace. Scientific achievements are fantastic, advances in medicine are phenomenal, and the probings of the inner secrets of earth and the outer limits of space leave one amazed and in awe.

In our science-oriented age we conquer space, but cannot control self; hence, we forfeit peace.

Through modern science, man has been permitted to fly through space at great speeds and to silently and without effort cruise sixty days under water in nuclear-powered ships. Now that man can fly like a bird and swim like a fish, if only he could learn to walk on earth like a man.

Amazing as has been man's exploration of space, his achievements on earth have been scarcely less remarkable.

"The computer," says *Time* magazine, "is in fact the largely unsung hero of the thrust into space. Computers carefully check out all systems before launch, keep track of the spacecraft's position in the heavens, plot trajectories and issue precise commands to astronauts. These fabulous machines are changing the world of business, they have given new horizons to the fields of science and medicine, changed the techniques of education and improved the efficiency of government."

Could it be that these machines which can add, multiply, divide, sort, eliminate, and remember will someday be able to think? The answer is definitely negative. While the computer is an advance in man's thinking processes as radical as the invention of writing, it is neither the symbol of the millennium nor a flawless rival of the human brain. There are limits to human genius. Man can devise the most complex machines, but he cannot give them life or bestow upon them the powers of reason and judgment.

Why? Because these are divine gifts, bestowed solely at God's discretion.

God made a computer once, constructing it with infinite care and precision exceeding that of all the scientists combined. Using clay for the main structure, he installed within it a system for the continuous intake of information of all kinds and descriptions, by sight, hearing, and feeling; a circulatory system to keep all channels constantly clean and serviceable; a digestive system to preserve its strength and vigor in perpetuity; and a nervous system to keep all parts in constant communication and coordination. Lying there on the ground in the Garden of Eden, it far surpassed the finest modern computer and was equally dead. It was equipped to memorize and calculate and work out the most complex equation, but there was something lacking.

Then God drew near and "breathed into his nostrils the breath of life; and man became a living being." (Genesis 2:7.)

This is why man has powers no modern computer possesses or ever will possess. God gave man life and with it the power to think and reason and decide and love. With such power given to you and to me, mastery of self becomes a necessity if we are to have the abundant life.

4. Joy in service

To find real happiness, we must seek for it in a focus outside ourselves. No one has learned the meaning of living until he has surrendered his ego to the service of his fellowmen. Service to others is akin to duty, the fulfillment of which brings true joy.

Winston Churchill, as he addressed the people of the British Commonwealth as peace dawned on a weary world, said:

> The unconditional surrender of our enemies was a signal for the greatest outburst of joy in the history of mankind. The Second World War had indeed been fought to the bitter end in Europe. The vanquished as well as the victors felt inexpressable relief. But for us in Britain and the British Empire, who had alone been in the struggle from the first day to the last and staked our existence on the result, there was a sublime meaning behind it all. Weary and worn, impoverished but undaunted and now triumphant, we had a moment that was sublime. We gave thanks to God for the noblest of all His blessings—the sense that we had done our duty.

Each of us can be a leader. May I remind you that the mantle of leadership is not the cloak of comfort, but the role of responsibility. Perhaps our service is to youth. If so, I caution: "Youth needs fewer critics and more models." One hundred years from now it will not matter what kind of a car we drove, what kind of a house we lived in, how much we had in the bank account, nor what our clothes looked like. But the world may be a little better because we were important in the life of a boy or a girl.

Dr. Hans Selye says wisely in his book *The Stress of Life,* "Neither wealth, nor force, nor any other instrument of power can ever be more reliable in assuring our security and peace of mind than the knowledge of having inspired gratitude in a great many people."

This is the joy which comes through service.

Our training, our experience, our knowledge are tools to be skillfully used. They have been self-acquired. Our conscience, our love, our faith are delicate and precious instruments to guide our destiny. They have been God given.

May each realize a full measure of success in his

The abundant life

personal quest for the abundant life through

> *Obedience to law,*
> *Respect for others,*
> *Mastery of self,*
> *Joy in service.*

And in so doing, may the peace proffered by Jesus Christ, the author of the abundant life, ever be ours.

Adapted from a baccalaureate address delivered at Utah State University.

16

"Return with honor"

ave you ever contemplated just how many words relevant to life commence with the letter "M"? Let me name but a few: Men, Money, Morals, Mission, Marriage, Military. May I illustrate my theme by telling of an experience related to this last word, *military.*

I enlisted in the navy just ten days before I would have been drafted into the army. Navy boot camp was a never-to-be-forgotten experience. For the first three weeks I was convinced my very life was in jeopardy. The navy didn't seem to be trying to train, but rather to kill me. Finally came Sunday and the welcome news that all recruits would go to church.

Standing at attention in a brisk California breeze, I heard the words of the Chief Petty Officer: "Today, everybody goes to church. Those of you who are Catholic, you meet in Camp Decatur. Forward, march!" A rather sizeable contingent moved out. "Those of you who are Jewish, forward, march!" A somewhat smaller group marched on. "The rest of you Protestants, you meet in Camp Farragut. Forward, march!"

Instantly there flashed through my mind the thought:

Monson, you aren't Catholic. Monson, you aren't Jewish; Monson, you aren't Protestant. You are a Mormon. I stood fast.

Then came the perplexed comment of the Petty Officer. Sweeter words I have not heard. "Just what do you guys call yourselves?"

For the first time I knew there were others standing behind me on that drill grinder. In unison we replied, "We're Mormons."

He queried, "Mormons? Well, go find somewhere to meet."

We marched proudly by, almost to the cadence of the Primary rhyme our children recite:

> *Dare to be a Mormon;*
> *Dare to stand alone;*
> *Dare to have a purpose firm;*
> *Dare to make it known.*

Our company had no particular slogan or symbol. One fighting unit in the war was known as "The Fighting Irish," another as "Uncle Sam's Hellcats." Some Naval Air Corps squadrons painted on their planes the words "Remember Pearl Harbor" or "Back from Bataan." The motto I remember best was that adopted by an air wing stationed in Britain and involved almost daily with bombing and strafing runs over the continent. The words were simple, yet packed with pride and power: "Return with Honor."

These words connoted courage to fight fear and meet death. They reminded each man to do his duty, without flinching. They implied, "Better to die a man than return a coward."

Then, as now, there were those who would "cop out," fake mechanical trouble, pull up too suddenly from a dive, or skip-drop a bomb load to avoid heavily concentrated anti-aircraft fire.

To most, that motto "Return with Honor" became a

way of life. I wonder if it may not be a most desirable motto for each of us.

Many of us have left our childhood homes, our close families, our old friends, our home communities. One day we will return to that port called home. Have we determined to *return with honor?* Unfortunately, some do not. There are those who return a cheater, a loafer, a procrastinator—even a sinner.

I shall never forget such a one with whom I studied business law. On the football field he was the Saturday afternoon hero; in the classroom, just a phony. Oh, he was clever, all right. Perhaps too much so. During the final examination all books were to be closed. Now was the moment of truth. My friend came to class that morning in sandals. As the examination began, he placed his textbook on the floor, removed his bare feet from the sandals, and, with toes saturated with glycerine, opened his textbook and skillfully, with those educated toes, turned the pages, that he might find the answers to the questions asked. He received an A grade, as he did in other classes. Nominated for honors, praised for his intellectual acumen, he passed the examinations of school but failed the test of manhood. Don't be a cheater.

In a similar class is the loafer or procrastinator. Content with mediocrity, he becomes an underachiever in life and loses perhaps forever that reward of excellence which, with concentrated effort, would have become his precious prize.

Along the road of life are many who are eager to help and advise us. We must not lend a listening ear to the persuasive voice of that evil one who would entice us to depart from our standards, our home-inspired teachings and philosophy of life. We must remember, rather, that gentle and ever-genuine invitation from the Redeemer, "Behold, I stand at the door, and knock: if any man hear

my voice, and open the door, I will come in to him. . . ."
(Revelation 3:20.) He speaks to each of us. Will we respond? As we do, our lives will be blessed, our education
enhanced, our happiness assured. We will *return with honor.*

Many young men today interrupt their formal schooling to fill a mission or to serve their country. Such an
experience should not be feared, but cherished. They have
the privilege of standing before the world as a beacon on
a hill—even a light unto the world. Will they falter? Will
they fail? Or will they *return with honor?* The choice is theirs.
Their attitude will make the difference.

Ella Wheeler Wilcox, the poet, had keen insight into
life when she penned the lines:

> *One ship drives East and another drives West*
> *With the self-same winds that blow.*
> *'Tis the set of the sails and not the gales*
> *Which tells us the way to go.*
>
> *Like the winds of the sea are the ways of fate,*
> *As we voyage along through life.*
> *'Tis the set of the soul that decides the goal,*
> *And not the calm or the strife.*

Three capsule illustrations may be helpful.

First, from a serviceman, this letter:

Dear Brother Monson: Today I arrived in Vietnam. It is raining, dull,
and frustrating. Yet I am happy, for I know this experience can be a
great missionary opportunity. Already I have participated in gospel
discussions with six interested persons not yet members of the Church.
This assignment is called a tour of duty, but to me it is a missionary
privilege.

Second, from a missionary.

Dear Brother Monson: Today was the greatest day in my life. I am the
happiest man in the world. You remember I spend much of my time in
a wheelchair and have done since a bout with polio long years ago. At
7:00 p.m., in this glorious state of California, my companions wheeled

me to the edge of the baptism font. I lifted myself from the wheelchair and, with effort, lowered my weak legs and crippled body into the font. I took the hand of one who had found the truth and pledged to live it and repeated the baptism prayer, then immersed him in those waters which cleanse soiled and troubled lives. He thanked me. I thanked God.

Third, from a cold—even an old—city of eastern Canada. The missionaries called it stony Kingston. There had been but one convert in six years, even though missionaries had been continuously assigned during that entire interval. No one baptized in Kingston. Just ask any missionary who labored there. Days in Kingston were marked on the calendar like days in prison. A missionary transfer to another place—anyplace—would be uppermost in thoughts, even in dreams.

While praying and pondering this sad dilemma, for my responsibility as a mission president required that I pray and ponder about such things, my wife called to my attention an excerpt from *A Child's Story of the Life of Brigham Young,* by Deta Petersen Neeley. She read: "Brigham Young entered Kingston, Ontario, on a cold and snow-filled day. He labored there thirty days and baptized forty-five souls." Here was the answer. If the missionary Brigham Young could accomplish this harvest, so could the missionary of today. Without explanation I withdrew the missionaries from Kingston, that the continuity of defeat might be broken. Then the carefully circulated word: "Soon a new city will be opened for missionary work, even the city where Brigham Young proselyted and baptized forty-five persons in thirty days." The missionaries speculated as to the location. Their weekly letters pleaded for the assignment to this "Shangri-la." More time passed. Then four carefully selected missionaries—two of them new, two of them experienced—were chosen for this high adventure. The members of the small branch pledged their support. The missionaries pledged their lives. The Lord honored both. In the space of three months, Kingston became the most productive city of the Canadian Mission. The city was the same, the population constant. The change was one of attitude.

Consider the serviceman in Vietnam, the crippled elder in California, the missionaries in Kingston. Like a silver thread running through the fabric of their lives is the spirit, "I will go and do the things which the Lord hath commanded. . . ." (1 Nephi 3:7.) Such will indeed *return with honor.*

Departure for school, entrance into military or missionary life—these are indeed significant journeys. Yet all of us commenced a more awesome and vital undertaking when we left the spirit world and entered the stage of mortality. Loving parents made us welcome. Inspired teachers taught us truth. True friends provided counsel. Yet life's choices remain for each to make.

A favorite hymn counsels:

> *Choose the right! there is peace in righteous doing;*
> *Choose the right! there's safety for the soul;*
> *Choose the right in all labors you're pursuing;*
> *Let God and heaven be your goal.*

Do you remember the game of childhood "Run, Sheepie, Run"? He who would look for the carefully hidden sheep would announce his search, "Ready or not, here I come!" So it is with the challenges of daily living—"Ready or not, here they come." How will we meet them? Bravely or cowardly? How will they leave us? Victorious or defeated? The outcome depends largely on these seven guideposts:

1. *Our perspective.* After the big London fire of long ago, the great English architect, Sir Christopher Wren, volunteered his services to plan and superintend the building of one of the world's greatest cathedrals. Unknown to

most of the workmen, he passed among them often, watching the construction.

To three stonecutters one day he put the same question: "What are you doing?" One of them answered, "I am cutting this stone." Another answered, "I am earning my three shillings per day." But the third stood up, squared his shoulders, and proudly said, "I am helping Sir Christopher Wren build this magnificent cathedral to our God."

2. *Our determination.* Let our creed be: I am a son of God. I am a daughter of God. I *will* endure!

3. *Our courage.* Courage becomes a living and attractive virtue when it is regarded not as a willingness to die manfully, but as the determination to live decently. A moral coward is one who is afraid to do what he thinks or knows is right because other men will disapprove or mock.

4. *Our love.* We must never lose sight of that marvelous lesson of the Savior of the world: "Thou shalt love the Lord thy God with all thy heart, and with all thy soul, and with all thy mind." (Matthew 22:37.)

5. *Our wisdom.* "Wisdom is the principal thing; therefore get wisdom: and with all thy getting get understanding." (Proverbs 4:7.)

6. *Our humility.* I speak not of a groveling posture before one's Maker, but rather a true appreciation of our own potential as worthy sons or daughters of God and knowledge of our total dependence upon him. One can't be one person and pretend to be another. Samuel Clemens, better known as Mark Twain, had Huckleberry Finn teach us this vital lesson. Huckleberry Finn is talking:

> It made me shiver. And I about made up my mind to pray and see if I couldn't try to quit being the kind of boy I was and be better. So I kneeled down. But the words wouldn't come. Why wouldn't they? It weren't no use to try and hide it from Him: . . . I knowed very well why they wouldn't come. It was because I was playing double. I was letting on to give up sin, but away inside of me I was holding on to the

biggest one of all. I was trying to make my mouth say I would do the right and the clean thing. But deep down in me, I knowed it was a lie, and He knowed it. YOU CAN'T PRAY A LIE. . . . I found that out.

7. Finally, *our faith*—faith in ourselves, faith in our future, faith in the Lord. Few examples of faith equal that of our pioneer forebears as they turned their backs on beautiful Nauvoo and, trusting in Divine Providence, faced west. Bancroft, in his *History of Utah,* described this faith: "And now, putting upon their animals and wagons such of their household effects as they could carry, in small detachments the migratory saints began to leave Nauvoo. Before them was the icebound river, and beyond that the wilderness."

These seven points of reference—perspective, determination, courage, love, wisdom, humility, and faith—will guide us, as they have ever guided faithful travelers on life's journey, back to our celestial home. At that time, may each of us hear the welcome salutation: ". . . thou hast been faithful over a few things, I will make thee ruler over many things: enter into the joy of the lord." (Matthew 25:23.) Thou hast indeed *returned with honor!*

Adapted from a Brigham Young University devotional assembly address.

17

Faces of failure vs. attitudes of accomplishment

ach evening as daylight departs and darkness comes to New York's famed Broadway or London's Drury Lane, the bright lights of the theatre bid welcome to the native and to the tourist. Some productions are poor and play for but an abbreviated season. Others are splendid and continue to attract hosts of patrons. Both Broadway and Drury Lane have boasted of one marvelous musical that has set a new record each time the curtain has been raised. *Fiddler on the Roof,* by Joseph Stein, is in a class by itself.

One laughs as he observes the old-fashioned father of a Jewish family in Russia as he attempts to cope with the changing times brought forcibly home to him by his beautiful daughters. With abandon they sing "Matchmaker, Matchmaker, Make Me a Match." Tevye, the father, replies with "If I Were a Rich Man." Tears come to the viewer as he hears the beautiful strains of "Sunrise, Sunset," and he seems to appreciate Tevye's love of his native village when the cast sings "Anatevka."

The gaiety of the dance, the rhythm of the music, the excellence of the acting all fade in significance when Tevye speaks what to me becomes the message of the musical. He gathers his lovely daughters to his side and, in the simplicity of his peasant surroundings, counsels them as they ponder their future. *"Remember,"* cautions Tevye, *"in Anatevka each one of us knows who he is and what God expects him to become."*

Contemplating our earthly life, could not each of us well consider Tevye's statement and respond, "Here, each one of us knows who he is and what God expects him to become."

Oh, the records may indicate one's name to be Mary Jane Roberts or John S. Marshall; they may show one to be from Boston, Atlanta, or Portland. The revealed word of God tells us much more. In chapter one of the first book of Moses, called Genesis, we read: "In the beginning God created the heaven and the earth. And the earth was without form, and void; and darkness was upon the face of the deep. . . . And God said, Let there be light: and there was light. . . . And God said, Let there be a firmament. . . ," and it was so. God created the beasts of the field, the fowl of the air, and the creatures of the deep. "And God said, Let us make man in our image, after our likeness. . . . So God created man in his own image, in the image of God created he him; male and female created he them. And God blessed them. . . ." (Genesis 1:1-3, 6, 26-28.) Heaven reflects his handiwork; earth echoes his skill; man becomes his masterpiece.

As Latter-day Saints we know that we lived before we came to earth, that mortality is a probationary period wherein we might prove ourselves obedient to God's command and thus worthy of celestial glory.

Our individual journey through life will be marked by sorrow and joy, sickness and health—even by *failure* and *accomplishment*. Failure, that monstrous scoundrel that would thwart our progress, stifle our initiative and destroy our dreams, has many faces. Can we recognize them?

There is the *Face of Fear*. Fear erects barriers that separate us from our objectives. We become content with mediocrity, when in reality excellence is within our grasp. The comment of the crowd causes us to withdraw from the race, and we retreat to the supposed safety of a sheltered life. A question from the movie *Shenandoah* points up our cowardice: "If we don't try, we don't do; and if we don't do, then why are we here?"

Failure has yet another face, even the *Face of Idleness.* To daydream, to loaf, to wish without work is to fall into the power of its hypnotic trance. So subtle, so inviting is the appeal of idleness that one does not know he has yielded his powers to such a deceitful face. "There has never lived a person who was an idler in his own eyes."

Consider the *Face of Doubt.* It too is one of failure's many masks. Doubt destroys. It chips away at our confidence, undermines our testimony and erodes our resistance to evil. Shun its winsome smile.

No enumeration of failure's many faces would be complete without the *Face of Sin.* This culprit plays for keeps. The stakes are high. Paul declared, "The wages of sin is death." (Romans 6:23.) And who can disregard the word of the Lord: "That which breaketh a law, and abideth not by law, but seeketh to become a law unto itself, and willeth to abide in sin, and altogether abideth in sin, cannot be sanctified by law, neither by mercy, justice, nor judgment. . . ." (D&C 88:35.)

Thus are the faces of failure: the *Face of Fear,* the *Face of Idleness,* the *Face of Doubt* and the *Face of Sin.* Let us never for a moment cast even a glance toward such a face. Rather, may we determine our destiny by incorporating into our lives the *Attitudes of Accomplishment.*

First, the *Attitude of Faith.* Whereas doubt destroys, faith fulfills. Such an attitude brings one closer to God and to his purposes. President David O. McKay often mentioned, "Man's earthly existence is but a test as to whether he will concentrate his efforts, his mind, his soul upon things which contribute to the comfort and gratification of his physical nature, or whether he will make as his life's pursuit the acquisition of spiritual qualities." Faith implies a certain trust, even a reliance, upon the word of our Creator.

An attitude of faith can convert a doubter to a doer. When Joseph Smith approached the doubting John E. Page with a call to fill a mission in Canada, Brother Page replied, "I cannot go on a mission to Canada, Brother Joseph. I haven't even a coat to wear." The Prophet removed his own coat, handed it to him, and said, "Here, wear this and the Lord will bless you." John E. Page had faith in the Prophet's promise. He labored two years in Canada, walked 5,000 miles, and baptized 600 souls.

Second, the *Attitude of Work.* Formula W is interesting: "Work will win when wishy-washy wishing won't." An attitude of work results in the capacity to make continuous effort toward the accomplishment of a given goal.

I'm an ardent sports fan. Long will I remember a TV sportscaster as he lauded the outstanding performance of Y. A. Tittle, one of the all-time great professional football quarterbacks. He said: "This will be the key play of the game. Tittle has the snap from center; he fades to throw, but his line cannot hold. It appears the game is over. Wait, Tittle has eluded his tacklers; he has fallen deep behind the line. He cocks his arm to throw, and the pass is away and caught in the end zone for a touchdown. That was a great second effort by Y. A. Tittle."

In the game of life a second effort is often required. The happy life is not ushered in at any age to the sound of drums and trumpets. It grows upon us year by year, little by little, until at last we realize that we have it. It is achieved in individuals not by flights to the moon or Mars, but by a body of work done so well that we can lift our heads with assurance and look the world in the eye. Of this be sure: You do not find the happy life—you make it.

Third, the *Attitude of Courage.* I've seen courage in the military. I've witnessed courage in the classrooms of learning and the factories of industry. Never have I observed its beauty more radiant than reflected from the service of a missionary. As a member of the Missionary Executive Committee of the Church, I often interview prospective missionaries who have physical impairments or other shortcomings. In considering the recommendation of one such candidate, the bishop of the ward had written: "Brother _____ is badly scarred due to an automobile accident. However, if courage will help, he'll lead the lot." I made an appointment to visit with the lad. My initial reaction upon meeting him was one of mixed surprise and pity. His face was badly scarred. He had been trapped in a burning automobile. Gone were his eyebrows, eyelashes, portions of his nose and face. "Son," I responded, "if you were in the mission field, there would be those who would reject your message and you may feel that they were rejecting you. This would be unbearable."

"Brother Monson," he replied, "I have become accustomed to that challenge. It doesn't bother me anymore. I so much want to serve the Lord and to preach the gospel. Please let me be called." The courage of his spirit bore witness to me of his faith. He received a call. After two years of outstanding missionary activity, his president wrote, upon the occasion of his honorable release:

> The bearer of this letter has served in this mission for two years. He has been one of the finest missionaries in our mission over the whole time that he has been here. He has been effective as a leader, as a proselyting missionary, as the liaison between the mission office and the several stakes in which he has served, and in all respects his performance has been without flaw.
>
> He has handled his personal problem, his severe scarring, in a way which has discouraged or affronted no one. It has been on a basis that "this is my problem; don't worry about it."

Failure vs. accomplishment

We love him dearly. We are grateful for his services; and if you have any more just like him, send them along.

Fourth, the *Attitude of Obedience.* All of us have an opportunity to live the commandments of our Heavenly Father, to love him with all our heart, mind, and strength and to demonstrate this love by how we serve. We receive callings in his kingdom. How well do we obey his bidding? How do we magnify our calling from the Lord?

The Prophet Joseph was often asked, "Brother Joseph, what do you mean by magnifying a calling?" Joseph replied: "What does it mean to magnify a calling? It means to build it up in dignity and importance, to make it honorable and commendable in the eyes of all men, to enlarge and strengthen it, to let the light of heaven shine through it to the view of other men. And how does one magnify a calling? Simply by performing the service that pertains to it. An elder magnifies the ordained calling of an elder by learning what his duties as an elder are and then by doing them."

Finally, the *Attitude of Love.* Such an attitude characterized the mission of the Master. He gave sight to the blind, legs to the lame, and life to the dead. Perhaps when we face our Maker, we will not be asked, "How many positions did you hold," but rather, "How many people did you help?" In reality, one can never love the Lord until he serves him by serving his people.

Do you recall the experience of John Weightman from Van Dyke's immortal "The Mansion"? He lived a life of wretched selfishness. He gave only those coins which would be seen of men and honor thus accorded him. Then one night he dreamed that he visited the Celestial City. He was given a dilapidated, old house in which to live. Feeling that this was unjust, because he felt he had lived a successful life, he inquired of the keeper of the Celestial City:

Failure vs. accomplishment

"What is it that counts here?" The answer: "Only that which is truly given. Only that good which is done for the love of doing it. Only those plans in which the welfare of others is the master thought. Only those labors in which the sacrifice is greater than the reward. Only those gifts in which the giver forgets himself."

Like John Weightman, we may be called upon to demonstrate an attitude of love. It may not take place in a Celestial City, but closer to home and nearer to the heart.

Our task is to recognize our opportunities and to pursue them successfully.

Thus, we have but a sampling of the attitudes of accomplishment: the *Attitude of Faith,* the *Attitude of Work,* the *Attitude of Courage,* the *Attitude of Obedience,* and the *Attitude of Love.* Such will overcome the faces of failure and permit us to respond affirmatively to old Tevye from *Fiddler on the Roof.* Each of us knows who he is and what God expects him to become. And with a loving Heavenly Father's ever-present help, we shall become even sons and daughters of the most high God.

Adapted from a Brigham Young University devotional assembly address.

THE PATHWAY OF

LOVE

". . . Thou shalt love the Lord thy God with all thy heart,
and with all thy soul, and with all thy mind.
This is the first and great commandment. And the second
is like unto it, Thou shalt love thy neighbour as thyself."

MATTHEW 22:37-39

18

Hands

hen Jesus of Nazareth taught and ministered among men, he spoke not as did the scribes and scholars of the day but rather in language understood by all. Jesus taught through parables. His teachings moved men and motivated them to a newness of life. The shepherd on the hillside, the sower in the field, the fisherman at his net all became subjects whereby the Master taught eternal truths.

The divinely created human body, with its truly marvelous powers and intricate parts, acquired new meaning when the Lord spoke of eyes that were not blinded but did really see, ears that were not stopped but did truly hear, and hearts that were not hardened but did know and feel. In his teachings he referred to the foot, the nose, the face, the side, the back. Significant are those occasions when he spoke of yet another part—even the human hand. Considered by artists and sculptors the most difficult member of the human body to capture on canvas or form in clay, the hand is a wonder to behold. Neither age, color, size, nor shape distorts this miracle of creation.

First, let us consider *the hand of a child.* Who among us has not praised God and marveled at his powers when an infant is held in one's arms. That tiny hand, so small yet so perfect, instantly becomes the topic of conversation. No one can resist placing his little finger in the clutching hand of an infant. A smile comes to the lips, a certain glow comes to the eyes, and one appreciates the tender feelings which prompted the poet to pen the lines:

A baby . . . that sweet new blossom of humanity, fresh fallen from God's own home to flower on earth.

As the child grows, the tightly clutched hand opens in an expression of perfect trust. "Take me by the hand, Mother; then I won't be afraid," bespeaks this confidence. The delightful song the little children sing so beautifully at once becomes a plea for patience, an invitation to teach— even an opportunity to serve:

I have two little hands folded snugly and tight.
  They are tiny and weak, yet they know what is right.
During all the long hours till daylight is through,
  There is plenty indeed for my two hands to do.

Kind Father, I thank thee for two little hands,
  And ask thee to bless them till each understands
That children can only be happy all day
  When two little hands have learned how to obey.

The sentiments such love and faith arouse should ever draw forth from each parent a pledge of fidelity—even a determination to do that which is right.

Should added emphasis be required, we need but refer to that account where the disciples came unto Jesus, saying:

Who is the greatest in the kingdom of heaven?
And Jesus called a little child unto him, and set him in the midst of them,
And said, Verily I say unto you, Except ye be converted, and become as little children, ye shall not enter into the kingdom of heaven.

Hands

And whoso shall receive one such little child in my name receiveth me.

But whoso shall offend one of these little ones which believe in me, it were better for him that a millstone were hanged about his neck, and that he were drowned in the depth of the sea. (Matthew 18: 1-3, 5-6.)

Second, may we turn our attention to *the hand of youth.* This is the training period when busy hands learn to labor —and labor to learn. Honest effort and loving service become identifying features of the abundant life. Each was effectively taught the girls in the Mutual Improvement Association class when cookies were baked and taken by them to elderly women residing in a neighborhood rest home. The aged hand of a lonely grandmother clasped that of the thoughtful teenager. No word was spoken. Heart spoke to heart. The hand that baked the cookies was raised to wipe a tear. Such hands are clean hands. Such hearts are pure hearts.

Then comes that day when the hand of a boy takes the hand of a girl, and parents suddenly realize their children have grown. Never is the hand of a girl so delicately displayed as when there glistens on her finger a ring denoting a sacred pledge. Her step becomes quicker, her countenance brighter, and all is well with the world. Courtship has come. Marriage follows. And once again two hands are clasped, this time in a holy temple. Cares of the world are for a brief moment forgotten. Thoughts turn to eternal values. The clasped hands speak of promised hearts. Heaven is here.

Time passes. The hand of a bride becomes *the hand of a mother.* Ever so gently she cares for her precious child. Bathing, dressing, feeding, comforting—there is no hand like mother's. Nor does its tender care diminish through the years. Ever shall I remember the hand of one mother— the mother of a missionary. Some years ago at a worldwide seminar for mission presidents, the parents of missionaries were invited to meet and visit briefly with each mission president. Forgotten are the names of each who extended a greeting and exchanged a friendly handshake. Remembered are the feelings which welled up within me as I took in my hand the calloused hand of one mother from Star Valley, Wyoming. "Please excuse the roughness of my hand," she apologized. "Since my husband has been ill, the work of the farm has been mine to do, that our boy may, as a missionary, serve the Lord." Tears could not be restrained nor should they have been. Such tears produce a certain cleansing of the soul. That boy continues to be very special to me, as he does to her. A mother's labor sanctified a son's service.

Not to be overlooked is *the hand of a father.* Whether he be a skilled surgeon, a master craftsman, or a talented teacher, his hands support his family. There is a definite dignity in honest labor and tireless toil. During the period of the great depression I was a small boy. Fortunate were those men who had work. Jobs were few, hours long, pay scant. On our street was a father who, though old in years, supported with the labor of his hands his rather large family of girls. His firm was known as the Spring Canyon Coal Company. It consisted of one old truck, a pile of coal, one shovel, one man, and his own two hands. From early morning to late evening he struggled to survive. Yet during the monthly fast and testimony meeting, I remember specifically his expressing his thanks to the Lord for his family, for his work, and for his testimony. The fingers of those rough, red, chapped hands turned white as they gripped the back of the bench on which I sat as Brother James Farrell bore witness of a boy who, in a grove of trees near Palmyra, New York, knelt in prayer and beheld the heavenly vision of God, the Father, and Jesus Christ, the Son. That boy was Joseph Smith. The memory of those hands of a father serve to remind me of his abiding faith, his honest conviction, and his testimony of truth.

Hands

On a Friday morning in the historic Tabernacle in October 1972, and in the homes of Church members viewing or listening to the conference session, hands were raised to sustain a prophet, a seer, and a revelator—even the president of The Church of Jesus Christ of Latter-day Saints. Our upraised hands were an outward expression of our inward feelings. As we raised our hands, we pledged our hearts. Could I for a moment mention the hands of that prophet, even President Harold B. Lee? I do so humbly and with his permission.

Some years ago, President Lee, directed by inspiration and revelation, called Dewitt J. Paul to serve as patriarch in one of the eastern stakes of the Church. The call humbled beyond words both Brother and Sister Paul. They wondered. They worried. They prayed for assurance and heavenly confirmation.

The vote of the people demonstrated their supporting approval. Then came the time for ordination. In a basement room situated in the stake meeting house, DeWitt Paul sat nervously on a chair and said a silent prayer. Seated next to Sister Paul was a dear friend in whom she had confided her concern. This trusted friend related a most unusual and inspiring account: "When Elder Lee, who stood behind Brother Paul who was seated, raised his hands to put them on Brother Paul's head, a very bright light like sunshine, as if coming through a high window about twelve inches square, suddenly focused on the crown of Elder Lee's head." She continued: "What a rare coincidence that the sun should begin to shine with a clear, bright light just at the moment Elder Lee was to place his hands upon the head of Brother Paul to pronounce a blessing and ordination! The experience was a confirmation of a sacred call. Suddenly I realized there was no window in that basement room through which the sun might beam its rays." Peace had replaced turmoil. Faith had overcome doubt. Precious are the hands of a prophet.

Finally, may we speak of yet another hand—even *the hand of the Lord*. This was the hand which guided Moses, which strengthened Joshua—the hand promised to Jacob when the Lord declared: "Fear thou not; for I am with thee: be not dismayed; for I am thy God: . . . I will uphold thee with the right hand of my righteousness." (Isaiah 41:10.) This was the determined hand which drove from the temple the money changers. This was the loving hand that blessed little children. This was the strong hand that opened deaf ears and restored vision to sightless eyes. By this hand was the leper cleansed, the lame man healed —even the dead Lazarus raised to life. With the finger of his hand there was written in the sand that message which the winds did erase but which honest hearts did retain. The hand of the carpenter. The hand of the teacher. The hand of the Christ. One called Pontius Pilate washed his hands of this man called King of the Jews. Oh foolish, spineless Pilate! Did you really believe that water could cleanse such guilt?

> *I think of his hands pierced and bleeding to pay the debt!*
> *Such mercy, such love, and devotion can I forget? . . .*
> *Oh, it is wonderful that he should care for me, enough to*
>   *die for me!*
> *Oh, it is wonderful, wonderful to me!*

Pitied is the hand that sins. Envied is the hand that paints. Honored is the hand that builds. Appreciated is the hand that helps. Respected is the hand that serves. Adored is the hand that saves—even the hand of Jesus Christ, the Son of God, the Redeemer of all mankind. With that hand he knocks upon the door of our understanding. "Behold, I stand at the door, and knock: if any man hear my voice and open the door, I will come in to him. . . ." (Revelation 3:20.)

Shall we listen for his voice? Shall we open the doorway of our lives to his exalted presence? Each must answer for himself.

In this journey called mortality, clouds of gloom may appear on the horizon of our personal destiny. The way ahead may be uncertain, foreboding. In desperation we may be prompted to ask, as did another:

> *I said to the man who stood at the gate of the year:*
> *"Give me a light, that I may tread safely into the unknown."*
> *And he replied:*
> *"Go out into the darkness and put your hand into the hand*
>   *of God.*
> *That shall be to you better than a light and safer than a*
>   *a known way."*

—M. LOUISE HASKINS,
"THE GATE OF THE YEAR"

19

Lost battalions

One November I stood on a very old bridge which spans the River Somme as it makes its steady but unhurried way through the heartland of France. Suddenly, I realized more than 50 years had come —then gone—since the signing of the Armistice of 1918 and the termination of the Great War. I tried to imagine what the River Somme looked like more than half a century before. How many thousands of soldiers had crossed this same bridge? Some came back. For others, the Somme was truly a river of no return. For the battlefields of Vimy Ridge, Armentieres, and Nueve Chappelle took a hideous toll of human life. Acres of neat, white crosses serve as an unforgettable reminder.

> *In Flanders fields the poppies blow*
> *Between the crosses, row on row,*
> > *That mark our place; and in the sky*
> > *The larks, still bravely singing, fly*
> *Scarce heard amid the guns below.*
>
> *We are the Dead. Short days ago*
> *We lived, felt dawn, saw sunset glow,*
> > *Loved and were loved, and now we lie*
> > *In Flanders fields.*
>
> —JOHN McCRAE

Lost battalions

I found myself saying softly, "How strange that war brings forth the savagery of conflict, yet inspires brave deeds of courage—some prompted by love."

As a boy, I enjoyed reading the account of the "lost battalion." The "lost battalion" was a unit of the 77th Infantry Division in World War I. During the Meuse-Argonne offensive, a major led this battalion through a gap in the enemy lines, but the troops on the flanks were unable to advance. An entire battalion was surrounded. Food and water were short; casualties could not be evacuated. Hurled back were repeated attacks. Ignored were notes from the enemy requesting the battalion to surrender. Newspapers heralded the battalion's tenacity. Men of vision pondered its fate. After a brief but desperate period of total isolation, other units of the 77th Division advanced and relieved the "lost battalion." Correspondents noted in their dispatches that the relieving forces seemed bent on a crusade of love to rescue their comrades in arms. Men volunteered more readily, fought more gallantly, and died more bravely. A fitting tribute echoed from that ageless sermon preached on the Mount of Olives: "Greater love hath no man than this, that a man lay down his life for his friends." (John 15:13.)

Forgotten is the plight of the "lost battalion." Unremembered is the terrible price paid for its rescue. But let us turn from the past and survey the present. Are there "lost battalions" even today? If so, what is our responsibility to rescue them? Their members may not wear clothes of khaki brown nor march to the sound of drums. But they share the same doubt, feel the same despair, and know the same disillusionment that isolation brings.

There are the "lost battalions" of the handicapped, even the lame, the speechless, and the sightless. Have you experienced the frustration of wanting but not knowing how to help the individual who walks stiffly behind his seeing-eye canine companion, or moves with measured step to the tap, tap, tap of a white cane? There are many who are lost in this trackless desert of darkness.

If you desire to see a rescue operation of a "lost battalion," visit your city's center for the blind and witness the selfless service of those who read to those who can't. Observe the skills which are taught the handicapped. Be inspired by the efforts put forth in their behalf to enable them to secure meaningful employment.

Those who labor so willingly and give so generously to those who have lost so tragically find ample reward in the light which they bring into the lives of the sightless.

Do we appreciate the joy of a blind person as his nimble fingers pass quickly over the pages of the Braille edition of the New Testament? He pauses at the twelfth chapter of John and contemplates the depth of meaning in the promise of the Prince of Peace: "I am come a light into the world, that whosoever believeth on me should not abide in darkness." (John 12:46.)

Consider the "lost battalions" of the aged, the widowed, the sick. All too often they are found in the parched and desolate wilderness of isolation called loneliness. When youth departs, when health declines, when vigor wanes, when the light of hope flickers ever so dimly, the members of these vast "lost battalions" can be succored and sustained by the hand that helps and the heart that knows compassion.

In Brooklyn, New York, there presides in a branch of the Church a young man who, as a boy of thirteen, led a successful rescue of such persons. He and his companions lived in a neighborhood in which resided many elderly widows of limited means. All the year long, the boys had saved and planned for a glorious Christmas party. They were thinking of themselves, until the Christmas spirit prompted them to think of others. Frank, as their leader, suggested to his companions that the funds they had accumulated so carefully be used not for the planned party, but rather for the benefit of three elderly widows who resided together.

The boys made their plans. As their bishop, I needed but to follow.

With the enthusiasm of a new adventure, the boys purchased a giant roasting chicken, the potatoes, the vegetables, the cranberries, and all that comprises the traditional Christmas feast. To the widows' home they went carrying their gifts of treasure. Through the snow and up the path to the tumbledown porch they came. A knock at the door, the sound of slow footsteps, and then they met.

In the unmelodic voices characteristic of thirteen-year-olds, the boys sang "Silent night, holy night; all is calm, all is bright." They then presented their gifts. Angels on that glorious night of long ago sang no more beautifully, nor did wise men present gifts of greater meaning. I gazed at the faces of those wonderful women and thought to myself: "Somebody's mother." I then looked on the countenances of those noble boys and reflected: "Somebody's son." There then passed through my mind the words of the immortal poem by Mary Dow Brine:

> *The woman was old and ragged and gray*
> > *And bent with the chill of the Winter's day.*
> *The street was wet with a recent snow,*
> > *And the woman's feet were aged and slow.*
> *She stood at the crossing and waited long,*
> > *Alone, uncared for, amid the throng*
> *Of human beings who passed her by*
> > *Nor heeded the glance of her anxious eye.*
>
> *Down the street, with laughter and shout,*
> > *Glad in the freedom of "school let out,"*
> *Came the boys like a flock of sheep,*

Lost battalions

Hailing the snow piled white and deep.
[One] paused beside her and whispered low,
"I'll help you cross, if you wish to go? . . .
She's somebody's mother, boys, you know,
For all she's aged and poor and slow.

"And I hope some fellow will lend a hand
To help my mother, you understand,
If ever she's poor and old and gray,
When her own dear boy is far away."
And "somebody's mother" bowed low her head
In her home that night, and the prayer she said
Was, "God be kind to the noble boy,
Who is somebody's son, and pride and joy."

There are other "lost battalions" comprised of mothers and fathers, sons and daughters who have, through thoughtless comment, isolated themselves from one another. An account of how such a tragedy was narrowly averted occurred in the life of a lad we shall call Jack.

Throughout Jack's life, he and his father had many serious arguments. One day, when he was seventeen, they had a particularly violent one. Jack said to his father: "This is the straw that breaks the camel's back. I'm leaving home, and I shall never return." So saying, he went to the house and packed a bag. His mother begged him to stay, but he was too angry to listen. He left her crying at the doorway.

Leaving the yard, he was about to pass through the gate when he heard his father call to him: "Jack, I know that a large share of the blame for your leaving rests with me. For this I am truly sorry. I want you to know that if you should ever wish to return home, you'll always be welcome. And I'll try to be a better father to you. I want you to know that I'll always love you." Jack said nothing, but went to the bus station and bought a ticket to a distant point. As he sat in the bus watching the miles go by, he commenced to think about the words of his father. He began to realize how much love it had required for him to do what he had done. Dad had apologized. He had invited him back and had left the words ringing in the summer air, "I love you."

It was then that Jack realized that the next move was up to him. He knew that the only way he could ever find peace with himself was to demonstrate to his father the same kind of maturity, goodness, and love that Dad had shown toward him. Jack got off the bus. He bought a return ticket to home and went back.

He arrived shortly after midnight, entered the house, and turned on the light. There in the rocking chair sat his father, his head in his hands. As he looked up and saw Jack, he rose from the chair and they rushed into each other's arms. Jack often said, "Those last years that I was home were among the happiest of my life."

We could say, "Here was a boy who overnight became a man. Here was a father who, suppressing passion and bridling pride, rescued his son before he became one of that vast 'lost battalion' resulting from fractured families and shattered homes." Love was the binding band, the healing balm. Love—so often felt; so seldom expressed.

From Mount Sinai there thunders in our ears, "Honour thy father and thy mother. . . ." And later, from that same God, the injunction, ". . . live together in love. . . ."

There are other "lost battalions." Some struggle in the jungles of sin, some wander in the wilderness of ignorance. In reality, each one of us is numbered in what could well have been the lost battalion of mankind, even a battalion doomed to everlasting death.

". . . by man came death. . . . For as in Adam all die. . . ." (1 Corinthians 15:21-22.) Each of us is a partaker of the experience called death. None escapes. Were we to remain unrescued, lost would be paradise sought. Lost would be family loved. Lost would be friends remembered. Realizing this truth, we begin to appreciate the supreme joy which accompanied the birth of the Savior of the world. How glorious the pronouncement of the angel: Behold a virgin "shall bring forth a son, and thou shalt call his name JESUS: for he shall save his people from their sins." (Matthew 1:21.)

While the rivers of France witnessed the advance of those who rescued the "lost battalion" in World War I, so did yet another river witness the commencement of the formal ministry of a universal rescuer, even a Divine Redeemer. The scripture records, "And there came a voice from heaven, saying, Thou art my beloved Son, in whom I am well pleased." (Mark 1:11.)

Today, only ruins remain of Capernaum, that city by the lakeshore, heart of the Savior's Galilean ministry. Here he preached in the synagogue, taught by the seaside, and healed in the homes.

On one significant occasion, Jesus took a text from Isaiah: "The Spirit of the Lord God is upon me; because the Lord hath anointed me to preach good tidings unto the meek; he hath sent me to bind up the brokenhearted, to proclaim liberty to the captives, and the opening of the prison to them that are bound" (Isaiah 6:1), a clear pronouncement of a divine plan to rescue the "lost battalion" to which we belong.

But Jesus' preaching in Galilee had been merely prelude. The Son of Man had always had a dread rendezvous to keep on a hill called Golgotha.

Arrested in the Garden of Gethsemane after the Last Supper, deserted by his disciples, spat upon, tried, and humiliated, Jesus staggered, under his great cross, toward Calvary. He progressed from triumph—to betrayal—to torture—to death on the cross.

In the words of the hymn, ". . . the scene was changed; the morn was cold and chill, as the shadow of a cross arose upon a lonely hill." For us our Heavenly Father gave his Son. For us our Elder Brother gave his life.

At the last moment the Master could have turned back. But he did not. He passed beneath all things that he might save all things—the human race, the earth, and all the life that ever inhabited it.

No words in Christendom mean more to me than those spoken by the angel to the weeping Mary Magdalene and the other Mary as they approached the tomb to care for the body of their Lord: "Why seek ye the living among the dead? He is not here, but is risen." (Luke 24:5-6.)

With this pronouncement, the "lost battalion" of mankind—those who have lived and died, those who now live and one day will die, and those yet to be born and yet to die—this battalion of humanity lost had just been rescued.

Of him who delivered each of us from endless death, I testify he is a teacher of truth—but he is more than a teacher. He is the exemplar of the perfect life—but he is more than an exemplar. He is the great physician—but he is more than a physician. He who rescued the "lost battalion" of mankind is the literal Savior of the world, the Son of God, the Prince of Peace, the Holy One of Israel, even the risen Lord, who declared, "I am the first and the last; I am he who liveth, I am he who was slain; I am your advocate with the Father." (D&C 110:4.)

As his witness I testify to you that he lives.

20
Only a teacher

ften we hear the expression, "Times have changed." And perhaps they have. Our generation has witnessed enormous strides in the fields of medicine, transportation, communication, and exploration, to name but a few. But there are those isolated islands of constancy amid the vast sea of change. For instance, boys are still boys. And they continue to make the same boyish boasts.

Some time ago I overheard what I am confident is an oft-repeated conversation. Three very young boys were discussing the relative virtues of their fathers. One spoke out: "My dad is bigger than your dad," to which another replied, "Well, my dad is smarter than your dad." The third boy countered: "My dad is a doctor"; then, turning to one boy, he taunted in derision, "and your dad is only a teacher."

The call of a mother terminated the conversation, but the words continued to echo in my ears. Only a teacher. Only a teacher. Only a teacher. One day, each of those small boys will come to appreciate the true worth of inspired teachers and will acknowledge with sincere gratitude the indelible imprint such teachers will leave on their personal lives.

"A teacher," as Henry Brook Adams observed, "af-

fects eternity; he can never tell where his influence stops."
This truth pertains to each of our teachers: first, the teacher in the home; second, the teacher in the school; third,
the teacher in the Church.

Perhaps the teacher you and I remember best is the
one who influenced us most. She may have used no chalk-
board nor possessed a college degree, but her lessons were
everlasting and her concern genuine. Yes, I speak of mother. And in the same breath, I also include father. In reality,
every parent is a teacher.

President David O. McKay reminded us that "the
proper training of childhood is man's most sacred obligation. . . . a child comes from the Father pure and sweet; a
creature undefiled by the taint of the world, unvexed by its
injustice, unwearied by its hollow pleasures, a being fresh
from the source of light, with something of its universal
luster in it. If childhood be this, how holy the duty to see
that in its onward growth it shall be no other."

Such a thought may have prompted the poet to pen
the words:

I took a piece of plastic clay
And idly fashioned it one day—
And as my fingers pressed it, still
It moved and yielded to my will.

I came again when days were past;
The bit of clay was hard at last.
The form I gave it, still it bore,
And I could change that form no more!

I took a piece of living clay,
And gently fashioned it day by day,
And moulded with my power and art
A young child's soft and yielding heart.

Only a teacher

I came again when years were gone:
It was a man I looked upon.
He still that early impress bore,
And I could fashion it never more.

Prime time for teaching is fleeting. Opportunities are perishable. The parent who procrastinates the pursuit of his responsibility as a teacher may, in years to come, gain bitter insight to Whittier's expression: ". . . of all sad words of tongue and pen, The saddest are these: 'It might have been.'" (John Greenleaf Whittier, "Maud Muller.")

Dr. Glen Doman, a prominent author and renowned scientist, reported a lifetime of research in the statement: "A newborn child is almost the exact duplicate of an empty electronic computer, although superior to one in almost every way. What is placed in the child's brain during the first eight years of its life is probably there to stay. If you put misinformation into his brain during this period, it is extremely difficult to erase it. The most receptive age in human life is that of two or three years."

Children display uncanny understanding. I remember hearing an account of a little boy who came up to his father. Dad had just come home from work and he was tired. Little Johnny came up to Dad and said, "Daddy, tell me a story," as he tugged his pant leg.

But you and I know what we tell little Johnny. Dad said, "Johnny, you run on for a little while, and after I have read the sports page you come back and then I'll tell you a story."

You don't get rid of little Johnny that way. He tugged again, "Daddy, tell me a story, now."

Dad looked down at Johnny and wondered what in the world he could do to shake him just for a few minutes. Then he looked on the end table and there was a magazine, and he had an idea. On the front cover of that magazine was a picture of the world, similar to the unisphere symbol of the New York World's Fair. He tore the cover off that magazine and shredded it in about sixteen pieces. He handed it to little Johnny and said, "Johnny, let's play a game. You take these pieces and go in the other room and get the Scotch tape and you put this world together, and when you do and put it together properly, then I will tell you a story."

Johnny accepted the challenge and off he ran, and Dad settled back very pleased with himself. He knew that he could now read the sports page. But only a moment had passed and here was Johnny again tugging at his pant leg.

"Daddy," said Johnny, "I have put it together."

Dad looked down and saw those sixteen pieces, each one in its proper place, and he felt that he had a genius in the household. He turned to that little boy of his, and he said, "John, my boy, how in the world did you do it?"

Johnny sort of ducked his head and said, "Well, it wasn't too hard, Dad. Turn the picture of the world over."

And as Dad turned the magazine cover over, Johnny said, "You see, on the back of the cover is the picture of a home. I just put the home together, and the world took care of itself."

When we put our homes together, the world will largely take care of itself. Fathers, we may be the head of the home. Mothers, you are the heart of the home, and the heart of the home is where the pulse of the home is. And I would trust with all my heart that you recognize your significant position in the home.

Recently while I was traveling on a plane, I read an article in the most prominent ladies magazine in this land, wherein the author declared that the women of America were tired of their role as homemakers, that mothers were tired of being Joey's mother, John's wife. This image was an old-fashioned image, and the article seemed to indicate that the popular thing today was to rear our children until they are in school and then to leave the responsibility of their instruction to the schoolteachers, and mother could then fulfill her purpose of working outside the home. Such was the tenor of this article.

Ann Landers, the popular columnist and human relations adviser, receives many letters from persons asking advice. Perhaps none so vividly illustrates the weakness of parents with respect to the tobacco habit as the following letter she received:

Dear Ann Landers: A year ago our two-year-old son, Earl, had difficulty breathing, so we took him to a doctor. We learned Earl is allergic to cigarette smoke. My husband said we both had to quit smoking right then and there. He hasn't touched a cigarette since. I went back to smoking that same night.

My husband doesn't know I smoke. I have to sneak around and smoke in the basement. And it is making a nervous wreck of me. Do you think it would be wrong if we let a nice couple adopt little Earl—a nice couple who don't smoke?

The only problem is that my husband is crazy about the boy. I love him, too, but I am more the practical type. What do you think, Ann?

Dear Mrs. _____: I think a lot of people who read this letter are going to say I made it up. It's utterly fantastic that a mother would put cigarettes ahead of her own child. Don't present your wild idea to your husband. I wouldn't blame him if he decided to keep little Earl and unload *you.*

Mothers, may I declare that your children need you. They have questions to ask. Why, I think of the little boy just four years of age. It is a spring day, early in the morning. He is out in the garden and he sees a bumblebee buzzing in the lilac blooms, or perhaps he notices the tiny ant making its tedious way across the hot pavement. In his own childlike way, he says, "Mother, Mother, come quickly.

Look what I have found." Is Mother at home to answer his call?

A little ten-year-old girl, having successfully competed in a hopscotch tournament, fairly flies home from school. She bursts into the kitchen and says, "Mother, Mother, I won, I won!" Is Mother at home to share her joy?

Mothers and fathers, do we realize that we are making the mold into which the lives of our youngsters will be cast? To teach our children, we must be close to our children, and the place to get close to our children is in the home. We have a responsibility to set before them the proper example. I think that I have never read a more scathing denunciation by the Lord than that found in the Book of Jacob in the Book of Mormon, wherein the Lord said: "Behold, ye have . . . broken the hearts of your tender wives, and lost the confidence of your children, because of your bad examples before them. . . ." (Jacob 2:35.)

If our Heavenly Father would give unto us such a denunciation for a poor example, isn't it logical to assume that he would give us his approbation if we set before our children a proper example? And then we can look back, as did John, when he declared: "I have no greater joy than to hear that my children walk in truth." (3 John 4.)

If any parent needs added inspiration to commence his God-given teaching task, let him remember that the most powerful combination of emotions in the world is not called out by any grand cosmic events nor found in novels or history books—but merely by a parent gazing down upon a sleeping child. "Created in the image of God," that glorious biblical passage, will acquire new and vibrant meaning as a parent repeats this experience. Home will become a haven called heaven, and loving parents will teach their children "to pray and walk uprightly before the Lord." (D&C 68:28.) Never will such an inspired parent fit the description, "Only a teacher."

Let us consider next the teacher in the school. Inevitably, there dawns that tearful morning when home yields to the classroom part of its teaching time. Johnny and Nancy join the happy throng which each day wends its way from the portals of home to the classrooms of school. There a new world is discovered. Our children meet their teacher.

The teacher not only shapes the expectations and ambitions of her pupils, but she also influences their attitudes toward their future and themselves. If she is unskilled, she leaves scars on the lives of youth, cuts deeply into their self-esteem, and distorts their image of themselves as human beings. But if she loves her students and has high expectations of them, their self-confidence will grow, their capabilities will develop, and their future will be assured.

In the present turmoil of events, with crisis following crisis, it is especially important that master teachers look ahead and exercise their important functions as builders of the future. In two fleeting decades, those who are now kindergarten children will be young men and young women who are either assets to society or liabilities. The influence of teachers in fashioning personality and in shaping careers can hardly be overestimated. It makes no difference whether or not she is teaching literature or mathematics or science or any other subject of the curriculum. She must win from her students the faith that moves mountains. When she succeeds, near miracles happen. Suddenly a pupil is awakened to an enthusiastic interest in some aspect of learning and begins to read widely without being urged. Another discovers in himself powers that he did not know he had. Another decides to seek better companions. In a flash of inspiration, still another makes a decision that leads to a lifetime career.

The impelling force, the dynamo, in that room, is very often a quiet, gracious personality with love in her heart for her young charges, a love never directly referred to, but there always. A citation to such a teacher could well read:

Only a teacher

"She created in her room an atmosphere where warmth and acceptance weave their magic spell; where growth and learning, the soaring of the imagination, and the spirit of the young are assured."

Unfortunately, there are exceptions to such teachers. There are those who delight to destroy faith rather than build bridges to the good life.

In the words of President J. Reuben Clark: "He wounds, maims, and cripples a soul who raises doubts about or destroys faith in the ultimate truths. God will hold such an one strictly accountable; and who can measure the depths to which one shall fall who fitfully shatters in another the opportunity for celestial glory?"

Since we cannot control the classroom, we can at least prepare the pupil. You ask "How?" I answer: "Provide a guide to the glory of the celestial kingdom of God, even a barometer to distinguish between the truth of God and the theories of men."

Several years ago I held in my hand such a guide. It was a volume of scripture we commonly call the Triple Combination, containing the Book of Mormon, Doctrine and Covenants, and Pearl of Great Price. The book was a gift from a loving father to a beautiful, blossoming daughter who followed carefully his advice. On the flyleaf page her father had written these inspired words:

April 9, 1944

To My Dear Maurine:

That you may have a constant measure by which to judge between truth and the errors of man's philosophies, and thus grow in spirituality as you increase in knowledge, I give you this sacred book to read frequently and cherish throughout your life.

Lovingly your father,
Harold B. Lee

I ask the question: "Only a teacher?"

Finally, let us turn to the teacher we usually meet on Sunday—the teacher in the Church. In such a setting, the history of the past, the hope of the present, and the promise of the future all meet. Here especially, the teacher learns it is easy to be a Pharisee, difficult to be a disciple. The teacher is judged by his students—not alone by what and how he teaches, but also by how he lives.

The apostle Paul counseled the Romans: "Thou . . . which teachest another, teachest thou not thyself? thou that preachest a man should not steal, dost thou steal? Thou that sayest a man should not commit adultery, dost thou commit adultery? . . ." (Romans 2:21-22.) Paul, that inspired and dynamic teacher, provides us a good example. Perhaps his success secret is revealed through his experience in the dreary dungeon which held him prisoner. Paul knew the tramp, tramp of the soldiers' feet and the clank, clank of the chains which bound him captive. When the prison warden, who seemed to be favorably inclined toward Paul, asked him whether he needed advice as to how to conduct himself before the emperor, Paul said he had an adviser—the Holy Spirit.

This same Spirit guided Paul as he stood in the midst at Mars Hill, read the inscription "TO THE UNKNOWN GOD," and declared, "Whom therefore ye ignorantly worship, him declare I unto you. God that made the world and all things therein . . . dwelleth not in temples made with hands; . . . he giveth to all life, and breath, and all things; . . . For in him we live, and move, and have our being; . . . For we are also his offspring." (Acts 17:23-25, 28.)

Again the question, "Only a teacher?"

In the home, the school, or the house of God, there is one teacher whose life overshadows all others. He taught of life and death, of duty and destiny. He lived not to be served, but to serve; not to receive, but to give; not to save his life, but to sacrifice it for others. He described a love more beautiful than lust, a poverty richer than treasure. It was said of this teacher that he taught with authority and not as did the scribes. In today's world, when many men are greedy of gold and of glory and are dominated by a teaching philosophy of "publish or perish," let us remember that this teacher never wrote—once only he wrote on the sand, and wind destroyed forever his handwriting. His laws were not inscribed upon stone, but upon human hearts. I speak of the Master Teacher, even Jesus Christ, the Son of God, the Savior and Redeemer of all mankind.

When dedicated teachers respond to his gentle invitation, "Come learn of me," they learn, but they also become partakers of his divine power.

It was my experience as a small boy to come under the influence of such a teacher. In our Sunday School class, she taught us concerning the creation of the world, the fall of Adam, the atoning sacrifice of Jesus. She brought to her classroom as honored guests Moses, Joshua, Peter, Thomas, Paul, and even Christ. Though we did not see them, we learned to love, honor, and emulate them.

Never was her teaching so dynamic nor its impact more everlasting as one Sunday morning when she announced sadly to us the passing of a classmate's mother. We had missed Billy that morning but knew not the reason for his absence. The lesson featured the theme, "It is more blessed to give than to receive." Midway through the lesson, our teacher closed the manual and opened our eyes and our ears and our hearts to the glory of God. She asked, "How much money do we have in our class party fund?"

Depression days prompted a proud answer: "Four dollars and seventy-five cents."

Then ever so gently she suggested: "Billy's family is hard-pressed and grief-stricken. What would you think of the possibility of visiting the family members this morning and giving to them your fund?"

Ever shall I remember the tiny band walking those three city blocks, entering Billy's home, greeting him, his brother, sisters, and father. Noticeably absent was his mother. Always I shall treasure the tears which glistened in the eyes of all as the white envelope containing our precious party fund passed from the delicate hand of our teacher to the needy hand of a grief-stricken father. We fairly skipped our way back to the chapel. Our hearts were lighter than they had ever been; our joy more full; our understanding more profound. A God-inspired teacher had taught her boys and girls an eternal lesson of divine truth. "It is more blessed to give than to receive."

Well could we have echoed the words of the disciples on the way to Emmaus: "Did not our heart burn within us, . . . while [she] opened to us the scriptures?" (Luke 24:32.)

I return to the dialogue mentioned earlier. When the boy heard the taunts: "My dad is bigger than yours," "My dad is smarter than yours," "My dad is a doctor," well could he have replied: "Your dad may be bigger than mine; your dad may be smarter than mine; your dad may be a pilot, an engineer, or a doctor; but my dad, *my dad is a teacher.*"

May each of us ever merit such a sincere and worthy compliment!

21

We should love as Jesus loves

As Jesus, our Lord and Savior, ministered among men, he was constantly beset by groups such as the Sadducees or the Pharisees who would direct leading questions to him in an effort to confound him. Such was the inquiring lawyer who stepped forward and asked boldly: "Master, which is the great commandment in the law?" I suppose Jesus could have been weary by this time, having answered query after query, and perhaps we would be critical of the impetuous lawyer; yet I am grateful that this cardinal question was asked.

Matthew records that Jesus said unto him, "Thou shalt love the Lord thy God with all thy heart, and with all thy soul, and with all thy mind. This is the first and great commandment. And the second is like unto it, Thou shalt love thy neighbour as thyself." (Matthew 22:36-39.) And Mark concludes the account with the Savior's statement, "There is none other commandment greater than these." (Mark 12:31.)

Not one could find fault with the Master's answer. His very actions gave credence to his words of instruction. He demonstrated genuine love of God by living the perfect life, by honoring the sacred mission that was his. Never was he haughty. Never was he puffed up with pride. Never was he disloyal. Ever was he humble. Ever was he sincere. Ever was he true.

Though he was led up of the Spirit into the wilderness

to be tempted by that master of deceit, even the devil; though he was physically weakened from fasting forty days and forty nights and was an hungered, yet when the evil one proffered Jesus the most alluring and tempting proposals, he gave to us a divine example of true love for God by refusing to deviate from what he knew was right.

When faced with the agony of Gethsemane where he endured such pain that his sweat was as it were great drops of blood falling down to the ground, he exemplified the epitome of true love, the pinnacle of perfection by saying, "Father, if thou be willing, remove this cup from me: nevertheless not my will, but thine, be done." (Luke 22:42.)

Jesus, throughout his ministry, blessed the sick, restored sight to the blind, made the deaf to hear and the halt and maimed to walk. He taught forgiveness by forgiving. He taught compassion by being compassionate. He taught devotion by giving of himself. Jesus taught by example.

As we survey the life of the Master, each of us could echo the words:

> *I stand all amazed at the love Jesus offers me,*
> *Confused at the grace that so fully he proffers me;*
> *I tremble to know that for me he was crucified,*
> *That for me, a sinner, he suffered, he bled and died.*

To demonstrate our gratitude, is it required that we too lay down our lives as did he? Some have.

Some time ago, under assignment of the First Presidency, I visited the stakes and missions in the South Pacific. During my stay at Melbourne, Australia, President and Sister Richard S. Tanner took me on a visit to the great War Memorial that stands on an imposing setting in that beautiful city. In that edifice, as one walks through its silent corridors, there are tablets that note the deeds of valor and acts of courage of those who made the supreme sacrifice. One could almost hear the roar of the cannon, the sound of the caissons, the piercing scream of the rocket, the cry of the wounded. One could feel the exhilaration of victory and at the same time the despair of defeat.

In the center of the main hall, inscribed for all to see, was the message of the memorial. The skylight overhead permitted easy reading, and once per year, at the eleventh hour of a November day, the sun shines directly upon that message, and it fairly stands up and speaks. "Greater love hath no man than this, that a man lay down his life for his friends." (John 15:13.)

The challenge of today is not necessarily that we should go forth upon the battlefield and lay down our lives, but rather that we should let our lives reflect our love of God and our fellowmen by the obedience we render his commandments and the service we give mankind.

Jesus instructed us, "If ye love me, keep my commandments." (John 14:15.) "He that hath my commandments, and keepeth them, he it is that loveth me: and he that loveth me shall be loved of my Father, and I will love him, and will manifest myself to him." (John 14:21.)

Years ago we danced to a popular song, the words of which were, "It's easy to say I love you, it's easy to say I'll be true, easy to say these simple things, but prove it by the things you do."

Yes, the oft-repeated statement is yet ever true: "Actions speak louder than words." And the actions whereby we demonstrate that we truly do love God and our neighbor as ourselves will rarely be such as to attract the gaze and admiration of the world. Usually our love will be shown in our day-by-day associations with one another.

I think of the seminary students at Highland High School in Salt Lake City who launched a program to help a family receive the blessings of the temple. They contributed modest amounts themselves and worked most diligently on various projects over a period of time until their goal had been accomplished. The proceeds were sent to the president of the Samoa Mission with a letter that asked only that the funds be used to assist the members of a family to receive their temple blessings. Those students never missed the money they contributed. They never suffered as a result of the service rendered in the projects undertaken. Rather, they were blessed and felt privileged to, in this small way, show their love of their fellowmen. These students will, in all probability, never meet the Samoan family that was benefited by their kindness. They will never hear their soft-spoken but meaningful "thank you," nor see the tears of gratitude of hearts too full to speak. Yet I was privileged with my own eyes to see this family and with my own ears to hear their eloquent "thank you" and with my own heart to feel their gratitude expressed. Oh, that these seminary students could have seen and heard a teenage young lady bear her testimony and tell how her family of ten, with the funds made available by this project, purchased tickets from Samoa to New Zealand. For days and nights they sailed the broad expanse of the Pacific Ocean, sleeping on the open deck of the vessel. They weren't worried about storm nor comfort of body. Their thoughts were riveted on the blessings which awaited them in God's holy house. The mission was accomplished. Temple ordinances were performed. A small sacrifice by seminary students had resulted in eternal blessings for others. They loved as Jesus loves.

Brigham Young counseled us: "Go on until we are perfect; loving our neighbor more than we love ourselves." It is folly in the extreme for persons to say that they love God when they do not love their brethren. And the Prophet Joseph Smith advised: "A man filled with the love of God is not content with blessing his family alone, but ranges through the whole world, anxious to bless the whole human race."

This is the kind of love which fills the hearts of our missionaries who, in response to a call from God's prophet, leave the comfort of their own families and homes and go into the world to share the most precious message given to man.

I saw a typical missionary rendering faithful service far off in the islands of the sea. I know his mother and father and his family. I know that there is love in their home. Father was a bishop in the Holladay Stake. This young man could have remained home with his family in their lovely home; he could have continued to pursue his education at the university; he could have chosen to advance his community standing and enjoyed the association of his friends and, incidentally, the good cooking of his mother. But the call came. He answered. He has learned how to live on coconuts, taro, boiled green bananas, and other items he never before heard of. He has learned how to walk miles on end in a downpour of torrential rain. He has learned to endure all kinds of deprivations. Yet is he unhappy? When I asked him how he was getting along he answered, "I've never worked harder, nor longer hours, nor under such unfavorable circumstances. But I have never been happier in my entire life. Tell my Mom and Dad that I love them, I love this people, and I love my mission." Does he love as Jesus loves?

We must not feel that the only way we can show our love for God and our fellowmen is to serve in distant lands. Our opportunities may be right in our own backyards.

One day I congratulated a friend of mine who together with his wife and family was preparing to visit the Manti Temple. I asked him to recount to me the experience of his conversion. I believe you will find it of interest.

Sharman Hummel and his wife, Anne Marie, lived in the eastern part of the United States and enjoyed a typical American family life with their three lovely daughters. They worked together, they attended their church together, and had but the most vague idea concerning The

Church of Jesus Christ of Latter-day Saints. And then the day came for their lives to change. A transfer of employment came and Dad went on to the West Coast to prepare for the arrival of his family. The bus ride across the continent was beautiful but rather insignificant until that bus stopped at Salt Lake City. A young lady boarded the bus and sat next to Sharman Hummel. She was en route to Reno to visit an aunt.

Knowing that he was in Mormon country, Sharman asked the young lady if she were a Mormon. When she answered "Yes," he inquired, "What do you Mormons believe?" The young lady then described what the Church of Jesus Christ meant to her. She mentioned doctrine, but the emphasis was upon testimony and feelings. She described the simplicity of the Church, its teachings, its chapels, its youth program. Said Brother Hummel, "I don't remember everything she said, but I do remember the spirit in which she said it." The young lady left the bus at Reno, but all the way to San Francisco, Brother Hummel could think of nothing other than what he had learned from this young lady. He investigated immediately the teachings of the gospel and, through the aid of members and missionaries alike, he, his wife, and their children were converted and baptized.

Sharman Hummel is today a seventy in the Melchizedek Priesthood, he has served a successful stake mission, he and his family are happy as they never before have been. He has often confided to me that he has but one regret in his life. He never obtained the name of the young lady who sat next to him on the bus, who in her humble way taught him what she believed and the importance of acquiring a personal testimony. Though this young girl will perhaps never know that she helped to bring precious souls unto the Lord, yet she surely demonstrated by her actions that she loved as Jesus loves, for didn't he, too, bring others to a knowledge of the truth? And what about her mother and father who taught her the gospel in their home? They too loved as Jesus loves, for didn't he ask that we teach our children to pray and walk uprightly before the Lord? And let us not forget the faithful and diligent Primary and Sunday School teachers who each week during all those formative years taught this young lady the teachings of the gospel and taught so well that she in turn could teach others. These teachers, too, loved as Jesus loves, for didn't he say, "Feed my sheep. Feed my lambs."

As we engage in the activities of our lives, may each one of us love as Jesus loves, remembering that "True Christianity is love in action."

22

The precious gift of sight

When Jesus walked and taught among men, he spoke in language easily understood. Whether he was journeying along the dusty way from Perea to Jerusalem, addressing the multitude on the shore of the Sea of Galilee, or pausing beside Jacob's well in Samaria, he taught in parables. Jesus spoke frequently of having hearts that could know and feel, ears that were capable of hearing, and eyes that could truly see.

One not so blessed with the gift of sight was the blind man who, in an effort to sustain himself, sat day in and day out in his usual place at the edge of a busy sidewalk in one of our large cities. In one hand he held an old felt hat filled with pencils. A tin cup was extended by the other hand. His simple appeal to the passer-by was brief and to the point. It had a certain finality to it, almost a tone of despair. The message was contained on the small placard held about his neck by a string. It read, "I am blind."

Most did not stop to buy his pencils or to place a coin in the tin cup. They were too busy, too occupied by their own problems. That tin cup never had been filled nor even half-filled. Then one beautiful spring day a man paused and, with a marking crayon, added several new words to the shabby sign. No longer did it read, "I am blind."

Now the message read, "It is springtime, and I am blind." The compassion of human feelings could not now be restrained. The cup was soon filled to overflowing. Perhaps the busy people were touched by Charles L. O'Donnel's exclamation: "I have never been able to school my eyes against young April's blue surprise." To each, however, the coins were a poor substitute for the desired ability to actually restore sight.

Did you happen to notice in our local newspapers a few years ago the United Press International dispatch from Sicily? "Five brothers blind since birth got their first dim glimpse of the world Tuesday and cried with delight." The Rotolo brothers were operated on for removal of congenital cataracts. As the surgeon, Luigi Picardo, in a darkened room removed their bandages, how he hoped and prayed that his work had been successful.

The first to speak was four-year-old Calogero, the youngest of the brothers. "The necktie," he cried, tugging at the surgeon's tie. "I can see, I can see." The removal of the bandages from the others' eyes was accompanied by shouts of joy. The boys' father could hardly believe it when he held thirteen-year-old Carmelo's face in his hands and asked tenderly, "Can you see, my son? Can you really see?"

By now, Mother Rotolo, the doctors, everyone was weeping for joy. Dr. Picardo replaced the bandages and walked slowly out of the room. Then he sat down on a bench and wept. "Never," he said, "have I felt such extraordinary serenity, such happiness." Thus a skilled surgeon actually brought the gift of sight to five little boys who had been blind.

Each of us knows those who do not have sight. We also know many others who walk in darkness at noonday. Those in this latter group may never carry the usual white cane and carefully make their way to the sound of its familiar tap, tap, tap. They may not have a faithful seeing-eye dog by their side nor carry a sign about their neck which reads, "I am blind." But blind they surely are. Some have been blinded by anger, others by indifference, by revenge, by hate, by prejudice, by ignorance, by neglect of precious opportunities.

Of such the Lord said, ". . . their ears are dull of hearing, and their eyes they have closed; lest at any time they should see with their eyes, and hear with their ears, and should understand with their heart, and should be converted, and I should heal them." (Matthew 13:15.)

Well might such lament, "It is springtime, the gospel of Jesus Christ has been restored, and yet I am blind." Some like the friend of Philip of old call out, "How can I [find my way] except some man should guide me?" (Acts 8:31.) Others are too shy, too fearful to ask for needed help that their precious vision might be restored.

The case of the Rotolo brothers made national headlines. In literally thousands of other instances, the transition from the dense darkness of despair to glorious spiritual light is accomplished without fanfare, without publicity, without the recognition of the world.

In Price, Utah, seventy-six men, together with their wives and children, walked from darkness into the light of understanding and truth and journeyed to the Manti Temple, there to participate for the first time in sacred, holy ordinances. More than three hundred such men, women, and children came to the Salt Lake Temple from Denver, Colorado, for the same purpose. In Rigby, Idaho; Cardston, Alberta, Canada; and numerous other areas the account has been the same. Hundreds are seeing springtime for the first time.

Let me share with you two typical comments from those who were once blind but who now walk in light and truth, thanks to faithful home teachers and concerned leaders.

From a family in central Utah: "Before our newly found church activity, we thought we were living average, normal lives. We had our problems, our ups and downs. But there was one thing missing in our home and that was a togetherness that only the priesthood can bring. Now we have that blessing, and our love for one another is greater than we ever dreamed it could be. We are truly happy."

From another family: "We thank our Heavenly Father every night for our bishopric and our home teachers who have helped us to achieve blessings that seemed so far away, so impossible to obtain. We now have a peace of mind beyond description."

Those who have felt the touch of the Master's hand somehow cannot explain the change which comes into their lives. There is a desire to live better, to serve faithfully, to walk humbly, and to live more like the Savior. Having received their spiritual eyesight and glimpsed the promises of eternity, they echo the words of the blind man to whom Jesus restored sight: ". . . one thing I know, that, whereas I was blind, now I see." (John 9:25.)

How can we account for these miracles? Why the upsurge of activity in men long dormant? The poet, speaking of death, wrote, "God touched him, and he slept." I say, speaking of this new birth, "God touched them, and they awakened."

Two fundamental reasons largely account for these changes of attitudes, of habits, of actions.

First, men have been shown their eternal possibilities and have made the decision to achieve them. Men cannot really long rest content with mediocrity once they see excellence is within their reach.

Second, other men and women and, yes, young people have followed the admonition of the Savior and have loved their neighbors as themselves and helped to bring their neighbors' dreams to fulfillment and their ambitions to realization.

The catalyst in this process has been the principle of

love, described as the noblest attribute of the human soul.

Frequently the love of a child can stir a man's heart to action and bring a change into his life. Last winter in a large department store, a little boy walked hand in hand with his mother and father to the toy department to see Santa Claus. As the little one climbed upon his knee, old Santa asked cheerfully, "What do you want for Christmas?" Santa had no ready answer when the lad replied, "Just for my daddy to love my mommy like he used to." Could a father hear such a plea and not be moved? Could a mother? ". . . a little child shall lead them." (Isaiah 11:6.)

Often it is the love of a patient, forgiving, and understanding wife that awakens within a man the desire to live a better life, to be the husband and the father he knows he should and can be.

Recently I had the privilege of performing a sealing ceremony in the temple for a family I have known for many years. The scene was one of tranquillity. The cares of the outside world had been temporarily discarded. The quiet and peace of the house of the Lord filled the heart of each one assembled in the room. I knew that this particular couple had been married for eighteen years and had never before been to the temple. I turned to the husband and asked, "Jack, who is responsible for bringing this glorious event to fulfillment?"

He smiled and pointed silently to his precious wife who sat by his side. I seemed to sense that this lovely woman was never more proud of her husband than at that particular moment. Jack then directed my attention to one of the brethren serving as witness to this ceremony and likewise acknowledged the great influence for good that he had had upon his life.

As the three beautiful children were sealed to their parents, I could not help noticing the tears which welled up in the eyes of the teenage daughter and then coursed in little rivulets down her cheeks, finally tumbling upon clasped hands. These were sacred tears, tears of supreme joy, tears that expressed silent but eloquent gratitude of a tender heart too full to speak.

I found myself thinking, *Oh, that such men and women would not wait eighteen long years to receive this priceless blessing.*

Yet there are those who feel that their own neglect, their bad habits, their shunning of the righteous life have caused God to abandon them, that he will no longer hear their pleadings, nor see their plight, nor feel compassion toward them. Such feelings are not compatible with the word of the Lord. He said:

> A certain man had two sons:
>
> And the younger of them said to his father, Father, give me the portion of goods that falleth to me. And he divided unto them his living.
>
> And not many days after the younger son gathered all together, and took his journey into a far country, and there wasted his substance with riotous living.
>
> And when he had spent all, there arose a mighty famine in that land; and he began to be in want.
>
> And he went and joined himself to a citizen of that country; and he sent him into his fields to feed swine.
>
> And he would fain have filled his belly with the husks that the swine did eat: and no man gave unto him.
>
> And when he came to himself, he said, How many hired servants of my father's have bread enough and to spare, and I perish with hunger!
>
> I will arise and go to my father, and will say unto him, Father, I have sinned against heaven, and before thee.
>
> And am no more worthy to be called thy son: make me as one of thy hired servants.
>
> And he arose, and came to his father. But when he was yet a great way off, his father saw him, and had compassion, and ran, and fell on his neck, and kissed him.
>
> And the son said unto him, Father, I have sinned against heaven, and in thy sight, and am no more worthy to be called thy son.
>
> But the father said to his servants, Bring forth the best robe, and put it on him; and put a ring on his hand, and shoes on his feet:

Gift of sight

And bring hither the fatted calf, and kill it; and let us eat, and be merry:

For this my son was dead, and is alive again; he was lost, and is found. . . . (Luke 15:11-24.)

Should there be anyone who feels he is too weak to change the onward and downward moving course of his life, or should there be those who fail to resolve to do better because of that greatest of fears, the fear of failure, there is no more comforting assurance to be had than the words of the Lord: ". . . my grace is sufficient for all men that humble themselves before me; for if they humble themselves before me, and have faith in me, then will I make weak things become strong unto them." (Ether 12:27.)

There are men and women everywhere who would be made better by our helping hand. They may be our neighbors, our friends, our business associates. All are our brothers and sisters.

The prayer of my heart is that such persons everywhere will respond to the kind invitation and gentle touch of the Master's hand and faithfully serve our Lord and our Savior, who so willingly died that we might forever live, hopefully having eyes that really see, ears that truly hear, and responsive hearts that know and feel.

23

The miracle of the Friendly Islands

oday is actually tomorrow in the Tongan Islands, which lie some 2700 miles southwest from Hawaii. The Tongan capital, Nuku'alofa, is situated twenty minutes east of the International Date Line, thereby giving Tonga the title "the place where time begins." Tongans take delight in the thought that of all the people whom God has created and placed over the expanse of this marvelous world, they are the first to greet the new day, the first to be upon their knees in morning prayer to thank a loving Heavenly Father for his abundant blessings.

Captain James Cook, one of the early explorers of the Pacific, was greatly impressed with the friendliness of the native people. On his charts he designated Tonga as the Friendly Islands. His designation could not have been more descriptive. Tongans are good humored, polite, outgoing, and, above all, friendly.

Perhaps the Friendly Islands didn't quite live up to their name in the estimation of those first Mormon missionaries who arrived on the island of Tongatabu July 15, 1891. A full year was to transpire before a frame meetinghouse could be erected, a humble and modest school opened, and the first new member baptized. Frustration followed frustration until progress halted. After a twenty-year lull, the work was recommenced with the establishment of the Tonga Mission.

Once again, men of faith and called of God left behind home and family and sailed for Tonga. Success came more readily, but not without exacting a price. Typhoid fever took its toll. Today, six well-kept graves mark the resting places of those who were willing to give all in the cause of truth. The words of the Lord provide a fitting epitaph to their lives and to the service of these early missionaries: "Wherefore, be not weary in well-doing, for ye are laying the foundation of a great work. And out of small things proceedeth that which is great." (D&C 64:33.)

From that small frame school has proceeded the Liahona College and a Church-administered school system that blesses the lives of the choice youth of the Friendly Islands. Teachers, both Tongan and American, with a common bond of faith, not only provide training for the mind, but also preparation for life.

Well could they say:

> *We are building in sorrow or joy*
> *A temple the world may not see;*
> *Which time cannot mar nor destroy—*
> *We build for eternity.*

—N.B. SARGENT

On a visit to Tonga, I witnessed such a building project. Entering a typical classroom, I noticed the rapt attention that the children gave their native instructor. His textbook and theirs lay closed upon the desks. In his hand he held a strange-appearing lure fashioned from a round stone and large seashells. This I learned was a *maka-feke* or octopus trap.

Tongan fishermen glide over the reef, paddling their outrigger canoes with one hand and dangling the *maka-feke* over the side. Octopuses dash out from their rocky lairs and seize the lure, mistaking it for an ocean crab. So tenacious is their grasp and so firm is their instinct not to relinquish the precious prize that fishermen can flip them right into the canoe.

It was an easy transition for the teacher to point out to eager and wide-eyed youth that the evil one, even Satan, often fashions a *maku-feke* to ensnare unsuspecting persons and to take possession of their destiny.

Before some he dangles the *maka-feke* of tobacco with the cunning call, "This is the way to social ease." He who grasps, like the octopus, finds it difficult to relinquish the bait.

Before others he presents the *maka-feke* of alcohol with the chant: "Here is the way to unwind and forget your cares." The unsuspecting victim finds himself not carefree, but held captive.

The "new morality" is a cleverly designed *maka-feke*. In a headlong dash for what they envision will be social acceptance, the weak-willed, deceived by a counterfeit bait, discover not social acceptance, but experience social rejection.

What prompted this inspired teacher to close the traditional textbook and for a brief moment teach an unforgettable lesson? Love is the answer—a love for his students and a genuine concern for their welfare.

This same spirit of abiding love and genuine concern has characterized the growth of the Church in Tonga from that humble beginning in 1891 even to the present time.

Today one in seven Tongans is a member of The Church of Jesus Christ of Latter-day Saints. Beautiful chapels dot the landscape. The full program of the Church is pursued in a vigorous and successful manner. Together with Elder Howard W. Hunter, I had the privilege to be a part of the creation of a stake of Zion at Nuku'alofa. We found a prepared people. We discovered that from "small things there had proceeded that which is great."

In their journey to greatness, the Tongans have not neglected nor forgotten a great source of their strength— this abiding love and genuine concern one for another.

Some time ago a baby boy was born to the Tonga Mission president and his wife, President and Mrs. John H. Groberg. Little John Enoch was their first son, the beloved brother of five sisters and the delight of the Tongan members. At first the little one did well, but then came illness. Doctors worked their skill, parents exercised their faith, but the baby did not improve.

Late one evening there came a knock at the door. From the Tongan visitor, President Groberg learned that on every island, in every home, and in every heart of every member of the Church, fervent prayer and faithful fasting became a united appeal to Almighty God that John Enoch Groberg would live. Visiting Tonga at the time, I witnessed this faith. I testify to the result. The cause of the illness was discovered; the deterioration was arrested. Today the baby is robust in strength. He is a living testimony of the power of prayer and the miracle of love.

During that same visit to Tonga, I accompanied President Groberg to the Royal Palace, where we were granted an interview with His Royal Majesty King Tupou IV. Our welcome was cordial and most pleasant. At the conclusion of the interview, the prompting of the Holy Spirit guided President Groberg as he bore fervent testimony to the king concerning the truth of the everlasting gospel and the blessings it provides the faithful. No more eloquent nor moving words have resounded in those royal chambers. No greater courage have I seen displayed.

To my mind came the apostle Paul's inspired defense before another king, even Agrippa. Here in Tonga was one called of God who was "not disobedient unto the heavenly vision." Here was uttered a testimony that "Christ should suffer, and that he should be the first that should rise from the dead, and should shew light unto the people, and to the Gentiles." (Acts 26:19, 23.) I could envision King Tupou saying with King Agrippa, "Almost thou persuadest me."

We exchanged greetings, departed the palace, but I did not, nor will I, forget that experience. What prompted such courage, such faith, such conviction in a young mission president? The answer: the miracle of love. John H. Groberg loves the Tongan people—all of them.

As a lad just twenty, called to the Tonga Mission, he was assigned to an outer island with a native missionary as his companion. After eight seasick days and sleepless nights on a storm-tossed sea, they reached their destination. Not one soul on the island spoke English. Here he acquired his gift of the language. Then came a devastating hurricane which struck the isolated island with tropical intensity, destroying the food crop and contaminating the water supply. There was no means of communication with the outside world. The supply boat was not due for almost two months. After four weeks the scant store of food, mainly taro, a native vegetable, was severely rationed. Four additional weeks passed. All food was gone. No help arrived. Bodies became emaciated, hope dwindled, confidence waned, some died. In desperation, John Groberg waded into the swampland where insects covered his face and, with a sweep of his hand, entered his mouth—his only nourishment.

The end drew near. The island's inhabitants sat in an idle stupor. One morning, nine weeks from the time of the hurricane, John Groberg felt a gentle hand upon his shoulder. He turned his head and gazed into the eyes of an elderly Tongan man. Slowly and with meticulous care, the old man unwrapped a precious prize, even his most treasured possession—a small can of berry jam. He spoke: "I am old; I think I may die. You are young; you may live. Accept my gift."

What was the declaration of the Savior: "Inasmuch as ye have done it unto one of the least of these my brethren, ye have done it unto me." (Matthew 25:40.)

Then came that speck on the horizon and a shout of joy as the supply ship came into view. John H. Groberg was no longer a boy. His faith had been tried; his life had been spared; his love for the Tongan people forever assured.

The Holy Scripture records that in the hushed quiet of the still night the boy Samuel heard the Lord call and answered, "Here am I." (1 Samuel 3:4.) On the bleak hill of Moriah, Abraham demonstrated his willingness to sacrifice all—even his only son. He heard the angel of the Lord call and answered, "Here am I." (Genesis 22:11.) On the morning of a beautiful spring day in a sacred grove at Palmyra, New York, the boy Joseph Smith beheld a heavenly vision and the appearance of the Father and the Son. He received his call, and his life demonstrated his answer, "Here am I."

On a distant Pacific Isle a faithful missionary, John H. Groberg, had answered, "Here am I."

So often the call to serve is not accompanied by the sound of a marching band, the cheering crowd, or the applause of those whose favor is deemed so great. Such distractions were not to be found on Damascus way, in Palmyra's grove, on Moriah's mount, in Gethsemane's garden, nor atop Golgotha's hill.

With a never-waning confidence in the people of Tonga, John H. Groberg has taught them not to pray for tasks equal to their powers, but rather to pray for powers equal to their tasks. Then the doing of their work shall be no miracle, but they shall be the miracle.

I found it difficult to bid goodbye to Tonga and its precious people. Here were men of faith, women of patience, even children of promise.

We boarded the plane. Slowly it taxied to the grass runway, and with a roar gained speed and lifted gently into the blue sky. I looked at the crowd who had bid us farewell; in the distance I saw the great school complex. In my memory I thought of the six graves of those early missionaries. Quietly I repeated a verse from Kipling's "Recessional":

> *The tumult and the shouting dies,*
> *The captains and the kings depart;*
> *Still stands thine ancient sacrifice,*
> *An humble and a contrite heart;*
> *Lord God of hosts, be with us yet,*
> *Lest we forget, lest we forget.*

From the cabin window I took a last fond glance at Nuku'alofa, which interpreted means "the abode of love." I realized that love is not only the miracle of the Friendly Islands; love is the guide to mortal happiness and a requisite for eternal life.

God so loved the world that he gave his Son. The Redeemer so loved mankind that he gave his life. To you and to me he declared, "A new commandment I give unto you, that ye love one another; as I have loved you. . . .

"By this shall all men know that ye are my disciples." (John 13:34-35.)

24

The lighthouse of the Lord

Gracing the entrance to the harbor of New York there stands a massive statue of copper and iron, a gift from the people of France. The statue is a famous lady, a torch held aloft in her right hand, a tablet securely held in her left. Her name is Liberty. Through the years, she has beckoned to many hundreds of thousands of human souls and held out to them a promise of opportunity; the blessing of a new beginning; the vision of a new life.

Inspired by this sight, the American writer, Emma Lazarus, wrote the immortal lines which are now emblazoned on a stone tablet at the main entrance to the Statue of Liberty.

> *Give me your tired, your poor,*
> *Your huddled masses yearning to breathe free;*
> *The wretched refuse of your teeming shore.*
> *Send these, the homeless, tempest-tossed to me,*
> *I lift my lamp beside the golden door.*
> —"THE NEW COLOSSUS"

Today, on the western side of the continent, within sight of the entrance to America's greatest Pacific port, there stands completed and dedicated a lamp beside the Golden Gate. The world refers to this imposing edifice as the Oakland Temple of The Church of Jesus Christ of Latter-day Saints. People marvel at the beauty of this stately building, the well-manicured lawns and shrubs which adorn the grounds, and the lofty spires thrusting upward to the heavens. But to those assembled who know and appreciate the true purpose of the temple, we could say to the world, "That famous Statue of Liberty which marks the entrance to America's Atlantic port may depict and symbolize the opportunities and blessings of this life, whereas this holy house brings the hope of eternal opportunities, eternal blessings, and eternal life."

True followers of the Savior, those who really love him and keep his commandments, are vitally concerned with eternity and eternal objectives. As Paul declared to the Corinthians: "If in this life only we have hope in Christ, we are of all men most miserable." (1 Corinthians 15:19.)

In this holy house, which by revelation must be "a house of prayer, a house of fasting, a house of faith, a house of learning, a house of glory, a house of order, a house of God" (D&C 88:119), two twin eternal principles go hand in hand: temple work for one's self and temple work for one's kindred dead.

A meaningful appreciation for these principles of temple work can best be taught in the family circle. Our homes are the laboratories of our lives; what we do there determines the course of our lives. Despite all new inventions and modern designs, fads and fetishes, no one has yet invented or will ever invent a satisfying substitute for one's own family.

Within the sanctity of the family circle, we can effectively develop an understanding and an insight into the faith and devotion which prompted our forefathers, in obedience to God's command, to give of their meager substance, the earnest labor of their hands, and, in some instances, the sacrifice of their lives, that the Lord's house might be properly built. It was so at Kirtland, at Nauvoo, and at Salt Lake City, where forty years were required in the building of that temple. It has been so elsewhere. When we truly appreciate the spirit of the pioneers, we desire to pattern our lives after their noble example. Would you like to be a pioneer? Would you desire to leave such a rich heritage to your posterity? Webster defines a pioneer as "one who goes before, showing others the way to follow." When we go worthily into the house of God and receive our endowments, our sealing blessings, and when we go there regularly to perform the work for our kindred dead, we become pioneers, because we literally go before our children and show them the way to follow.

As Latter-day Saints, a great deal is expected of us. Marriage after the way of man might be satisfactory to the world, but not to Latter-day Saints, for the Lord told the Prophet Joseph, "For of him unto whom much is given, much is required; and he who sins against the greater light shall receive the greater condemnation.

"I, the Lord, am bound when ye do what I say; but when ye do not what I say, ye have no promise." (D&C 82: 3, 10.)

How I hope that all of our young people will come to a realization that the temple is the place where we should marry. This is the place where we should do the work for our dead. This is the place where we should receive our endowments and our blessings. When we truly understand and appreciate the purpose for which temples are built, we will not want to be deprived of the blessings of coming herein. When our family units are blessed by eternal covenants, we can avoid the pitfalls and the quicksands that bring to ruin many marriages. For temple marriage, eternal marriage, is based on true love.

Our lives will have some days that will be glorious, full of hope and opportunity, and others, perhaps, that may be dismal and filled with discouragement. But through it all there is no need for any one of us to lose his way.

Recently I was reading an account of Francis Chichester and his crossing of the Atlantic Ocean in mid-1962. He was all alone in his twenty-eight-foot sailboat, and all around him the sea met the sky in an unmarked horizon. But he was not lost; he had a compass. His course was charted. The stars were overhead.

The holy endowment that we receive in our temples can well be the compass for our lives. Our course, our eternal course, is charted by the scriptures; and the voice that has come and continues to come from the heavens to God's prophets and in answer to humble, personal, and family prayer will ever guide us back to our eternal home. We need but to do our part. However, that ancient principle is still true that nothing can be had for nothing. All blessings are predicated on obedience to law. "For all who will have a blessing at my hands [saith the Lord] shall abide the law which was appointed for that blessing, and the conditions thereof as were instituted from before the foundation of the world." (D&C 132:5.)

Yet today, in the very shadows of our temples, many of our young Latter-day Saints are failing to choose temple marriage. I am afraid that some of our young people are caught in the whirlpool of status seeking. While fathers drive stately cars and mothers open their homes to admiring inspection, some lose their sons and their daughters, for they learn to judge by the symbols people display, rather than by people's individual worth.

An appreciation for the temple endowment and the sealing ordinances will bring the members of our families closer together and there will be quickened within each family member a desire to make available these same blessings to our loved ones who have gone beyond. We will come to say with George Elliott, "I desire no future that would break the ties of the past, for heaven would not be heaven without family and friends."

This vicarious work performed in our temples must be carried forth in the same spirit of selfless devotion and sacrifice that characterized the life of the Master. When we remember him, it becomes easier for us to do our individual parts in this vital work. Each time we gaze upon one of these holy houses, may we be reminded of the eternal opportunities which are found inside, not only for ourselves, but for our dead. Let us be mindful that decisions pertaining to the temple are eternal decisions with eternal consequences.

In one of Christopher Marlowe's plays, *The Tragical History of Dr. Faustus,* there is portrayed an individual, Dr. Faustus, who chose to ignore God and follow the pathway of Satan. At the end of his wicked life and facing the frustration of opportunities lost and punishment certain to come, he lamented, "There is a more searing anguish than flaming fire—eternal exile from God."

Just as eternal exile from God is the most searing anguish, so eternal life in the presence of God is our most cherished goal. With all my heart and soul I pray that we might persevere in the pursuit of this most precious prize.

Address delivered at the dedication of the Oakland Temple.

25

"Can there any good thing come out of Nazareth?"

wo thousand years ago the Son of Man was born into a world like ours—asunder. Sixty-three years had passed since Roman legions under Pompey had conquered Palestine and taken Jerusalem. The helmets, broadswords, and eagles of the Roman legionary were everywhere to be seen. The oppressive yoke of the Caesars was universally felt.

Deep in the depths of human hearts there dwelt a longing, even a yearning, for the advent of the promised Messiah. When will he come? This was the unanswered question on the lips of the righteous.

Generations had lived and died since the Prophet Isaiah had declared: "Behold, a virgin shall conceive, and bear a son. . . ." (Isaiah 7:14.) ". . . the government shall be upon his shoulder: and his name shall be called Wonderful, Counseller, The mighty God, The everlasting Father, The Prince of Peace." (Isaiah 9:6.)

With such a promise ringing in his ears, can you and I appreciate the supreme joy and overwhelming exultation that coursed through one called Philip when he heard the Savior of the world speak unto him those immortal words, that divine injunction, "Follow me"? The dawn of promise had dispelled the night of despair. The King of kings, the Lord of lords had come.

Such knowledge could not be hidden, nor could Philip of Bethsaida keep to himself such glad tidings. "Philip findeth Nathanael, and saith unto him, We have found him, of whom Moses in the law, and the prophets, did write, Jesus of Nazareth, the son of Joseph.

"And Nathanael said unto him, Can there any good thing come out of Nazareth? Philip saith unto him, Come and see." (John 1:45-46.)

Shall we, too, join Nathanael? Come and see.

Could Nazareth be so honored? Nazareth, the most disregarded valley in a despised province of a conquered land?

Nazareth, just eighty miles from Jerusalem, was situated on the main trade route which ran from Damascus through the Galilean cities to the Mediterranean coast at Acre. This, however, was not to be the village's claim to fame. Nor was its glory to be found in the beauty of its environs. Nazareth was the scene of more lasting events and profound consequence than routes of trade or landscapes of beauty.

To a city of Galilee, called Nazareth, came the angel Gabriel, sent from God. To a virgin whose name was Mary, he declared, "Fear not, Mary: for thou hast found favour with God.

"And, behold, thou shalt conceive in thy womb, and bring forth a son, and shalt call his name Jesus.

"He . . . shall be called the Son of . . . God." (Luke 1:30-32.)

After the birth of the Christ child, and following the flight into Egypt, the sacred record reveals, "And he came and dwelt in a city called Nazareth: that it might be fulfilled which was spoken by the prophets, He shall be called a Nazarene." (Matthew 2:23.)

In Nazareth, the boy Jesus grew "in wisdom and stature, and in favour with God and man." (Luke 2:52.)

From Nazareth came he who made blind men see, lame beggars walk—even the dead to live. He set before us an example to emulate. He lived the perfect life. He taught the glad tidings which changed the world. Let us examine more closely and individually these epochal events, that we may know for ourselves if any good thing came out of Nazareth.

First let us turn to him of whom Jesus himself spoke: "Verily I say unto you, among them that are born of women there hath not risen a greater than John the Baptist. . . ." (Matthew 11:11.) John, "the Baptist," stands forth like a colossus from the bleakness and confusion—the "wilderness" of his own age. Knowing that one "mightier than he" was coming, he threw himself with superhuman fervor into the task of "making straight the way." His was the agony, and the distinction, of being both an end and a beginning.

Astride the watershed of time, he could look back on a long line of prophets—his spiritual forebears. Letting his eye range over the fertile plains ahead, he was the first to see that Light to which he would bear witness.

"And it came to pass in those days, that Jesus came from Nazareth of Galilee, and was baptized of John in Jordan." (Mark 1:9.)

"And John bare record, saying, I saw the Spirit descending from heaven like a dove, and it abode upon him.

". . . he that sent me to baptize with water, the same said unto me, Upon whom thou shalt see the Spirit descending, and remaining on him, the same is he which baptizeth with the Holy Ghost.

"And I saw, and bare record that this is the Son of God." (John 1:32-34.)

From Nazareth came the perfect one to be baptized—an example for all.

Second, let us turn to Judea and examine the testi-

211

mony of one who was born blind—him for whom it was always night. No day—just night. But let him provide his own account—how darkness was turned to light. Astonished neighbors, noting his newly acquired vision, asked: "Is not this he that sat and begged? . . .

". . . others said, He is like him: but he said, I am he.

"Therefore said they unto him, How were thine eyes opened?

". . . A man that is called Jesus made clay, and anointed mine eyes, and said unto me, Go to the pool of Siloam, and wash: and I went and washed, and I received sight." (John 9:8-11.)

When the disbelievers urged, "Give God the praise: we know that this man is a sinner," he rejoined: "Whether he be a sinner or no, I know not; one thing I know, that, whereas I was blind, now I see." (John 9:24-25.)

From Nazareth came sight.

Next, let us journey to Bethesda to inquire of him who now walks, but who for thirty-eight long years walked not. "When Jesus saw him lie, and knew that he had been now a long time in that case, he saith unto him, Wilt thou be made whole?" The impotent man's reply of frustration, mingled with hope, was met with the gentle, yet divine command, "Rise, take up thy bed, and walk." (John 5:6, 8.)

From Nazareth to a withered body came new strength.

Jesus of Nazareth restored sight, removed lameness, but could it be true that he raised the dead to life?

In Capernaum, Jairus, a ruler of the synagogue, came to the Master, saying, "My little daughter lieth at the point of death: I pray thee, come and lay thy hands on her, that she may be healed; and she shall live." Then came the news from the ruler's house, "Thy daughter is dead," to which the Christ replied: "Be not afraid, only believe." He came to the house, passed by the mourners, and said to them,

"Why make ye this ado, and weep? the damsel is not dead, but sleepeth."

And they laughed him to scorn, knowing that she was dead. And he put them all out, and took her by the hand, and called, saying, "Maid, arise."

"And straightway the damsel arose, and walked. . . . And they were astonished. . . ." (See Mark 5:23-43.) *From Nazareth came life where once there was death.* And with that miracle came the perfect pattern whereby our own lives may be made fruitful: *"Be not afraid, only believe."* (Mark 5:36. Italics added.)

Out of Nazareth and down through the generations of time come his excellent example, his welcome words, his divine deeds.

They inspire patience to endure affliction, strength to bear grief, courage to face death, and confidence to meet life. In this world of chaos, of trial, of uncertainty, never has our need for such divine guidance been more desperate.

Lessons from Nazareth, Capernaum, Jerusalem, Galilee transcend the barriers of distance, the passage of time, the limits of understanding, and bring to troubled hearts a light and a way.

With sorrow we read each day of young men and those not so young who bravely die, who give their all upon the altar of freedom.

In a hurried moment, one such took in hand a stubby pencil, a scrap of paper and wrote to anxious love, "Soon we go into battle. The enemy is well fortified; loss of life will be heavy. Mom, I hope I live, but I'm not afraid to die, for I'm square with God."

Mother received the precious note. On the same day another message arrived. "We regret to inform you that your son has been killed in action."

Friends visited, loved ones comforted, but peace came only from him who called Nazareth his home.

Out of Nazareth

All battles are not waged on foreign soil. Nor do the participants bear arms, hurl grenades, or drop bombs.

A few months ago I witnessed such a conflict—not in the steaming jungles of Viet Nam, but on the fourth floor of the Los Angeles Orthopedic Hospital. There were no shrill sounds of mortar fire to be heard, no disarray of men and equipment to be seen. Yet a life or death struggle was in progress. Happy, handsome Paul Van Dusen, age fifteen, had just lost the first skirmish with the dreaded foe called cancer.

Paul loved life. He excelled in sports. He and his parents hoped, then prayed that the doctors' fears would not be confirmed—that his precious right leg would not be amputated. Shattered and stunned, they accepted the sad news. To save his life, he must lose his leg.

The surgery completed, Paul rested.

Entering the room, I was attracted immediately by his cheerful and infectious grin. He breathed hope. He emanated goodness.

The crisp, white sheet lay noticeably flat where once there was a leg. Flowers from friends bedecked his bedside. Parents, grateful for his life, stood close by.

I noticed a cord strung along the exercise bar stretching the length of the bed. Gaily colored cards covered the entire span. Paul invited me to read them. One carried the message: "We love you, Paul. We're praying for you." It was signed by members of his Sunday School class. Another expressed the wish, "May you get well soon. We think you're great." This from his schoolmates at high school. Still another from home teachers had the inscription, "May God bless you. Tomorrow we'll visit you again."

What did the Carpenter from Nazareth say of such? "Inasmuch as ye have done it unto one of the least of these my brethren, ye have done it unto me." (Matthew 25:40.)

The spirit of prayer came easy that day. A perfect

peace filled the room. Smiles of confidence crept across lips moist with tears. From distant Capernaum we seemed to hear the echo, "Be not afraid, only believe." Then Paul said, "I'll be all right."

We beheld a faith-filled heart and a countenance which reflects gratitude. Faith in whom? Gratitude for what?

> *Jesus of Nazareth, Savior and King!*
> *Triumphant over death, Life thou didst bring.*
> *Leaving thy Father's throne, On earth to live,*
> *Thy work to do alone, Thy life to give.*

Can any good thing come out of Nazareth?

> From Nazareth came example.
> From Nazareth came sight.
> From Nazareth came strength.
> From Nazareth came life.
> From Nazareth came faith.
> From Nazareth came peace.
> From Nazareth came courage.
> From Nazareth came Christ.

To him Nathanael declared, ". . . thou art the Son of God; thou art the King of Israel." (John 1:49.) I testify that he is Lord of lords, King of kings, precious Savior, dear Redeemer. Jesus Christ of Nazareth. There is none other name under heaven given among men whereby we must be saved.

May we live his teachings, may we emulate his example, may we follow in his footsteps to life eternal.

26

With hand and heart

In our general, stake, and ward conferences, each person is given the privilege to raise his right hand to sustain, in the positions to which they have been called, the leadership of the church. The upraised hand is an outward expression of an inner feeling. As one raises his hand, he pledges his heart.

The Master frequently spoke of hand and heart. In a revelation given through the Prophet Joseph Smith at Hiram, Ohio, in March 1832, he counseled: ". . . be faithful; stand in the office which I have appointed unto you; succor the weak, lift up the hands which hang down, and strengthen the feeble knees. And if thou art faithful unto the end, thou shalt have a crown of immortality, and eternal life in the mansions which I have prepared in the house of my Father." (D&C 81:5-6.)

As I ponder his words, I can almost hear the shuffle of sandaled feet, the murmurs of astonishment from listeners as they echoed from Capernaum's peaceful scene. Here multitudes crowded around Jesus, bringing the sick to be healed. A palsied man picked up his bed and walked, and a Roman centurion's faith restored his servant's health.

Not only by precept did Jesus teach, but also by example. He was faithful to his divine mission. He stretched forth his hand that others might be lifted toward God.

At Galilee there came to him a leper who pleaded: "Lord, if thou wilt, thou canst make me clean. And Jesus put forth his hand, and touched him, saying, I will; be thou clean. And immediately his leprosy was cleansed." (Matthew 8:2-3.) The hand of Jesus was not polluted touching the leper's body, but the leper's body was cleansed by the touch of that holy hand.

In Capernaum, at the house of Peter, yet another example was provided. The mother of Peter's wife lay sick of a fever. The sacred record reveals that Jesus came "and took her by the hand, and lifted her up; and immediately the fever left her. . . ." (Mark 1:31.)

So it was with the daughter of Jairus, a ruler of the synagogue. Each parent can appreciate the feelings of Jairus as he sought the Lord, and, upon finding him, fell at his feet and pleaded, "My little daughter lieth at the point of death: I pray thee, come and lay thy lands on her, that she may be healed; and she shall live." (Mark 5:23.)

"While he yet spake, there cometh one from the [ruler's] house saying to him, Thy daughter is dead; trouble not the Master. But when Jesus heard it he answered him, saying, Fear not: believe only, and she shall be made whole." Parents wept. Others mourned. Jesus declared: "Weep not; she is not dead, but sleepeth. [He] . . . took her by the hand, and called, saying: Maid, arise. And her spirit came again, and she arose straightway. . . ." (Luke 8:49-50, 52, 54-55.) Once again, the Lord had stretched forth his hand to take the hand of another.

The beloved apostles noted well his example. He lived not so to be ministered unto, but to minister; not to receive, but to give; not to save his life, but to pour it out for others.

If they would see the star which should at once direct their feet and influence their destiny, they must look for it, not in the changing skies or outward circumstance, but each in the depth of his own heart and after the pattern provided by the Master.

Reflect for a moment on the experience of Peter at the gate Beautiful of the temple. One sympathizes with the plight of the man lame from birth who each day was carried to the temple gate that he might ask alms of all who entered. That he asked alms of Peter and John as these two brethren approached indicates that he regarded them no differently from scores of others who must have passed by him that day. Then Peter's majestic yet gentle command: "Look on us." (Acts 3:4.) The record states that the lame man gave heed unto them, expecting to receive something from them.

The stirring words Peter then spoke have lifted the hearts of honest believers down through the stream of time, even to this day: "Silver and gold have I none; but such as I have give I thee: In the name of Jesus Christ of Nazareth rise up and walk." Frequently we conclude the citation at this point and fail to note the next verse: "And he took him by the right hand and lifted him up: . . . he . . . stood, and walked, and entered with them into the temple. . . ." (Acts 3:6-8.)

A helping hand had been extended. A broken body had been healed. A precious soul had been lifted toward God.

Time passes. Circumstances change. Conditions vary. Unaltered is the divine command to succor the weak and lift up the hands which hang down and strengthen the feeble knees. Each of us has the charge to be not a doubter, but a doer; not a leaner, but a lifter. But our complacency tree has many branches, and each spring more buds come into bloom. Often we live side by side but do not communicate heart to heart. There are those within the sphere of our own influence who, with outstretched hands, cry out: "Is there no balm in Gilead. . . ?" Each of us must answer. Edwin Markham observed:

> *There is a destiny that makes us brothers;*
> *None goes his way alone:*
> *All that we send into the lives of others*
> *Comes back into our own.*
>
> —"A CREED"

"He that loveth not his brother abideth in death," wrote the apostle John 1900 years ago. (1 John 3:14.)

Some point the accusing finger at the sinner or the unfortunate and in derision say, "He has brought his condition upon himself." Others exclaim, "Oh, he will never change. He has always been a bad one." A few see beyond the outward appearance and recognize the true worth of a human soul. When they do, miracles occur. The downtrodden, the discouraged, the helpless become "no more strangers and foreigners, but fellowcitizens with the saints, and of the household of God." (Ephesians 2:19.) True love can alter human lives and change human nature.

This truth was stated so beautifully on the stage in *My Fair Lady*. Eliza Doolittle, the flower girl, spoke to one for whom she cared and who later was to lift her from such mediocre status: "You see, really and truly, apart from the things anyone can pick up [the dressing and the proper way of speaking, and so on], the difference between a lady and a flower girl is not how she behaves, but how she's treated. I shall always be a flower girl to Professor Higgins, because he always treats me as a flower girl, and always will; but I know I can be a lady to you, because you always treat me as a lady, and always will."[1]

Eliza Doolittle was but expressing the profound truth: When we treat people merely as they are, they will remain as they are. When we treat them as if they were what they should be, they will become what they should be.

In reality, it was the Redeemer who best taught this principle. Jesus changed men. He changed their habits and opinions and ambitions. He changed their tempers, dispositions, and natures. He changed their hearts. He lifted! He loved! He forgave! He redeemed! Do we have the will to follow?

Prison warden Kenyon J. Scudder has related this experience:

A friend of his happened to be sitting in a railroad coach next to a young man who was obviously depressed. Finally the man revealed that he was a paroled convict returning from a distant prison. His imprisonment had brought shame to his family, and they had neither visited him nor written often. He hoped, however, that this was only because they were too poor to travel and too uneducated to write. He hoped, despite the evidence, that they had forgiven him.

To make it easy for them, however, he had written them to put up a signal for him when the train passed their little farm on the outskirts of town. If his family had forgiven him, they were to put a white ribbon in the big apple tree which stood near the tracks. If they didn't want him to return, they were to do nothing; and he would remain on the train as it traveled west.

As the train neared his home town, the suspense became so great he couldn't bear to look out of his window. He exclaimed, "In just five minutes the engineer will sound the whistle indicating our approach to the long bend which opens into the valley I know as home. Will you watch for the apple tree at the side of the track?" His companion changed places with him and said he would. The minutes seemed like hours, but then there came the shrill sound of the train whistle. The young man asked, "Can you see the tree? Is there a white ribbon?"

Came the reply: "I see the tree. I see not one white

221

ribbon, but many. There is a white ribbon on every branch. Son, someone surely does love you."

In that instant all the bitterness that had poisoned a life was dispelled. "I felt as if I had witnessed a miracle," the other man said. Indeed, he had witnessed a miracle. We too can experience this same miracle when we, with hand and heart, as did the Savior, lift and love our neighbor to a newness of life.

---

[1]*My Fair Lady* as adapted from George Bernard Shaw's *Pygamalion, The Complete Plays of Bernard Shaw,* p. 260.

27

"Behold thy mother"

One summer day I stood alone in the quiet of the American War Memorial cemetery of the Philippines. A spirit of reverence filled the warm tropical air. Situated amidst the carefully mowed grass, acre upon acre, were markers identifying men, mostly young, who in battle gave their lives. As I let my eyes pass name by name along the many colonnades of honor, tears came easily and without embarrassment. As my eyes filled with tears, my heart swelled with pride. I contemplated the high price of liberty and the costly sacrifice many had been called upon to bear.

My thoughts turned from those who bravely served and gallantly died. There came to mind the grief-stricken mother of each fallen man as she held in her hand the news of her precious son's supreme sacrifice. Who can measure a mother's grief? Who can probe a mother's love? Who can comprehend in its entirety the lofty role of a mother? With perfect trust in God, she walks, her hand in his, into the valley of the shadow of death, that you and I might come forth into light.

> *The holiest words my tongue can frame,*
> *The noblest thoughts my soul can claim,*
> *Unworthy are to praise the name*
> *More precious than all others.*

"Behold thy mother"

An infant, when her love first came,
A man, I find it still the same;
Reverently I breathe her name,
The blessed name of mother.

In this spirit, let us consider mother. Four mothers come to mind: first, mother forgotten; second, mother remembered; third, mother blessed; and finally, mother loved.

"Mother forgotten" is observed all too frequently. The nursing homes are crowded, the hospital beds are full, the days come and go—often the weeks and months pass—but mother is not visited. Can we not appreciate the pangs of loneliness, the yearnings of mother's heart when hour after hour, alone in her age, she gazes out the window for the loved one who does not visit, the letter the postman does not bring. She listens for the knock that does not sound, the telephone that does not ring, the voice she does not hear. How does such a mother feel when her neighbor welcomes gladly the smile of a son, the hug of a daughter, the glad exclamation of a child, "Hello, Grandmother!"

There are yet other ways we forget mother. Whenever we fall, whenever we do less than we ought, in a very real way we forget mother.

Last Christmas I talked to the proprietress of a Salt Lake City nursing home. From the hallway where we stood, she pointed to several elderly women assembled in a peaceful living room. She observed, "There's Mrs. Hansen. Her daughter visits her every week, right at 3:00 P.M. on Sunday. To her right is Mrs. Peek. Each Wednesday there is a letter in her hands from her son in New York. It is read, then reread, then saved as a precious piece of treasure. But see Mrs. Carroll: her family never telephones, never writes, never visits. Patiently she justifies this neglect with words that are heard but do not convince or excuse: 'They are all so busy.' "

Shame on all who thus make of a noble woman "mother forgotten."

"Hearken unto thy father that begat thee," wrote Solomon, "and despise not thy mother when she is old." (Proverbs 23:22.) Can we not make, of a mother forgotten, a mother remembered?

Men turn from evil and yield to their better natures when mother is remembered. A famed officer from the Civil War period, Colonel Higgenson, when asked to name the incident of the Civil War that he considered the most remarkable for bravery, said that there was in his regiment a man whom everybody liked, a man who was brave and noble, who was pure in his daily life, absolutely free from dissipations in which most of the other men indulged.

One night at a champagne supper, when many were becoming intoxicated, someone in jest called for a toast from this young man. Colonel Higgenson said that he arose, pale but with perfect self-control, and declared: "Gentlemen, I will give you a toast which you may drink as you will, but which I will drink in water. The toast that I have to give is, 'Our mothers.' "

Instantly a strange spell seemed to come over all the tipsy men. They drank the toast in silence. There was no laughter, no more song, and one by one they left the room. The lamp of memory had begun to burn, and the name of "Mother" touched every man's heart.

As a boy, I well remember Sunday School on Mother's Day. We would hand to each mother present a small potted plant and sit in silent reverie as Melvin Watson, a blind member, would stand by the piano and sing "That Wonderful Mother of Mine." This was the first time I saw a blind man cry. Even today, in memory, I can see the moist tears move from those sightless eyes, then form tiny rivulets and course down his cheeks, falling finally upon the lapel of the suit he had never seen. In boyhood puzzlement I wondered why all the grown men were silent, why so many handkerchiefs came forth. Now I know. You see, mother was remembered. Each boy, each girl, all fathers and husbands seemed to make a silent pledge, "I will remember that wonderful mother of mine."

Some years ago I listened intently as a man well beyond middle age told me of an experience in his family history. The widowed mother who had given birth to him and his brothers and sisters had gone to her eternal and well-earned reward. The family assembled at the home and surrounded the large dining room table. The small metal box in which mother had kept her earthly treasures was opened reverently. One by one each keepsake was brought forth. There was the wedding certificate from the Salt Lake Temple. "Oh, now Mother can be with Dad." Then there was the deed to the humble home where each child had in turn entered upon the stage of life. The appraised value of the house had little resemblance to the worth Mother had attached to it.

Then there was discovered a yellowed envelope that bore the marks of time. Carefully the flap was opened and from inside was taken a homemade valentine. Its simple message, in the handwriting of a child, read, "I love you, Mother." Though she was gone, by what she held sacred mother taught yet another lesson. A silence permeated the room, and every member of the family made a pledge not only to remember, but also to honor mother. For them it was not too little and too late, as in the classic poem of Rose Marinoni entitled "At Sunrise":

> *They pushed him straight against the wall,*
> *The firing squad dropped in a row;*
> *And why he stood on tiptoe,*

"Behold thy mother"

Those men shall never know.
He wore a smile across his face
As he stood primly there,
The guns straight aiming at his heart,
The sun upon his hair.

For he remembered in a flash
Those days beyond recall,
When his proud mother took his height
Against the bedroom wall.

Now that we have considered "mother remembered," let us turn to "mother blessed." For one of the most beautiful and reverent examples, I refer to the holy scriptures.

In the New Testament of our Lord, perhaps we have no more moving account of "mother blessed" than the tender regard of the Master for the grieving widow at Nain.

"And it came to pass . . . that he went into a city called Nain; and many of his disciples went with him, and much people.

"Now when he came nigh to the gate of the city, behold, there was a dead man carried out, the only son of his mother, and she was a widow: and much people of the city was with her.

"And when the Lord saw her, he had compassion on her, and said unto her, Weep not.

"And he came and touched the bier: and they that bear him stood still. And he said, Young man, I say unto thee, Arise.

"And he that was dead sat up, and began to speak. And he delivered him to his mother." (Luke 7:11-15.)

What power, what tenderness, what compassion did our Master and Exemplar thus demonstrate! We, too, can bless if we will but follow his noble example. Opportunities are everywhere. Needed are eyes to see the pitiable plight; ears to hear the silent pleadings of a broken heart. Yes, and a soul filled with compassion, that we might communicate not only eye to eye or voice to ear, but in the majestic style of the Savior, even heart to heart. Then every mother everywhere will be "mother blessed."

Finally, let us contemplate "mother loved." Universally applicable is the poem recalled from childhood and enjoyed by children even today, "Which Loved Best?"

"I love you, Mother," said little John;
Then, forgetting his work, his cap went on
And he was off to the garden swing,
Leaving her the water and wood to bring.

"I love you, Mother," said rosy Nell.
"I love you better than tongue can tell."
Then she teased and pouted full half the day
Till her mother rejoiced when she went to play.

"I love you, Mother," said little Fan.
"Today I'll help you all I can.
How glad I am that school doesn't keep."
So she rocked the baby till it fell asleep.

Then, stepping softly, she fetched the broom
And swept the floor and tidied the room.
Busy and happy all day was she,
Helpful and happy as a child could be.

"I love you, Mother," again they said,
Three little children going to bed.
How do you think that Mother guessed
Which of them really loved her best?

One certain way each can demonstrate genuine love for mother is to live the truths mother so patiently taught. Such a lofty goal is not new to our present generation. On this continent, in the times described in the Book of Mormon, we read of a brave, a good and noble leader named

228

Helaman who did march in righteous battle at the head of 2,000 young men. Helaman described the activities of these young men:

". . . never had I seen so great courage . . . [as] they said unto me: Father, behold our God is with us, and he will not suffer that we should fall; then let us go forth. . . .

"Now they never had fought, yet they did not fear death; . . . yea, they had been taught by their mothers, that if they did not doubt, God would deliver them.

"And they rehearsed unto me the words of their mothers, saying: We do not doubt our mothers knew. it." (Alma 56:45-47.)

At the end of the battle, Helaman continued his description: "Behold, to my great joy there had not one soul of them fallen to the earth; yea, and they had fought as if with the strength of God; yea, never were men known to have fought with such miraculous strength; and with such mighty power. . . ." (Alma 56:56.)

Miraculous strength, mighty power—mother's love and love for mother had met and triumphed.

The holy scriptures, the pages of history, are replete with tender, moving, convincing accounts of "mother loved." One, however, stands out supreme, above and beyond any other. The place is Jerusalem, the period known as the meridian of time. Assembled is a throng of Roman soldiers. Their helmets signify their loyalty to Caesar, their shields bear his emblem, their spears are crowned by Roman eagles. Assembled also are natives to the land of Jerusalem. Faded into the still night, and gone forever, are the militant and rowdy cries, "Crucify him, crucify him."

The hour has come. The personal earthly ministry of the Son of God moves swiftly to its dramatic conclusion. A certain loneliness is here. Nowhere to be found are the lame beggars who, because of this man, walk; the deaf who, because of this man, hear; the blind who, because of this man, see; the dead who, because of this man, live.

There remained yet a few faithful followers. From his tortured position on the cruel cross he sees his mother and the disciple whom he loved standing by. He speaks: "Woman, behold thy son! Then saith he to the disciple, Behold thy mother!" (John 19:26-27.)

From that awful night when time stood still, when the earth did quake and great mountains were brought down—yes, through the annals of history, over the centuries of years and beyond the span of time, there echoes his simple yet divine words, "Behold thy mother."

As we truly listen to that gentle command and with gladness obey its intent, gone forever will be the vast legions of "mothers forgotten." Everywhere present will be "mothers remembered," "mothers blessed," and "mothers loved"; and, as in the beginning, God will once again survey the workmanship of his own hand and be led to say, "It is very good."

May each of us treasure this truth: "One cannot forget mother and remember God. One cannot remember mother and forget God." Why? Because these two sacred persons, God and mother, partners in creation, in love, in sacrifice, in service, are as one.

THE PATHWAY OF
PRAYER

*"Pray always, and I will pour out my Spirit upon you,
and great shall be your blessing . . ."*
D&C 19:38

28

"Finishers wanted"

On sunlit days during the noon hour, the streets of Salt Lake City abound with men and women who for a moment leave the confines of the tall office buildings and engage in that universal delight called window shopping. On occasion I, too, am a participant.

One Wednesday I paused before the elegant show window of a prestigious furniture store. That which caught and held my attention was not the beautifully designed sofa nor the comfortable appearing chair which stood at its side. Neither was it the beautiful chandelier positioned overhead. Rather, my eyes rested upon a small sign which had been placed at the bottom right-hand corner of the window. Its message was brief: "FINISHERS WANTED." The store had need of those persons who possessed the talent and the skill to make ready for final sale the expensive furniture the firm manufactured and sold. "Finishers Wanted." The words remained with me as I returned to the pressing activities of the day.

In life, as in business, there has always been a need for those persons who could be called finishers. Their ranks are few, their opportunities many, their contributions great.

From the very beginning to the present time, a fundamental question remains to be answered by each who runs the race of life. Shall I falter, or shall I finish? On the answer await the blessings of joy and happiness here in mortality and eternal life in the world to come.

We are not left without guidance to make this momentous decision. The Holy Bible contains those accounts, even those lessons which, if carefully learned, will serve us well and be as a beacon light to guide our thoughts and influence our actions. As we read, we sympathize with those who falter. We honor those who finish.

The apostle Paul likened life to a great race when he declared, "Know ye not that they which run in a race run all, but one receiveth the prize? So run, that ye may obtain." (1 Corinthians 9:24.)

And before the words of Paul fell upon the ears of his listeners, the counsel of the preacher, even the son of David, king in Jerusalem, cautioned, ". . . the race is not to the swift, nor the battle to the strong. . . ." (Ecclesiastes 9:11.)

Could the son of David have been referring to his own father? Judged by any standards, the greatest king Israel ever had was David. Anointed by Samuel, he was honored by the Lord.

In the first flush of his incredible triumphs, David rode the crest of popularity. As he achieved fresh victories, in adoration the people exclaimed: "Behold, we are thy bone and flesh." (2 Samuel 5:1.) Power he won. Peace he lost.

It happened late one afternoon when David was walking upon the roof of the king's house that he saw from the roof a woman bathing, and the woman was very beautiful. "And David sent and inquired after the woman. And one said, Is not this Bathsheba, . . . the wife of Uriah the Hittite?" So "David sent messengers, and took her. . . ." (2 Samuel 11:3-4.) The gross sin of adultery was followed by yet another: ". . . Set ye Uriah in the forefront of the hottest battle, and retire ye from him, that he may be smitten, and die." (2 Samuel 11:15.) Lust and power had triumphed.

David's rebuke came from the Lord God of Israel. ". . . thou hast killed Uriah the Hittite with the sword and hast taken his wife to be thy wife. . . . Now therefore the sword shall never depart from thine house. . . ." (2 Samuel 12:9-10.) David commenced well the race, then faltered and failed to finish his course.

Lest we lull ourselves into thinking that only the gross sins of life cause us to falter, consider the experience of the rich young man who came running to the Savior and asked the question: "Good Master, what good thing shall I do, that I may have eternal life?" Jesus answered him: "If thou wilt enter into life, keep the commandments. He saith unto him, Which?"

To Jesus' enumeration of the commandments, "the young man saith, . . . All these things have I kept from my youth up: what lack I yet?

"Jesus said unto him, If thou wilt be perfect, go and sell that thou hast, and give to the poor, . . . and come and follow me.

"But when the young man heard that saying, he went away sorrowful: for he had great possessions." (Matthew 19:16-18, 20-22.)

He preferred the comforts of earth to the treasures of heaven. He would not purchase the things of eternity by abandoning those of time. He faltered. He failed to finish.

So it was with Judas Iscariot. He commenced his ministry as an apostle of the Lord. He ended it a traitor. For thirty paltry pieces of silver, he sold his soul. At last, realizing the enormity of his sin, Judas, to his patrons and temptors, shrieked: "I have sinned in that I have betrayed the innocent blood." (Matthew 27:4.) Remorse had led to despair, despair to madness, and madness to suicide. He had succeeded in betraying the Christ. He had failed to finish the apostolic ministry to which he had been divinely called.

Lust for power, greed of gold, and disdain for honor have ever appeared as faces of failure in the panorama of life. Captivated by their artificial attraction, many noble souls have stumbled and fallen, thus losing the crown of victory reserved for the finisher of life's great race.

May we turn from the lives of those who faltered and consider for a moment some who finished and won the prize.

There was a man in the land of Uz whose name was Job, and that man was perfect and upright and one that feared God and eschewed evil. Pious in his conduct, prosperous in his fortune, Job was to face a test which would tempt any man. Shorn of his possessions, scorned by his friends, afflicted by his suffering, even tempted by his wife, Job was to declare from the depths of his noble soul: ". . . . behold, my witness is in heaven, and my record is on high." (Job 16:19.) ". . . I know that my redeemer liveth. . . ." (Job 19:25.) Job did not falter. Job became a finisher.

Following the earthly ministry of the Lord, there were many who, rather than deny their testimony of him, would forfeit their lives. Such was Paul the apostle. The impulse of his father to send him to Jerusalem opened the door to Paul's destiny. He would pass through it and help to shape a new world.

Gifted in his capacity to stir, move, and manage groups of men, Paul was a peerless example of one who nobly made the transition from sinner to saint. Though disappointment, heartache, and trial were to beset him, yet Paul, at the conclusion of his ministry, could say: "I have fought a good fight, I have finished my course, I have kept the faith." (2 Timothy 4:7.) Like Job, Paul was a finisher.

He admonished us to "lay aside . . . sin . . ." and to "run

with patience the race. . . , looking [for an example] unto Jesus the author and finisher of our faith. . . ." (Hebrews 12:1-2.)

Though Jesus was tempted by the evil one, yet he resisted. Though he was hated, yet he loved. Though he was betrayed, yet he triumphed. Not in a cloud of glory or chariot of fire was Jesus to depart mortality, but with arms outstretched in agony upon the cruel cross. The magnitude of his mission is depicted in the simplicity of his words. To his Father he prayed, ". . . the hour is come. . . . I have glorified thee on the earth; I have finished the work which thou gavest me to do." (John 17:1, 4.) ". . . into thy hands I commend my spirit. . ." (Luke 23:46.) Mortality ended. Eternity began.

Times change, circumstances vary, but the true marks of a finisher remain. Note them well, for they are vital to our success.

1. *The Mark of Vision.* It has been said that the door of history turns on small hinges and so do people's lives. We are constantly making small decisions. The outcome determines the success or failure of our lives. That is why it is worthwhile to look ahead, to set a course, and at least be partly ready when the moment of decision comes. True finishers have the capacity to visualize their objective.

2. *The Mark of Effort.* Vision without effort is daydreaming; effort without vision is drudgery; but vision, coupled with effort, will obtain the prize.

Needed is the capacity to make that second effort when life's challenges lay us low.

> *Stick to your task 'til it sticks to you;*
> *Beginners are many, but enders are few.*
> *Honor, power, place and praise*
> *Will always come to the one who stays.*

"Finishers wanted"

Stick to your task 'til it sticks to you;
Bend at it, sweat at it, smile at it, too;
For out of the bend and the sweat and the smile
Will come life's victories after a while.

—AUTHOR UNKNOWN

3. *The Mark of Faith.* Long years ago the psalmist wrote: "It is better to trust in the Lord than to put confidence in man: It is better to trust in the Lord than to put confidence in princes." (Psalm 118:8-9.) Recognize that faith and doubt cannot exist in the same mind at the same time, for one will dispel the other.

4. *The Mark of Virtue.* ". . . let virtue garnish thy thoughts unceasingly. . . ." (D&C 121:45.) This counsel from the Lord will provide staying power in the race we run.

5. *The Mark of Courage.* Have the courage—

To dream the impossible dream,
To fight the unbeatable foe,
To bear with unbearable sorrow,
To run where the brave dare not go.

To right the unrightable wrong,
To love, pure and chaste, from afar,
To try, when your arms are too weary,
To reach the unreachable star! [1]

And you will, thus becoming a finisher.

6. *The Mark of Prayer.* When the burdens of life become heavy, when trials test one's faith, when pain, sorrow, and despair cause the light of hope to flicker and burn low, communication with our Heavenly Father provides peace.

[1]©MCMLXV by Andrew Scott, Inc., Helena Music Corp., & Sam Fox Publishing Co., Inc. Sam Fox Publishing Company, Inc., Sole Agent. All rights reserved. International Copyright secured. Used by special permission of the publisher. Lyrics by Joe Darion, music by Mitch Leigh, from *Man of La Mancha.*

"Finishers wanted"

These, the marks of a true finisher, will be as a lamp to our feet in the journey through life. Ever beckoning us onward and lifting us upward is he who pleaded, ". . . come, follow me." (Luke 18:22.)

Frequently his help comes silently—on occasion with dramatic impact. Such was my experience of some years ago when, as a mission president, I was afforded the privilege to guide the activities of precious young men and women, even missionaries whom he had called. Some had problems, others required motivation; but one came to me in utter despair. He had made his decision to leave the mission field when but at the halfway mark. His bags were packed, his return ticket purchased. He came by to bid me farewell. We talked; we listened; we prayed. There remained hidden the actual reason for his decision to quit. As we arose from our knees in the quiet of my office, the missionary began to weep almost uncontrollably. Flexing the muscle in his strong right arm, he blurted out, "This is my problem. All through school my muscle power qualified me for honors in football and track, but my mental power was neglected. President Monson, I'm ashamed of my school record. It reveals that 'with effort' I have the capacity to read at but *the level of the fourth grade.* I can't even read the Book of Mormon. How then can I understand its contents and teach others its truths?"

The silence of the room was broken by my young nine-year-old son who, without knocking, opened the door and, with surprise, apologetically said, "Excuse me. I just wanted to put this book back on the shelf." He handed me the book. Its title: *A Child's Story of the Book of Mormon,* by Dr. Deta Petersen Neeley. I turned to the foreword and read these words: "This book has been written with a scientifically controlled vocabulary to *the level of the fourth grade.*" A sincere prayer from an honest heart had been dramatically answered.

"Finishers wanted"

My missionary accepted the challenge to read the book. Half laughing, half crying, he declared: "It will be good to read something I can understand." Clouds of despair were dispelled by the sunshine of hope. He completed an honorable mission. He became a finisher.

Today I think I shall once more walk by that furniture store in our city and again gaze at the small sign in the large show window, that I may indelibly impress upon my mind the true meaning of its words: "FINISHERS WANTED."

29

Building a house for eternity

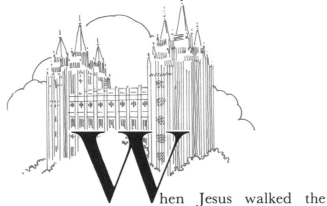

When Jesus walked the dusty pathways of towns and villages that we now reverently call the Holy Land and taught his disciples by beautiful Galilee, he often spoke in parables in language the people understood best. Frequently he referred to home building in relationship to the lives of those who listened.

He declared: ". . . every . . . house divided against itself shall not stand." (Matthew 12:25.) Later he cautioned: "Behold, mine house is a house of order, saith the Lord God, and not a house of confusion." (D&C 132:8.)

In a revelation given through the Prophet Joseph Smith at Kirtland, Ohio, December 27, 1832, the Master counseled: "Organize yourselves; prepare every needful thing; and establish a house, even a house of prayer, a house of fasting, a house of faith, a house of learning, a house of glory, a house of order, a house of God." (D&C 88:119.)

Where could any of us locate a more suitable blueprint whereby he could wisely and properly build a house to personally occupy throughout eternity?

Such a house would meet the building code outlined in Matthew—even a house built "upon a rock"; a house capable of withstanding the rain of adversity, the floods of opposition, and the winds of doubt everywhere present in our challenging world.

Perhaps if we considered these architectural guidelines on an individual basis, we would more readily appreciate this divine counsel from the Master Builder.

A house of prayer

Our Heavenly Father invites us to come to him in prayer. He appreciates the value of this raw material which we call life. "Remember the worth of souls is great in the sight of God." (D&C 18:10.) His pronouncement finds lodgment in our souls and inspires purpose in our lives.

During the final phases of World War II, I turned eighteen and was ordained an elder one week before I departed for active duty with the navy. A member of my ward bishopric was at the train station to bid me farewell. Just before train time, he placed two books in my hands. One was a popular satire in which I took interest. The other was entitled *The Missionary Handbook.* I laughed and commented, "I'm not going on a mission." He answered, "Take it anyway—it may come in handy."

It did. In basic training the quartermaster instructed us concerning how we might best pack our clothing in a large sea bag. He advised: "If you have some hard, rectangular object you can place in the bottom, your clothes will stay more firm." I suddenly remembered just the right rectangular object: *The Missionary Handbook.* Thus it served for sixteen weeks.

The night preceding our Christmas leave our thoughts were, as always, on home. The quarters were quiet. Suddenly I became aware that my buddy in the adjoining bunk, a Mormon boy, Leland Merrill, was moaning in pain. I asked, "What's the matter, Merrill?" He replied, "I'm sick. I'm *really* sick." I advised him to go to the base dispensary, but he answered knowingly that such a course would prevent him from being home for Christmas.

The hours lengthened, his groans grew louder. Suddenly he whispered, "Monson, Monson, aren't you an elder?" I acknowledged this to be so, whereupon he asked, "Give me a blessing."

Suddenly I became very much aware that I had never given a blessing, I had never received such a blessing, I had never witnessed a blessing being given. My prayer to God was a plea for help. The answer came: "Look in the bottom of the sea bag." Thus, at 2:00 A.M., I spilled the contents of the bag on the deck, took the book to the night light, and read how one blesses the sick. With about forty curious sailors looking on, I proceeded with the blessing. Before I could stow my gear, Leland Merrill was sleeping like a child.

The next morning Merrill smilingly turned to me and said: "Monson, I'm glad you have the priesthood." His gladness was only surpassed by my joy.

Our house must qualify as a house of prayer.

A house of fasting

Closely allied with prayer is the principle of fasting. The prophet Alma observed that the sons of Mosiah possessed the spirit of prophecy and the spirit of revelation and taught with power and authority of God. Why? Because "they had given themselves to much prayer, and fasting. . . ." (Alma 17:3.)

Isaiah described the proper fast by asking: "Is it not to deal thy bread to the hungry, and that thou bring the poor that are cast out to thy house? when thou seest the naked, that thou cover him; and that thou hide not thyself from thine own flesh?" He then promised, "Then shall thy light break forth as the morning, and thine health shall spring forth speedily: and thy righteousness shall go before thee: . . . and the Lord shall guide thee continually. . . ." (Isaiah 58:7-8, 11.)

Our house is to be a house of fasting.

A house of faith

Faith is a foundation stone in our eternal house. Throughout life many of us may be exposed to conflicting theories of men and science as opposed to the laws of God. Just say to those skeptical, disturbing, rebellious thoughts, "I propose to stay with my faith, with the faith of my people. I know that happiness and contentment are there, and I forbid you, agnostic, doubting thoughts, to destroy the house of my faith. I acknowledge that I do not understand the processes of creation, but I accept the fact of it. I grant that I cannot explain the miracles of the Bible, and I do not attempt to do so, but I accept God's word. I wasn't with Joseph, but I believe him. My faith did not come to me through science, and I shall not permit science to destroy it. When I change my mind about God and his work, only the inspiration of God will change it." (Stephen L Richards)

With such firm mortar, the faith stones of our house will be secure.

A house of learning

". . . seek ye out of the best books words of wisdom; seek learning, even by study and also by faith." (D&C 88: 118.) This is our day of preparation, that we might meet the days of decision which are before us.

Part of this seeking of wisdom pertains to our chosen field or profession. A sophisticated economy, based upon power tools and computer, upon engineer and the professional, has no room at the bottom for unskilled labor. "The uneducated need not apply" is the unseen sign on every employment door. "Out of school and out of work" could well

apply to those who interrupt a vital training program before its conclusion.

Academic learning is vital, but don't disregard the
knowledge that saves, even a knowledge of the Lord Jesus
Christ. Study habits acquired through the years help prepare us for a continuous program for improved gospel
scholarship.

Our house will glow brightly when we include learning.

A house of glory

For our house to be a house of glory, we need to be
square with God, fair with others, and honest with ourselves. One person who is striving to make of her house a
house of glory is a young woman not of our faith. Distressed
by the declining standards everywhere about her, she declared boldly, as reported in *Look* magazine:

> Our generation has been exposed through every means of com-
> munication to major and minor fears—the little threat of not finding a
> mate if one does not use a certain mouthwash, or fear of non-acceptance
> if one does not succumb to a low moral standard because it is the
> "nature of the beast."
> Many of us accept the premises that, "You can't fight City Hall,"
> "Live life to its fullest now; so eat, drink, and be merry, for tomorrow
> we will be destroyed by nuclear war." I am old-fashioned enough to
> believe in God, to believe in the dignity and potential of His creature
> —man, and I am realistic, not idealistic, enough to know that I am
> not alone in these feelings.
> Some say that, unlike other generations, we have no threat to
> our freedom, no cause to propagate, no mission in life—everything
> has been handed to us. We have not been pampered, but spiritually im-
> poverished. I don't want to live in the poverty of affluence, and I can-
> not live alone. (*Look*, January 12, 1965.)

Make every decision pass the test:

> *What does it do to me?*
> *What does it do for me?*

And let our code emphasize not "What will others

think?" but rather, "What will I think of myself?" Then our Father can say of us as Jesus said of Nathanael, "Behold an Israelite indeed, in whom is no guile!" (John 1:47.)

Such is a house of glory.

A house of order

For students today, there is no period in their lives where so many demands will confront them. Study requirements are heavy. Employment may necessarily be coupled with school. And what of church duties or family responsibilities?

An orderly scheduling of time is essential. Some foolish students, like the housebuilder who built upon sand, have said: "In this period of my life I have no time for God." To him I would unhesitatingly say, "Thou fool."

Other students take a reverse course and so complicate their available time with overly numerous church assignments that their studies suffer and dropout dangers threaten. Two familiar twins stand before us almost daily and demand that we favor one—not both. They are, "Do it now," and "Put it off." If we choose the first, we emerge weary but at peace. Select the second, and frustration is our constant companion.

In these busy times it is essential that our house is a house of order.

A house of God

Clean thoughts, noble purpose, a willing heart, and ready hands are all features of a house of God. He does not leave us to struggle alone, but stands ever ready to help.

A few years ago I was afforded the privilege to serve as a mission president and became intimately acquainted with almost four hundred missionaries. We had one young missionary who was very ill. After weeks of hospitalization, as the surgeon prepared to undertake extremely serious and complicated surgery, he asked that we send for the missionary's mother and father. He said that there was a great likelihood that Elder Davidson could not survive the surgery. The parents came; and late that evening, his father and I, in the hospital room in Toronto, Canada, placed our hands upon the head of that young missionary and gave him a blessing. What happened following that blessing was a testimony to me.

Elder Davidson was in a six-bed ward in the hospital. The other beds were occupied by five men with a variety of illnesses. The morning of Elder Davidson's surgery, his bed was empty. The nurse came into the room with the breakfast these husky men normally ate. She brought a tray over to bed number one and said, "Fried eggs this morning, and I have an extra portion for you." Bed number one was occupied by a man who was lying on his bed with his toe wrapped up in a bandage. He had suffered an accident with his lawnmower. Other than his injured toe, he was well physically. He said to the nurse, "I'll not be eating this morning."

"All right, we shall give your breakfast to your partner in bed number two!" As she went over to him, he said, "No, I think I'll not eat this morning."

She said, "That's two in a row. I don't understand you men, and there is no one this morning in bed three." She went on to bed four, bed five, and bed six; and the answer was the same. "No, this morning we're not hungry."

The young lady put her hands on her hips and said, "Every other morning you eat us out of house and home and today not one of you wants to eat. What is the reason?"

And then the man who occupied bed number six came forth with the answer. He said, "You see, bed number three is empty. Our friend, Davidson, is in the operating room under the surgeon's hands. He needs all the help he can get. He is a missionary for his church; and while he has been lying on that bed while we have been patients in this ward, he has talked to us about the principles of his church —principles of prayer, of faith, of fasting wherein we call upon the Lord for blessings." He said, "We don't know much about the Mormon Church, but we have learned a great deal about Davidson; and we are fasting for him today."

I might tell you that the operation was a success. In fact, when I attempted to pay the surgeon, he countered, "Why, that would be dishonest for me to accept a fee. I have never before performed surgery when my hands seemed to be guided by a power which was other than my own. No," he said, "I wouldn't take a fee for the surgery which Someone on high helped me to perform."

Elder Davidson's life was as a house of God.

This, then, is our building project. We are master builders of eternal houses, "even temples of God, which temples ye are."

"Organize yourselves; prepare every needful thing; and establish a house, even a house of prayer, a house of fasting, a house of faith, a house of learning, a house of glory, a house of order, a house of God." (D&C 88:119.)

Then the Lord, even our building inspector, may say to us, as he said as he appeared to Solomon, a builder of another day, ". . . I have hallowed this house, which thou hast built, to put my name there forever; and mine eyes and mine heart shall be there perpetually." (1 Kings 9:3.)

Adapted from an address delivered at a devotional assembly at the University of Utah Institute of Religon.

30

Pathway to life eternal

he Book of Genesis records: ". . . God created man in his own image, in the image of God created he him; male and female created he them. And God blessed them. . . ." (Genesis 1:27-28.)

As God blessed Adam and Eve, so he blesses us of a later generation—blesses us with the gift of free agency, the right to choose and determine our destiny.

In this significant preparatory period of life we seek a map to sail uncharted seas, a formula to insure success, a guide to guarantee achievement. Where will we look? How will we seek? To whom will we turn for help? Our decision is vital. Our day of decision is now.

To our youth, a chosen generation, I say: Turn your hearts and direct your thoughts to him who declared, "I am the way, the truth, and the light." His word is as an unfailing compass to chart safely a true course through the storms of life. He taught faith, love, charity, and hope. He spoke of devotion, courage, example, and fidelity. His life reflected his teachings.

To you his inviting voice repeats the call, "Come, follow me." By so doing, your generation will not fall victim to the evil one's cunning and to temptation's snare.

Your generation will not be that generation "that curseth their father and doth not bless their mother. . . ," that generation "that are pure in their own eyes, and yet is not washed from their filthiness." Nor shall you be that "perverse and crooked generation, a generation of vipers."

Rather, you can qualify as a "chosen generation, a royal priesthood, an holy nation, a peculiar people; that ye should shew forth the praises of him who hath called you out of darkness into his marvellous light." (1 Peter 2:9.)

You ask: "Are there codes of conduct to insure our success? How may we continue to qualify as a chosen generation?"

Since this is a day of the ready reference, the condensed version, the handy guide, may I offer brief suggestion, even steps for your pathway to the abundant life:

STEP 1: *Labor to learn.*
STEP 2: *Strive to serve.*
STEP 3: *Think to thank.*
STEP 4: *Pause to pray.*

First, labor to learn

As I look at you youth, I think not only of what you are, but of what you may become. I also remember who you are, and I plead with you to do likewise. You are the sons and daughters of Almighty God. Each of you has a destiny to fulfill, a life to live, a contribution to make, a goal to achieve. The future of the kingdom of God upon the earth will, in part, be determined by your devotion.

When this perspective is firmly in mind, you can appreciate the absolute necessity of diligence in this, your period of preparation. Neglect to prepare and you mortgage your future.

I chose the phrase "Labor to Learn," since these challenging times will require your finest efforts. A half-hearted effort will not suffice. You must labor with your might.

This is your world. Whether you like it or not, you are engaged in the race of your life. At stake is eternal life— yours. What shall be the outcome? Will you be a leader of men and a servant of God? Or will you be a servant of sin and a follower of Satan? Decisions determine destiny. In the quiet of your study, surrounded by books written by the finest minds of men, listen for and hearken to the Master's invitation: ". . . learn of me; for I am meek and lowly in heart: and ye shall find rest unto your souls." (Matthew 11:29-30.) Such learning transcends the classroom, it endures beyond graduation, it meets the test of experience.

Alma, the prophet, could well have been speaking to you when he counseled, "Oh, remember, my son, and learn wisdom in thy youth; yea, learn in thy youth to keep the commandments of God." (Alma 37:35.)

Second, strive to serve

Thomas Huxley advised: "The end of life is not knowledge, but action." When our testimonies are reflected by our service, they shine with unequaled brilliance. Unfortunately there are those who, turning to their academic pursuits, turn their back to God. You have heard their comment: "I will serve the Lord later—now I must study." This is shortsightedness and shallow thinking.

I am reminded of a highly successful business executive in Salt Lake City who served as a counselor in his ward bishopric while at the same time pursued his master's degree. During the hectic period preceding finals, the bishop asked him, "Lynn, I know you are facing the crisis in your schooling pursuits. Let us relieve you of your meeting schedule and some of the details of your assignments during the next two weeks." Lynn answered, "Bishop, I would ask that rather than relieving me of responsibility, you and your first counselor let me assume additional duties. I want to go to the Lord and ask his help by right, not by grace." He never slackened. He graduated among the highest in his class.

Your service to God and to your fellowmen will not be restricted to the pulpit, the classroom, or your home teaching visits. One found that his moment of decision, his determination to serve, came many thousands of miles from home.

One of two brothers fighting in the same company in a war now past fell mortally wounded from a detonated land mine. After an exchange of rifle fire which brought casualties to each side, the brother who escaped asked permission of his officer to go and bring his brother in.

"He is probably dead," said the officer, "and there is no use in your risking your life to bring in his body."

But after further pleading the officer consented. Just as the soldier returned to the lines with his brother on his shoulders, the wounded man died.

"There, you see," said the officer, "you risked your life for nothing."

"No," replied the soldier. "I did what he expected of me, and I have my reward. When I crept up to him and took him in my arms, he said, 'Dick, I knew you would come; I just felt you would come.' "

Third, think to thank

In these three words are the finest capsule course for a happy marriage, a formula for enduring friendships, and a pattern for personal happiness.

In our hectic, frantic pace for progress we can fall victim to the sin of ingratitude.

The United States Post Office dead-letter department receives annually thousands and thousands of children's pre-Christmas letters addressed to Santa Claus asking for things. After it was all over one year, a single, solitary letter thanking Santa Claus was received. Could this be one of the problems of this troubled world; that people think only of getting—not giving? Of receiving—and not even expressing their gratitude for that which they do receive?

Do you think to thank your mother and your father who have given you life and who rejoice in your accomplishments? To them no sacrifice is too great, no loneliness too acute if such opens the way for you to enjoy the blessings of life. Your thanks may be expressed in your letters but can more appropriately be mirrored by your lives.

A fitting tribute of gratitude was made by a young Latter-day Saint girl attending a Denver, Colorado, high school. The students in her class had been asked to prepare a letter to be written to a great man of their choice. Many addressed their letters to Mickey Mantle, the New York Yankee star of baseball; some to the governor of their state; others to the president of the United States and other celebrities. This young lady, however, addressed her letter to her father, and in the letter she stated: "I have decided to write this letter to you, Dad, because you are the greatest man that I have ever known. The overwhelming desire of my heart is that I might so live that I will have the privilege of being beside you and mother and other members of the family in the celestial kingdom." That father has never received a more cherished letter.

Finally, pause to pray

Perhaps there has never been a time when we had greater need to pray to that God who has given us life. One cannot help but compare our situation today with conditions at the time of Belshazzar, the king of the Chaldeans.

The prophet Daniel rebuked Belshazzar: "And thou . . . O Belshazzar, hast not humbled thine heart. . . . But hast lifted up thyself against the Lord of heaven; and they have brought the vessels of his house before thee, and thou, and thy lords, thy wives, and thy concubines, have drunk wine in them; and thou hast praised the gods of silver, and gold, of brass, iron, wood, and stone, which see not, nor hear, nor know: and the God in whose hand thy breath is, and whose are all thy ways, hast thou not glorified." (Daniel 5:22-23.)

He then interpreted the writing on the wall: "God hath numbered thy kingdom, and finished it. . . . Thou art weighed in the balances, and art found wanting." (Daniel 5:26-27.)

When we are weighed in the balances we will not be found wanting if we make personal prayer a pattern for our lives. When we remember that each of us is literally a spirit son or daughter of God, we will not find it difficult to approach our Father in heaven.

A boy, born in the year of our Lord one thousand eight hundred and five, on the twenty-third of December, in the town of Sharon, Windsor County, State of Vermont, paused to pray that bright day in the grove near Palmyra. Who can calculate the far-reaching effects of that one prayer by that one boy? Do you pause to pray? Your teachers do.

Consider Sister Hansen, the faithful teacher of a Laurel class of lovely young girls in a small mission branch. How she prayed for inspiration that she might teach well the precious girls in her class. Particularly did she pray for Betty, one who had been subjected to great stress and temptation to leave the pathway of truth and follow the detour of sin. Through the constant persuasions of her classmates at school, Betty had agreed that this would be her choice. The plan was designed. She would attend opening exercises of MIA, even the first portion of the class, that she might appear on the roll as being present; and then there would be the sound of an automobile horn to announce to her that her girl friend and their dates, who were older and far more experienced than Betty, were at hand and the night of the carefully arranged escapade of sin would begin. Then she would be one of the inner circle.

But before calling the roll that night, this humble, loving teacher announced to the class that a shipment from Church headquarters had arrived at her home that very day. She had opened the packages and found copies of a pamphlet by Elder Mark E. Petersen. Its subject: chastity. Sister Hansen then said: "I feel impressed to leave for another week our lesson scheduled for tonight and want, rather, to review with you the inspiration of this pamphlet. We will each read a paragraph or two aloud, that all might participate." Sister Hansen looked at each of her precious girls and then said, "Betty, will you begin?" Betty looked at the clock; just two minutes before the scheduled rendezvous. She began to read. Her heart was touched, her conscience awakened, her determination renewed. She scarcely heard the repeated sound of the automobile horn. She remained throughout the class and rode home with her teacher, her guide, her friend. The temptation to detour from God's approved way had been averted. Satan had been frustrated. A soul had been saved. A prayer had been answered.

To you, representatives of the most chosen generation ever to grace this glorious earth, I counsel:

Labor to learn
Strive to serve
Think to thank
Pause to pray

By so doing you will find that pathway which leads to life eternal. To you I bear a personal witness and testimony that God lives, that he hears the prayers of humble hearts. His son, our Savior and Redeemer, speaks to each of you this day: "Behold, I stand at the door, and knock. If any man hear my voice, and open the door, I will come in to him. . . ." (Revelation 3:20.)

Will you listen for that knock? Will you hear and heed that voice? Will you open that door to the Lord? With all my heart I pray that you will.

Adapted from a Brigham Young University devotional assembly address.

31

The search for Jesus

In the New Testament of our Lord, John describes a journey by those who would worship.

"And there were certain . . . among them that came up to worship at the feast; The same came therefore to Philip . . . and desired him, saying, *Sir, we would see Jesus.*" (John 12:20-21. Italics added.)

Little children have another way of expressing the same wish. Most often they say, "Tell me the stories of Jesus, I love to hear; things I would ask him to tell me if he were here." They seek after Jesus, and so it has ever been. No search is so universal. No undertaking so richly rewarding. No effort so enobling. No purpose so divine.

The search for Jesus is not new to this present period of time. In his touching and tender farewell to the Gentiles, Moroni emphasized the importance of this search: "And now I, Moroni, bid farewell. . . . And . . . I would commend you to seek this Jesus of whom the prophets and apostles have written. . . ." (Ether 12:38, 41.) For generations, enlightened mankind in the old and new worlds anxiously sought the fulfillment of prophecies uttered by righteous men inspired of Almighty God.

Then came that night of nights when the angel of the

Lord came upon shepherds abiding in the field, keeping watch over their flock, and the pronouncement, "For unto you is born this day in the city of David, a Saviour, which is Christ the Lord." (Luke 2:8, 11.)

Thus, personally invited to undertake a search for the babe wrapped in swaddling clothes and lying in a manger, did these shepherds concern themselves with the security of their possessions? Did they procrastinate their search for Jesus? The record affirms that the shepherds said to one another, ". . . Let us now go even unto Bethlehem. . . . And they came with haste. . . ." (Luke 2:15-16.)

Wise men journeyed from the East to Jerusalem, saying, "Where is he that is born King of the Jews? for we have seen his star in the east, and are come to worship him.

"When they saw the star, they rejoiced with exceeding great joy.

"And when . . . they saw the young child with Mary his mother, they fell down, and worshipped him: and when they had opened their treasures, they presented unto him gifts; gold, and frankincense, and myrrh." (Matthew 2:2, 10-11.)

With the birth of the babe in Bethlehem, there emerged a great endowment—a power stronger than weapons; a wealth more lasting than the coins of Caesar. This child was to be the King of kings and Lord of lords, the promised Messiah, even Jesus Christ, the Son of God.

Born in a stable, cradled in a manger, he came forth from heaven to live on earth as mortal man and to establish the kingdom of God. During his earthly ministry, he taught men the higher law. His glorious gospel reshaped the thinking of the world. He blessed the sick; he caused the lame to walk, the blind to see, the deaf to hear. He even raised the dead to life.

What was the reaction to his message of mercy, his

words of wisdom, his lessons of life? There were a precious few who appreciated him. They bathed his feet. They learned his word. They followed his example.

Then there were the many who denied him. When asked by Pilate, "What shall I do then with Jesus which is called Christ?" they cried, "Let him be crucified." (Matthew 27:22.) They mocked him. They gave him vinegar to drink. They reviled him. They smote him with a reed. They spat upon him. They crucified him.

Can we, in part, appreciate the suffering of God, the Eternal Father, as his Only Begotten Son in the flesh was placed on a cross and crucified? Is there a father or a mother who could not be moved to complete compassion if he or she heard a son cry out in his own Garden of Gethsemane, "Father, if thou be willing, remove this cup from me: nevertheless, not my will, but thine, be done." (Luke 22:42.)

All of us love the beautiful account of Abraham and Isaac found in the Holy Bible. How exceedingly difficult it must have been for Abraham, in obedience to God's command, to take his beloved Isaac into the land of Moriah, there to present him as a burnt offering. Can you imagine the heaviness of his heart as he gathered the wood for the fire and journeyed to the appointed place? Surely pain must have racked his body and tortured his mind as he bound Isaac and laid him on the altar upon the wood and stretched forth his hand and took the knife to slay his son. How glorious was the pronouncement, and with what wondered welcome did it come: "Lay not thine hand upon the lad, neither do thou any thing unto him: for now I know that thou fearest God, seeing thou hast not withheld thy son, thine only son from me." (Genesis 22:12.)

As God witnessed the suffering of Jesus, his Only Begotten Son in the flesh, and beheld his agony, there was no voice from heaven to spare the life of Jesus. There was no ram in the thicket to be offered as a substitute sacrifice. "For God so loved the world, that he gave his only begotten Son, that whosoever believeth in him should not perish, but have everlasting life." (John 3:16.)

Down through the generations of time, the message from Jesus has been the same. To Peter by the shores of beautiful Galilee, he said, "Follow me." To Philip of old came the call, "Follow me." To the Levite who sat a receipt of customs came the instructions, "Follow me." And to you and to me, if we but listen, shall come that same beckoning invitation, "Follow me."

But how do we follow him if first we don't find him? And how shall we find him if first we don't seek him? Where and how should we begin this search for Jesus?

Some have attempted to answer these questions by turning to idols; others by burning incense or lighting candles. In times past, great throngs journeyed in the crusades of Christianity, feeling that if only the Holy Land could be secured from the infidel, then Christ would be found in their lives. How mistaken they were. Thousands upon thousands perished; many others committed heinous crimes in the very name of Christianity. *Jesus will not be found by crusades of men.*

Still others searched for Jesus in councils of debate. Such was the historic council of Nicea in A.D. 325. There, with the help of the Roman Emperor, the delegates did away in Christendom with the concept of a personal God and a personal Son, the two separate and distinct glorified beings of the scriptures. The creed of Nicea, the "incomprehensible mystery" of which its originators seemed so proud, precisely because it could not be understood, substituted for the personal God of love and for Jesus of the New Testament an immaterial abstraction. The result was a maze of confusion and a compoundment of error. *Jesus will not be found in councils of debate.* Men of the world have modified his miracles, doubted his divinity, and rejected his resurrection.

The formula for finding Jesus has always been and ever will be the same—*the earnest and sincere prayer of a humble and pure heart.* The prophet Jeremiah counseled, ". . . ye shall seek me, and find me, when ye shall search for me with all your heart." (Jeremiah 29:13.)

Before we can successfully undertake a personal search for Jesus, we must first prepare time for him in our lives and room for him in our hearts. In these busy days there are many who have time for golf, time for shopping, time for work, time for play, but no time for Christ.

Lovely homes dot the land and provide rooms for eating, rooms for sleeping, playrooms, sewing rooms, television rooms, but no room for Christ.

Do we get a pang of conscience as we recall his own words: "The foxes have holes, and birds of the air have nests, but the Son of man hath not where to lay his head." (Matthew 8:20.) Or do we flush with embarrassment when we remember, "And she brought forth her firstborn son, and wrapped him in swaddling clothes, and laid him in a manger; because there was no room for them in the inn." (Luke 2:7.) No room. No room. No room. Ever has it been.

As we undertake our personal search for Jesus, aided and guided by the principle of prayer, it is fundamental that we have a clear concept of him whom we seek. The shepherds of old did seek Jesus the child. But we seek Jesus the Christ, our older brother, our mediator with the Father, our Redeemer, the Author of our salvation; he who was in the beginning with the Father; he who took upon himself the sins of the world and so willingly died that we might forever live. This is the Jesus whom we seek.

And when we find him, will we be prepared as were the wise men of old to provide gifts from our many treasures? They presented gold, frankincense, and myrrh.

These are not the gifts Jesus asks of us. From the treasure of our hearts Jesus asks that we give of ourselves: "Behold, the Lord requireth the heart and a willing mind. . . ." (D&C 64:34.)

In this marvelous dispensation of the fulness of times, our opportunities to give of ourselves are indeed limitless, but they are also perishable. There are hearts to gladden. There are kind words to say. There are gifts to be given. There are deeds to be done. There are souls to be saved.

As we remember that "when ye are in the service of your fellow beings ye are only in the service of your God" (Mosiah 2:17), we will not find ourselves in the unenviable position of Jacob Marley's ghost, who spoke to Ebenezer Scrooge in Dickens' immortal *A Christmas Carol.* Marley spoke sadly of opportunities lost. Said he, "Not to know that any Christian spirit, working kindly in its little sphere, whatever it may be, will find its mortal life too short for its vast means.of usefulness. Not to know that no space of regret can make amends for one life's opportunities misused. Yet, such was I. Oh, such was I."

Marley added, "Why did I walk through crowds of fellow beings with my eyes turned down, and never raised them to that blessed star which led wise men to a poor abode? Were there no poor homes to which its light would have conducted me?" In a vain effort to comfort Marley, Scrooge proffered: "But you were always a good man of business, Jacob." Lamented Marley: "Mankind was my business!"

Fortunately, the privilege to render service to others can come to each of us. If we but look, we too will see a bright, particular star which will guide us to our opportunity.

One who saw such a star and followed it was the late Boyd Hatch of Salt Lake City, Utah. Deprived of the use of his legs, faced with a lifetime in a wheelchair, Boyd could well have looked inward and, through sorrow for self, existed, rather than lived. However, Brother Hatch looked not inward, but rather outward into the lives of others and upward into God's own heaven; and the star of inspiration guided him not to one opportunity, but to literally hundreds. He organized Scout troops of handicapped boys. He taught them camping. He taught them swimming. He taught them basketball. He taught them faith. Some boys were downhearted and filled with self-pity and despair. To them he handed the torch of hope. Before them was his own personal example of struggle and accomplishment. With a courage which we shall never fully know or understand, these boys of many faiths overcame insurmountable odds and found themselves anew. Through it all, Boyd Hatch not only found joy, but by willingly and unselfishly giving of himself, he found Jesus.

Every member of The Church of Jesus Christ of Latter-day Saints, in the waters of baptism, has covenanted to stand as a witness of God "at all times and in all things, and in all places" (Mosiah 18:9), and has expressed a willingness to "bear one another's burdens that they might be light" (Mosiah 18:8).

By fulfilling this covenant in our lives, we will become acquainted with him who declared, "Behold, I am Jesus Christ, whom the prophets testified shall come into the world." (3 Nephi 11:10.) This is the Jesus whom we seek. This is our brother whom we love. This is Christ the Lord, whom we serve. I testify that he lives, for I speak as one who has found him.

32

Great expectations

Recently I reread an old favorite of mine by Charles Dickens entitled *Great Expectations*. Dickens described a little fellow by the name of Philip Pirrip, more commonly known as "Pip." Pip was born in unusual circumstances. He was an orphan boy. He never met his mother or his father. He never saw a picture of them. Yet he had all the normal desires of a boy. He wished with all his heart that he were a scholar. He wished that he were a gentleman. He wished that he were less ignorant. Yet all of his ambitions and all of his hopes seemed doomed to failure, until one day a London lawyer by the name of Jaggers approached little Pip and told him that an unknown benefactor had bequeathed a fortune to him. Then that lawyer put his arm around little Pip and said to him, *"My boy, you have great expectations."*

Today, as I contemplate our youth—who they are and what they are and whom they may become and what they may become—I say to them, as that lawyer said to Pip, "You have *great expectations*—not as a result of an unknown benefactor, but as a result of a known benefactor, even our Heavenly Father, and great things are expected of you. The race of life is so important, the prize so valued, that great emphasis must necessarily be placed on adequate and thorough preparation."

When we contemplate the eternal nature of our choices, preparation is a vital factor in our lives. The day will come when we will look upon our period of preparation and be grateful that we properly applied ourselves.

Some years ago I had the opportunity to address a business convention in Dallas, Texas, the city called "the city of churches." After the convention I took a casual sightseeing bus ride about the city's suburbs. As we would pass the beautiful churches our driver would comment, "On the left you see the Methodist Church," or, "There on the right is the Catholic Cathedral." As we passed a beautiful red brick building situated upon a hill, the driver exclaimed, "That building is where the Mormons meet." A lady's voice from the rear of the bus asked, "Driver, can you tell us something about the Mormons?" The driver pulled the bus over to the side of the road, turned about in his seat, and replied, "Lady, all I know about the Mormons is that they meet in that red brick building. Is there anyone on this bus who knows anything about the Mormons?"

I gazed at the expression on each person's face for some sign of recognition, some desire to comment. I found nothing—not a sign. Then I realized for the first time the truth of the statement, "When the time for decision arrives, the time for preparation is past." For the next fifteen minutes I had the privilege of sharing with others my testimony. Since that time I have developed a greater appreciation for the matter of preparation.

Actually the period of our preparation began long before we ever came into mortality, when we lived as spirits—spirit children of our Heavenly Father. I am so grateful that in his wisdom he has given us a record, in the book of Abraham, which tells us something of that existence.

> Now the Lord had shown unto me, Abraham, the intelligences that were organized before the world was; and among all these there were many of the noble and great ones;
> And God saw these souls that they were good, and he stood in the midst of them, and he said. These I will make my rulers; for he stood among those that were in spirits, and he saw that they were good; and he said unto me: Abraham, thou art one of them; thou wast chosen before thou wast born.
> And there stood one among them that was like unto God, and he said unto those who were with him· We will go down, for there is space there, and we will take of these materials, and we will make an earth whereon these may dwell;
> And we will prove them herewith, to see if they will do all things whatsoever the Lord their God shall command them;
> And they who keep their first estate shall be added upon; and they who keep not their first estate shall not have glory in the same kingdom with those who keep their first estate; and they who keep their second estate shall have glory added upon their heads for ever and ever. (Abraham 3:22-26.)

Then in the wisdom of our Heavenly Father, you and I were born into a home with loving parents, parents who welcomed us with open arms, and parents who understood the importance of those first formative years of life. The Lord tells us in the Doctrine and Covenants that during those first eight years power is not given unto Satan to tempt us as little children. (See D&C 29:46-47.) We had an eight-year head-start on Lucifer.

One might ask, "Why is Brother Monson emphasizing this? Our first eight-year period of learning is long past." But many of our Saints, not yet parents, are going to be parents one day, and they will want to emphasize the importance to their youngsters and to their future generations of that first eight-year period.

I know that we have all given our parents "fits," as it were, as they have attempted to rear us. When we consider some of the things we have done as children, some of the things that we contemplated doing as teenagers, some of the things we have done as young adults, I think it is a wonder at times that our parents retain their sanity. In fact, one woman said to her neighbor, "You know, I believe that insanity is hereditary—we get it from our children." She had just suffered a disappointing experience. Her little son had come to her and said brightly, "Mother, you remember that vase that your grandmother gave to your mother and she to you and which you worry that I am always going to break?" She said, "Yes, son." "Mother," he said, "you can quit worrying."

These are times when parents think of severely reprimanding their youngsters and perhaps would, but then they lovingly recall the expression of a little child as he defined the word *eternity*. He said, "Eternity to me is when my mother goes to the hospital."

From the home, we then enter into another great preparation period in order that we might qualify for the race of life. I speak of academic preparation. This is so important because it is here that we learn the lessons which will help us meet the challenges of this changing world in which we live.

Just a generation ago, if your father or my father were applying for a position of responsibility in the business world, a foreman would no doubt say to him, "Are you willing to work hard? Are you healthy?" And if the answers to these questions were to be "Yes," chances are Dad would be hired.

This is not so today. That foreman has long ago been replaced by a personnel director who sits in a modern office and rather quizzically looks at us while he asks, "What skills do you have? What advantage will you be to our firm? May we have a look at your transcript of credits and see your grades?" It is here that we have an immediate application of Alma's prophecy that we shall "have a bright recollection of all our guilt." (Alma 11:43.)

Some years ago, I had the opportunity to teach at the university level. I remember that some students seemed to know where they were going. They applied themselves; they had objectives; they had goals; and they worked toward the achievement of these objectives and goals. But other students could not care less. They seemed to be drifting on a sea of chance, with waves of failure threatening to engulf them. First they became lazy; then discouraged; then indifferent; and then they became dropouts.

One such student who dropped out of school went home to his mother and said, "Mother, I've quit school. I'm going out to make my own way in the world." Almost like the fairy tale, he packed his little knapsack and with it over his shoulder went out to meet life head-on. After two weeks of meeting life, he wrote a letter home to his mother. His letter went something like this: "Dear Mom: Remember when I left home and you told me that if I quit school I wouldn't be able to get a job? Mom, you were wrong. I've only been out on the road for two weeks, and I have had six jobs already."

But the kind of jobs that he found are not the kind of jobs that will enable us to make our mark upon life, for life is waiting for those who are prepared.

In the pursuit of excellence, real effort is required. Remember, "He which soweth sparingly shall reap also sparingly; and he which soweth bountifully shall reap also bountifully." (2 Corinthians 9:6.)

In professional, business, scientific, and technological life there is a rule which can be a very good rule for ambitious young persons. The rule is, "Find a vacuum and expand into it." Ask yourself, "What is there that needs doing and is not being done?" Then assess your capacity for doing things and let it be your ambition to do the work that you can do best, in an area where it is needed most, and then put all your mind into it.

Life is a sea upon which the proud are humbled; the shirker is exposed; and the leader is revealed: To sail it safely and reach our desired port, we need to keep our charts at hand and up to date. We need to learn by the experience of others, to stand firm for principles, to broaden our interests, to be understanding of the rights of others to sail the same sea, and to be reliable in our discharge of duty.

Excellence in school will have a notable effect on opportunities after we leave school. However, more significant than our period of academic preparation is the matter of spiritual preparation—we must acquire for ourselves a testimony of the gospel of Jesus Christ, a testimony which President David O. McKay has described as an anchor to the soul.

In the inquiring, inquisitive, uncertain period of youth, some may ask, as did Pilate, "What is truth?" And again we turn to the revelations for guidance: "And that which doth not edify is not of God, and is darkness. That which is of God is light. . . ." (D&C 50:23-24.)

To those who humbly seek there is no need to stumble or falter along the pathway leading to truth. It is well marked by our Heavenly Father. We must first have a desire to know for ourselves. We must study. We must pray. We must do the will of the Father. And then we shall know the truth and the truth shall make us free. Divine favor will attend those who humbly seek it.

To those who are embarking on this great race of life, may I suggest some helpful hints that will assist you to achieve your *great expectations.*

Helpful hint number one: *Avoid the pitfalls in the track.*

Avoid the detours that will deprive you of your celestial reward. You can recognize them if you will. They may be labeled, "Just this once won't matter," or, "My parents are so old-fashioned." Bad habits also can be such pitfalls. First we could break them if we would. Later, we would break them if we could. John Dryden said: "Ill habits gather by unseen degrees—As brooks make rivers, rivers run to seas." Good habits, on the other hand, are the soul's muscles. The more you use them the stronger they grow.

Helpful hint number two: *Beware of the flashy start and the fade-out finish.*

Follow the example of Christopher Columbus. Take a leaf out of the log of his journal on his first voyage. Day after day as they hoped to find land and never found it, he wrote simply, "This day we sailed on."

Helpful hint number three: *Help others in their races of life.*

In a life or death setting, may I illustrate by relating the experience of one who helped and, in turn, one who thanked. More than twenty-five years ago, I saw a grown man cry. It wasn't his custom. The tears stemmed not from sorrow but from gratitude. My swimming coach, Charlie Welch, who perhaps aided more boys than did any other man to achieve their swimming skills and successfully earn their life-saving merit badge, was calling the roll of our swimming class at the University of Utah. His voice resounded and bounced back from the plaster walls. The gym door opened that day in 1944 during World War II, and there stood a young man in navy uniform. The sailor came up to Charlie and said: "Charlie, excuse me, but I want to thank you for saving my life." Charlie lifted his eyes from the roll card, put the pencil in his pocket, and asked, "What's that?" Again the sailor said, "I want to thank you for saving my life. You once told me, Charlie, that I swam like a lead ball, yet you patiently taught me to swim. Two months ago, far off in the Pacific, a Japanese torpedo sank my destroyer. As I swam my way through the murky waters and foul-tasting and ever-dangerous film of oil, I found myself saying, 'If I ever get out of this mess alive, I'm going to thank Charlie Welch for teaching me, as a Boy Scout, how to swim.' I came here today to say thank you."

Twenty athletes stood shoulder to shoulder and never uttered a word. We watched the great tears of gratitude well up in Charlie's eyes, roll down his cheeks, and tumble upon his familiar sweatshirt. Charlie Welch, a humble, prayerful, patient, and loving builder of boys, had just received his reward.

Helpful hint number four: *Seek the help of the Lord.*

Souls are precious—your soul and my soul. God himself has said so. Remember, we do not run alone in this great race of life—we can have the help of the Lord. However, before we can take Jesus as our companion, before we can follow him as our guide, we must find him. You ask, "How can we find Jesus?" Said the Lord: "He that seeketh me early shall find me, and shall not be forsaken." (D&C 88:83.) "For every one that asketh receiveth; and he that seeketh findeth; and to him that knocketh it shall be opened." (Luke 11:10.)

We must make room for the Lord in our homes and in our hearts. He will be a welcome companion. He will be by our side. He will teach us the way of truth. With his help, and with the preparation about which we have spoken, we can all go forward in this great race of life and achieve that which the lawyer Jaggers said to little Pip, our *great expectations.*

Adapted from a Brigham Young University devotional assembly address.

33

The race for eternal life

Our young people constitute the most valuable materials in the universe. Only master craftsmen with abiding faith and unyielding testimony should be permitted to shape their eternal destiny. May all of us remember:

> *Who touches a boy by the Master's plan*
> *Is shaping the course of a future man;*
> *Is dealing with one who is human seed,*
> *Who may be the man the world will need.*

And what an exciting, thrilling, adventuresome world is this in which we live! Why, things are moving so fast that all of us, living in such dynamic times, must occasionally feel the desire expressed in the words of the musical *Stop the World, I Want to Get Off.*

Dr. Wernher Von Braun, world-renowned space scientist, has told us the delightful story of the eighty-year-old woman who wrote him as follows: "Dear Dr. Von Braun, Why do we have to go to the moon? Why can't we stay on this earth and watch television the way the good Lord intended?"

Yet time marches on. It took man 5,000 years to go from the sailboat to the steamboat; a hundred years from the steamboat to the airplane. There were only forty years from the Air Age to the Atomic Age, and twelve years from the Atomic Age to the Space Age.

In the Space Age, the flow of knowledge is 'as relentless and in a real sense is as uncompromising as the spring flow of the rushing waters of the Snake River. It imposes on us the stiff, and in many ways new, requirement that we not merely adjust to, but that we anticipate the future.

Too many people shrink from reality and recoil from discomfort. The tendency of the discontented is to look back at everything with nostalgia and of the timid to look ahead at everything with fear. I hope you will join with the Roman poet and declare: "Let ancient times delight other folk; I rejoice that I was not born till now."

This is our day of opportunity. Are we prepared to grasp it? Our friends, our parents, our church are counting on us. In a way, each of us is engaged in a vital race.

The race of life is not optional—we are on the track and running whether we like it or not. Some see dimly the goal ahead and take costly detours that lead to disappointment and frustration. Others view clearly the prize for running well and remain steadfast in pursuit. This prize, this lofty and desirable goal, is none other than eternal life in the presence of God. May I suggest four guiding principles to help us win the prize:

1. *Prepare properly*
2. *Serve willingly*
3. *Live honorably*
4. *Pray earnestly*

1. Prepare properly

When we contemplate the eternal nature of our choices, preparation is a vital factor in our lives. The day will come when we will look back upon our period of preparation and be grateful that we properly applied ourselves.

Actually, the period of your preparation did not begin the day you walked into college. It began long before you ever came into mortality, when we lived as spirits—spirit children of our Heavenly Father.

Have we made preparations for life's journey? Do we know what is expected of us? Do we know the gospel? "And this is life eternal, that they might know thee the only true God, and Jesus Christ, whom thou hast sent." (John 17:3.)

Such knowledge will dispel that hidden and insidious enemy who lurks within and limits our capacity, destroys our initiative, and strangles our effectiveness. This enemy is *fear:* A fear to wholeheartedly accept a calling. A fear to provide direction. A fear to lead, to motivate, to inspire. Preparation eradicates fear.

Preparation precedes power. To obtain the knowledge and skill we require need not be an insurmountable task if we adopt for our pattern the experience of the sons of Mosiah. Alma was journeying from the land of Gideon southward, away to the land of Manti, when he met the sons of Mosiah journeying toward the land of Zarahemla. Alma rejoiced exceedingly to see his brethren; and what added more to his joy, they were still his brethren in the Lord; yea, and they had waxed strong in the knowledge of the truth; for they were men of a sound understanding and had searched the scriptures diligently that they might know the word of God. But this is not all; they had given themselves to much prayer, and fasting; therefore, they had the spirit of prophecy and the spirit of revelation, and when they taught, they taught with power and authority of God. (See Alma 17:1-3.)

2. Serve willingly

The Lord declared that he requires "the heart and a willing mind; and the willing and obedient shall eat the good of the land of Zion in these last days." (D&C 64:34.)

277

The race for eternal life

A wise man of experience observed: Men will work hard for money. They will work harder for other men. But men will work hardest of all when they are dedicated to a cause. Until willingness overflows obligation, men fight as conscripts rather than following the flag as patriots. Duty is never worthily performed until it is performed by one who would gladly do more if only he could.

Man does not by himself run the race of life. When we help another in his race of life, we really serve our God. King Benjamin stated the principle so beautifully, ". . . when ye are in the service of your fellow beings ye are only in the service of your God." (Mosiah 2:17.)

Balanced service is a virtue to be cherished. There is to be time in our life to serve God, to serve our family, to serve our country and community, to serve our employer. Wise persons budget available time so that no significant area of one's life falls into a state of neglect. An axiom to follow: "When you play—play hard. When you work—don't play at all."

Service with a smile is far more than a department store slogan. It is a way of life and a path to happiness.

The book of Judges teaches a powerful lesson concerning willing and obedient service and in a life or death setting. The example features a famous general named Gideon. Gideon faced his most crucial test. He and his army came upon an overwhelmingly superior force of Midianites and Amalekites. The enemy lay along in the valley like grasshoppers for multitude, and their camels without number as the sand by the seaside for multitude. Gideon needed knowledge to extricate himself from this frightful situation.

To his amazement the Lord said unto him:

The people that are with thee are too many for me to give the Midianites into their hands, lest Israel vaunt themselves against me, saying, Mine own hand hath saved me.

Now therefore go to, proclaim in the ears of the people, saying, Whosoever is fearful and afraid, let him return and depart early from mount Gilead. And there returned of the people twenty and two thousand; and there remained ten thousand. (Judges 7:2-3.)

Again the Lord ruled that Gideon had too many followers and instructed Gideon to take them to water to observe the manner in which they should drink of the water. Those that lapped the water were placed in one group, and those who bowed down upon their knees to drink were placed in another. The Lord said unto Gideon, "By the three hundred men that lapped will I save you, and deliver the Midianites into thine hand: and let all the other people go every man unto his place." (Judges 7:7.)

A battle plan was provided. The force was to be divided into three companies. Trumpets were to be taken in the right hand and a pitcher containing a lamp within the other hand. Gideon said, "When I blow with a trumpet, I and all that are with me, then blow ye the trumpets also on every side of all the camp, and say, The sword of the Lord, and of Gideon." (Judges 7:18.) "As I do, so shall ye do." (Judges 7:17.)

At the leader's signal, the host of Gideon did blow on the trumpets and did break the pitchers and did shout, "The sword of the Lord, and of Gideon." The scripture records the outcome of this decisive battle: "And they stood every man in his place," and the battle was won. (Judges 7:20-21.)

Willing service, obedient service, had triumphed.

3. Live honorably

Each of us has received from the Savior the divine charge to "let your light so shine before men, that they may see your good works, and glorify your Father which is in heaven." "Ye are the light of the world." (Matthew 5:16, 14.)

To glow with brilliance, develop a tried and proven set of Be Attitudes:

> *Be honest.*
> *Be clean.*
> *Be true.*
> *Be kind.*
> *Be obedient.*

Values are lived—not talked about. Let us then place our trust in a personal God.

We can best insure our compliance with God's law by remembering that our actions are preceded by our thoughts. Our thinking will automatically improve when we remember the words of Paul: "Know ye not that ye are the temple of God, and that the Spirit of God dwelleth in you?" (1 Corinthians 3:16.)

4. Pray earnestly

As we pursue our quest for eternal life, we will come to many forks and turnings in the road. We cannot venture into the uncertainties of the future without reference to the certainties of the past. Our challenge is to join the forces of the old and the new—experience and experiment, history and destiny, the world of man and the new world of science —but always in accordance with the never-changing word of God. In short, he becomes our pilot on this eternal journey. He knows the way. His counsel can keep us from the pitfalls threatening to engulf us and lead us rather to the way of life eternal.

As we face the temptations of time, the confusion of choice, the embarrassment of error, the pursuit of perfection, our Heavenly Father is there to listen, to love, to inspire. Our Father to whom we earnestly pray is not an ethereal substance or a mysterious and incomprehensible being. Rather, he has eyes with which to view our actions, lips with which to speak to us, ears to hear our plea, and a heart to understand our love.

Prayer is the soul's sincere desire. It is the compass to guide our lives.

Many years ago I was called and sustained to preside in a large ward in Salt Lake City. One prominent couple with a son in the mission field had become somewhat offended in their hearts. An offhand remark was made by them that they would not darken the door of the chapel again. This became a pledge. The weeks turned to months and the months approached a year. The resolve hardened. One Sunday evening we planned to hear from a returning missionary who had been a friend of the son of our offended couple. I remember how my heart yearned for this fine couple to return to activity. I had explored my every avenue of hope—personal visits, personal pleadings, personal prayer. This particular Sunday I returned to a private place and poured out my feelings to my Heavenly Father. As I arose from my knees I felt certain peace beyond description fill my soul. I knew that this couple would attend sacrament meeting that very evening.

The appointed hour arrived—there was no sign of them. My counselors went to the stand. My watch showed but two minutes remaining. I peered out the window in the entranceway toward the street where the family lived. Just then the family automobile appeared and proceeded along its way to the chapel. With hesitation they came up the stairway. I greeted them: "Welcome home. We've missed you. We need you." The mother handed me a wire which read: "Be at church this Sunday. I know you won't let me down. Signed, Your missionary son." I noted the time—4:00 P.M.—the exact moment I had been upon my knees. Man's extremity had become God's opportunity.

The race for eternal life

May each of us prepare properly, serve willingly, live honorably, and above all, pray earnestly.

I testify that God does live, that Jesus is the Christ, our older brother, our mediator with the Father, our Lord and our Savior, our Redeemer. I know that he lives, and I bear this solemn witness to you. May you have this same testimony in your hearts to guide you well throughout your sojourn on this planet in mortality and into the eternal worlds of our Heavenly Father.

Adapted from a baccalaureate address delivered at Ricks College in Rexburg, Idaho.

34

"Mrs. Patton, Arthur lives"

The flight from Brisbane, Australia, to San Francisco is a long one. There is time to read, time to sleep, and time to ponder and think. As a passenger on this flight, I was awakened by the calm, resonant sound of the pilot's voice as he announced: "Ladies and gentlemen, we're now passing over the Coral Sea, scene of the great sea battle of World War II."

Through the cabin window I could see billowy, white clouds and far below the azure blue of the vast Pacific. My thoughts turned to the events of that fateful eighth day of May in 1942 when the mammoth aircraft carrier *Lexington* slipped to its final resting place on the ocean floor. Twenty-seven hundred and thirty-five sailors scrambled to safety. Others were not so fortunate. One who went down with his ship was my boyhood friend, Arthur Patton.

May I tell you about Arthur? He had blond, curly hair and a smile as big as all outdoors. Arthur stood taller than any boy in the class. I suppose this is how he was able to fool the recruiting officers and enlist in the navy at the tender age of fifteen. To Arthur and most of the boys, the war was a great adventure. I remember how striking he appeared in his navy uniform. How we wished we were older, or at least taller, so we too could enlist.

"Mrs. Patton, Arthur lives"

Youth is a very special time of life. As Longfellow wrote:

> *How beautiful is youth! How bright it gleams*
> *With its illusions, aspirations, dreams!*
> *Book of Beginnings, Story without End,*
> *Each maid a heroine, and each man a friend!*
>
> —"MORITUS SALUTAMUS"

Arthur's mother was so proud of the blue star which graced her living room window. It represented to every passerby that her son wore the uniform of his country. When I would pass the house she often opened the door and invited me in to read the latest letter from Arthur. Her eyes would fill with tears, and I would then be asked to read aloud. Arthur meant everything to his widowed mother. I can still picture Mrs. Patton's coarse hands as she would carefully replace the letter in its envelope. These were honest hands which bore the worker's seal. Mrs. Patton was a cleaning woman—a janitress for a downtown office building. Each day of her life except Sundays, she could be seen walking up the sidewalk, pail and brush in hand, her gray hair combed in a tight bob, her shoulders weary from work and stooped wth age.

Then came the Battle of the Coral Sea, the sinking of the *Lexington,* and the death of Arthur Patton. The blue star was taken from its hallowed spot in the front window. It was replaced by one of gold. A light went out in the life of Mrs. Patton. She groped in utter darkness and deep despair.

With a prayer in my heart, I approached the familiar walkway to the Patton home, wondering what words of comfort could come from the lips of a mere boy. The door opened and Mrs. Patton embraced me as she would her own son. Home became a chapel as a grief-stricken mother and a less-than-adequate boy knelt in prayer.

"Mrs. Patton, Arthur lives"

Arising from our knees, Mrs. Patton gazed into my eyes and spoke: "Tom, I belong to no church, but you do. Tell me, will Arthur live again?"

Time dims the memory of that conversation. The present whereabouts of Mrs. Patton are not known to me; but, Mrs. Patton, wherever you are, from the backdrop of my personal experience, I should like to once more answer your question, "Will Arthur live again?"

I suppose we could say that this is a universal question, for who has not at a time of bereavement pondered the same thought?

Death leaves in its cruel wake shattered dreams, unfulfilled ambitions, crushed hopes. In our helplessness, we turn to others for assurance. Men of letters and leaders of renown can express their beliefs, but they cannot provide definitive answers.

The dim light of belief must yield to the noonday sun of revelation. We turn to Jesus.

The plan of life and an explanation of its eternal course come to us from the Master of heaven and earth, even Jesus Christ the Lord. To understand the meaning of death, we must appreciate the purpose of life.

In this dispensation, the Lord declared: "And now, verily I say unto you, I was in the beginning with the Father, and am the Firstborn." (D&C 93:21.) "Man was also in the beginning with God. . . ." (D&C 93:29.) Jeremiah the prophet recorded, ". . . the word of the Lord came unto me, saying, Before I formed thee . . . I knew thee; and before thou camest forth . . . I sanctified thee, and ordained thee a prophet unto the nations." (Jeremiah 1:4-5.)

From that majestic world of spirits we enter the grand stage of life even to prove ourselves obedient to all things commanded of God. During mortality we grow from helpless infancy to inquiring childhood and then to reflective maturity. We experience joy and sorrow, fulfillment and

285

disappointment, success and failure; taste the sweet, yet sample the bitter. This is mortality.

Then to each life comes the experience known as death. None is exempt. All must pass its portals. Death claims the aged, the weary and worn. It visits the youth in the bloom of hope and glory of expectation. Nor are the little children kept beyond its grasp. In the words of the apostle Paul: ". . . it is appointed unto men once to die. . . ." (Hebrews 9:27.)

To most, there is something sinister and mysterious about this unwelcome visitor called death. Perhaps it is a fear of the unknown which causes many to dread his coming.

Arthur Patton died quickly. Others linger. Not long ago I held the thin hand of a youth as he approached the brink of eternity. "I know I am dying," he said touchingly. "What follows death?" I turned to the scriptures and read to him: "Then shall the dust return to the earth as it was: and the spirit shall return unto God who gave it." (Ecclesiastes 12:7.) ". . . there is a time appointed unto men that they shall rise from the dead; and there is a space between the time of death and the resurrection. . . . concerning the state of the soul between death and the resurrection—Behold, . . . the spirits of all men, as soon as they are departed from this mortal body . . . are taken home to that God who gave them life." (Alma 40:9, 11.)

To me, the lad said, "Thank you." To my Heavenly Father I said silently, "Thank thee, oh God, for truth."

Mrs. Patton, do not grieve as you think of your boy in the depths of the Pacific or question how God's purposes can be fulfilled. Remember the words of the Psalmist: "If I take the wings of the morning, and dwell in the uttermost parts of the sea; Even there shall thy hand lead me, and thy right hand shall hold me." (Psalm 139:9-10.)

God has not forsaken you, Mrs. Patton. He sent his

Only Begotten Son into the world to teach us by example the life we should live. His Son died upon the cross to redeem all mankind. His words to the grieving Martha and to his disciples today bring comfort to you: "I am the resurrection, and the life: he that believeth in me, though he were dead, yet shall he live: And whosoever liveth and believeth in me shall never die." (John 11:25-26.) "In my Father's house are many mansions; if it were not so, I would have told you. I go to prepare a place for you. . . . I will come again, and receive you unto myself; that where I am, there ye may be also." (John 14:2-3.)

Mrs. Patton, the testimonies of John the revelator and Paul the apostle are also significant to you. John recorded: ". . . I saw the dead, small and great, stand before God. . . . And the sea gave up the dead which were in it. . . ." (Revelation 20:12-13.) Paul declared: ". . . as in Adam all die, even so in Christ shall all be made alive." (1 Corinthians 15:22.)

Until the glorious resurrection morning, we walk by faith. "For now we see through a glass, darkly, but then face to face. . . ." (1 Corinthians 13:12.)

Jesus invites you, Mrs. Patton, "Come unto me, all ye that labour and are heavy laden, and I will give you rest. Take my yoke upon you, and learn of me; for I am meek and lowly in heart: and ye shall find rest unto your souls." (Matthew 11:28-29.)

Such knowledge will sustain you in your heartache. You will never be in the tragic situation of the disbeliever who, having lost a son, was heard to say as she watched the casket lowered into mother earth: "Goodbye, my boy. Goodbye forever." Rather, with head erect, courage undaunted, and faith unwavering, you can lift your eyes as you look beyond the gently breaking waves of the blue Pacific and whisper, "Goodbye, Arthur, my precious son. Goodbye—until we meet again."

And the words of Alfred, Lord Tennyson may come to
you as though spoken by your boy:

> *Sunset and evening star,*
>   *And one clear call for me;*
> *And may there be no moaning of the bar,*
>   *When I put out to sea.*
>
> *Twilight and evening bell,*
>   *And after that the dark!*
> *And may there be no sadness of farewell*
>   *When I embark;*
>
> *For tho' from out our bourne of time and place*
>   *The flood may bear me far,*
> *I hope to see my Pilot face to face*
>   *When I have crossed the bar.*

To the words of the poet I add the testimony of a witness. Mrs. Patton, God our Father is mindful of you.
Through sincere prayer you can communicate with him.
He, too, had a Son who died, even Jesus Christ the Lord.
He is our advocate with the Father, the Prince of Peace,
our Savior and Divine Redeemer. One day we shall see him
face to face.

In his blessed name I declare to you the solemn and
sacred truth: Oh, Mrs. Patton, Arthur lives.

INDEX

Index

Index

K

L

Index

Index

Index

T

300

Index

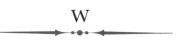

Index